Navigating New
Markets Abroad

Navigating New Markets Abroad

*Charting a Course for the
International Businessperson*

Second Edition

David M. Raddock

ROWMAN & LITTLEFIELD PUBLISHERS, INC.
Lanham • Boulder • New York • Oxford

ROWMAN & LITTLEFIELD PUBLISHERS, INC.

Published in the United States of America
by Rowman & Littlefield Publishers, Inc.
4720 Boston Way, Lanham, Maryland 20706
http://www.rowmanlittlefield.com

12 Hid's Copse Road
Cumnor Hill, Oxford OX2 9JJ, England

British Library Cataloguing in Publication Information Available

Library of Congress Cataloging-in-Publication Data

Raddock, David M.
    Navigating new markets abroad : charting a course for the international businessperson
  / by David M. Raddock ; with contributions by John P. Entelis ... [et al.].—2nd ed.
      p.   cm.
    "Revised edition for the 21st century."
    Includes index.
    ISBN 0-7425-0206-6 (alk. paper)
      1. International business enterprises—Management. 2. Corporations,
    American—Management. 3. Country risk. 4. Cross-cultural orientation—United States. I.
    Title.

    HD62.4 .R34 2001
    658'.049—dc21

                                                                    00-059061

Printed in the United States of America

♾™ The paper used in this publication meets the minimum requirements of American
National Standard for Information Sciences—Permanence of Paper for Printed Library
Materials, ANSI/NISO Z39.48-1992.

Contents

List of Tables

Acknowledgments

This book represents years of applying formal study to a very new and amorphous field. In these practical applications of the social sciences to business needs, I have learned a great deal from high-level foreign officials, journalists, and specialists within key departments of the U.S. government. Individual sources for this education are hard to pinpoint, let alone credit or blame.

I really learned my political science at Columbia University through my own efforts in reading for my doctoral examinations and through the practical experience to follow. A few of my professors sensitized me to key areas of political exploration and cross-cultural behavior. These include Franz Schurmann, the late A. Doak Barnett, Ted de Bary, the late Marty Wilbur, Milton Viederman (formerly at the Department of Politics and Science at Columbia), and the late Margaret Mead. Of my colleagues, the most supportive and helpful along the way have been Don Easum, Bill Overholt, John Dolfin, A. Lopez, Andy Nathan, Myron Cohen, Steve Levine, and June Teufel Dreyer who has kept me abreast of Chinese military affairs.

My work over nearly ten years at the Washington office of ENSERCH Corporation taught me a lot about corporate needs and corporate politics. The practice of applying social science principles to corporate planning problems gave rise to the sort of international environmental analysis construct that appears in this book. Widespread travel, for ENSERCH Corporation and as an academic with the support of the National Endowment for the Humanities and others, provided the critical seasoning.

Of all my careers—add acting, university teaching, and public affairs, I've enjoyed political risk analysis and writing the most. Perhaps, the most exciting dimension of the work has been on-site assessment of countries with which I've had some personal interaction, like Indonesia, China, or Zimbabwe. The more in-depth research, involving a lot of interviewing under sensitive conditions, was a bit like a manipulative sort of cultural anthropology. I am grateful to all the local figures who colored my reports and enriched my knowledge of their countries. Some are in prison now; some have been elected president or appointed to cabinet positions; and some—like me—are just muddling through!

I especially want to draw the reader's attention to the fact that my work on financial analysis in this book represents collaborative thinking with Fariborz Ghadar of George Washington University's School of Business. In the process of updating examples and offering new ones for this edition, I spoke with desk officers at the Department of State for Indonesia, Thailand, Peru, Burma, Venezuela, and Pakistan and with the international affairs office of the U.S. Treasury Department. I also thank Dr. Joel Barkin of the National Endowment for Democracy.

From start to finish, my wife Annette has encouraged me with this work, in all its permutations. In her own way, she faces cross-cultural risks on a daily basis and copes constructively with them.

Getting to the right source materials at the start of any important project is vitally important. I hope this book, written in revised form for the very beginning of a new century, will be helpful to the reader as a framework for decisions and as a reference tool. The expert case study contributors and I, respectively, take responsibility for our errors and our conclusions.

Preface to a Revised Edition for the Twenty-first Century

Political risk analysis came into its own as a result of a perceived need during the 1979 Iranian revolution to find ways to anticipate political and social turmoil that might harm U.S. business operations overseas. It represented the application then of principles from the social and behavioral sciences to doing business in third-world countries. The purpose at the time was to predict critical disruptions of stability in a host country and thereby avoid serious negative losses at the bottom line. Previously, the focus had been on examining macroeconomic variables for their effect on doing business. The first edition to this book treated such economic measures as indices and also *integrated them with political influences*.

The first edition recognized that the corporate planning need had evolved. Corporations also required research support in marketing and public policymaking. The key was to ascertain what variables would affect corporate operations in the broader political and economic environment and to show a corporation how to position itself accordingly in that market.

Cataclysms are few and social revolutions seldom succeed. International business planners and marketing managers needed less red flags and menacing numbers to scare them away from new markets. Instead, they needed a systematic framework for educating themselves about potential host countries: a way to understand the risks and disincentives, weigh them against opportunities, compare them to circumstances in alternative countries, and learn how to surmount the likely difficulties that might arise.

At the advent of a century, this new edition has had a chance to consider globalization—its homogenizing effects and its limitations. Simply looking at one country like the People's Republic of China, we see areas of the political culture that seem to have been unaffected by Westernization and the communications revolution. Although the central government in China has written new commercial laws and has made great strides toward privatization, it has been resistant to world standards of tolerance of civil freedoms and has reacted with a nationalistic backlash to international censure of its treatment of human rights. And it still behaves in traditional, statist, and bureaucratic ways.

This edition, replete with examples of the pitfalls along the way, informs the businessperson to be cautious. The businessperson from the United States or another advanced Western country whose vision has expanded beyond its shores must be all the more judicious in approaching strange developing or "newly independent" countries. Cultural differences and business practices might not appear to be glaring, but international corporate persons should not deceive themselves. Often, lurking beneath the surface are enough differences in point of view and custom to warrant proper attention. Moreover, resentments of the foreigner can emerge from the shadows of history to color negotiations, regulations, taxation, and regional behaviors.

Offered here are fresh illustrations of more recent episodes in the third world, the former Soviet Union, and Eastern Europe. We address two very important new issues: the rule of law and human rights. It is ironic that in a shrinking world, countries still arbitrarily change or ignore the written law. With many countries, like Russia, in a state of systemic flux, it is perhaps not surprising that privatized sectors of the economy only years later can be "renationalized" under pressure. However, it comes as a devastating shock to the western investor who plunged excitedly into the market that Mikhail Gorbachev and Boris Yeltsin first opened. This edition—including an in-depth case study of Russia and its treatment of its law—will be interesting to those who presume change to be inviolate.

When old ideologies die, new ones inexorably emerge. Two of these, the issue of environment/ecology and human rights, now have a global momentum all of their own. The human rights issue mainly was a means of political leverage in foreign policy during the cold war but now has a coterie of worldwide followers and has become political currency in all countries. An international corporation on shores where human rights abuses are common may become the target of activists and the local community in the host country, activists in the home country, sanctions from the home country government, and reprisals from the host country. The reader will find a whole section on this question in this new edition.

For me personally, globalization has some drawbacks. It has made the world a duller place. Whenever I see another McDonald's or Kentucky Fried Chicken on the landscape of Beijing or Bali, I bristle a little. I have to enter and check out the sauce to realize that it is different. Sometimes hot enough to burn the palate! In this difference, even the fast food retains its identity and should be swallowed with care.

David M. Raddock
Brooklyn Heights, New York

Introduction: The Business of Getting Global

The world seems to be shrinking; our own, expanding. Globalizing one's business interests ought to be a natural extension of the marketing process.

Territorial divisions now appear to be less of a barrier to the U.S. businessperson. The once forbidding Berlin Wall symbolically defined the boundary between the communist and "free worlds" in the Western Hemisphere. As the century entered its last decade, the Wall, over which countless refugees had climbed in search of a different way of life, was dismantled, and parts of it were broken into small pieces and sold as souvenirs in the West. This spectacle is certainly an invitation to all of us to redefine our operational boundaries. Enterprises in other countries have become more competitive internationally, and U.S. corporations must search for new markets and sources of supply or stagnate.

Terms like "globalization" and "internationalization," once the jargon of academic and multinational business circles for discussion of social and business planning, now have gained currency as a signal that our markets must be expanded overseas. By 2000, they have come to proclaim a *new universality of doing business worldwide.* International businesspeople now have come to expect (and advanced governments and lending institutions now demand) certain standards of doing business in foreign markets, such as enforcement of contract, transparency of corporate accounts, and political environmental safeguards of their legal position in the host market. The problem is that often a wide gap exists between expectations and realities, and sometimes the institutional vagaries and inconsistencies from one locality to another and one period to another are beyond the control of the contract negotiators and politicians of the moment. Entrenched local interests and bureaucratic defenses, economic and social trends, and the political cultural habits of the host country all can resist and undermine more progressive legal reforms and regulations. Old, intransigent practices persist in relatively personalized and interpersonal societies.

The science of business and management techniques, homegrown in the West, has evolved and spread to other places and cultures and presumably drawn them closer to the West. Telecommunications and computer technology have spawned linkages between country and country, bank and bank, and terminal and terminal. *But does this mean that, given an appealing business opportunity in this day and age, one should find Myanmar less daunting than Michigan?*

Even if it is now simpler to communicate globally, one has to work harder at having a viable and enduring relationship with those whose cultures, organizations, and practices vary so much from our own. Countries with varying levels of institutionalization and uncertain governing and business practices demand a special type of planning and adaptiveness. Although the world does seem suddenly smaller and more ideologically sanitized as we enter the twenty-first century, businesses should look before they leap.

Now indeed may be the critical time to look for offshore business opportunities, but not without a sense of cross-cultural as well as historical perspective. What we must do is learn how to incorporate such a perspective into our international corporate strategic planning.

Historically, the era of ideologies has not necessarily passed. If the cold war has ebbed, the North-South polarity (the developing world counterpoised against less developed countries) still does continue. And resurgent rivalries among nationalities portend more schisms, if not "isms."

Cataclysms that threaten foreign-owned equity and expatriate lives and the flow of normal international commerce are never farther behind us than the most recent local war, whether in the Persian Gulf, West Africa, or somewhere else in the third world or in the reborn ethnogeographical areas of eastern and central Europe.

POLITICAL RISK ANALYSIS: A PREMATURE BIRTH

The year 1978–1979 took all players by surprise!

At one time, when things seemed simpler and aggressive energies in the world seemed more focussed on a cold war, multinational corporations believed that they could cushion themselves against, or even transcend, most conflicts. In the United States, transnational corporate entities had followed the lead of the government or worked in advance of the U.S. government to build economic bridges.

Before 1979, the relatively few U.S. corporations with heavy international commitments could count countries like Iran among their more reliable hosts and partners. Former secretary of state Henry Kissinger had predicted that Mohammad Reza Pahlavi, the shah of Iran, would be an anchor for U.S. security interests in the Middle East. That year, the social revolution that shook Iran sent a wave of aftershocks through the international business community and under-mined a shared confidence that the U.S. government could show us the way.

The abrasiveness and inequities of Western-style modernization that U.S. for-eign direct investment had helped create in Iran had led to social ferment. A per-vasive Western presence that had cast a shadow on traditional values and had eroded a sense of identity there gave rise to a sandstorm that shook us out of our complacency.

After the dust had settled, a gaggle of experts, calling themselves "political risk analysts," emerged to clear the way for a new sort of confusion in international strategic planning. (Even Kissinger eventually took his place among these con-sultants.) Making their impression at Washington cocktail parties and behind closed doors of major international corporations were new experts with a diver-sity of backgrounds in applied areas of international politics—former covert op-eratives and overt analysts from the Central Intelligence Agency, former journal-ists, retired State Department country experts and policy planning staffers, and even former expatriate marketing executives called in from the cold by their home offices.

Add to this list a small coterie of academics, persons with a critical formal training in comparative politics/international relations and in geographical area studies. Drawing from this latter group represented a step in the right direction. But what the young academics and area specialists and the other groups of trained political observers lacked for the most part was an appreciation for the busi-nessperson's criteria for making decisions and formulating marketing strategies. Few seemed to grasp the international marketing executive's concerns and the pressures under which he or she had to operate.

The new breed of political risk analysts as a whole were slow to make the link-age between political variables and their potential for direct or indirect impact on the corporate bottom line.

To be effective, such analyses needed to be predicated on knowledge of the or-ganization's specific needs and sometimes even the characteristics of a specific project. The reality is that corporations have different objectives and criteria for investment and financial exposure. Specific projects themselves, like nuclear power plants and joint production sharing agreements for petroleum develop-ment, can vary in terms of their special conditions.

Corporate cultures also differ in their capacity to assimilate and utilize such in-formation. Before the Iranian revolution, a senior executive at a major consumer products multinational told the author: "We were one of the first American com-panies in Latin America. What can anyone tell us that our marketing people there don't already know?" Not many years passed before this manufacturing giant began to experience political difficulties from pressure groups and from the gov-ernment elite in one of its stronghold markets.

If smug ignorance and denial are an extreme corporate reaction, they are only the simplest defenses against innovation. A hard reality is that the introduction of new techniques of planning mechanisms needs the push of the chief executive officer (CEO) and a systematic effort toward promoting the service within the organization. Large corporations must *inform* line and staff at all levels of finance, marketing, and planning; *persuade* them of the utility of the service to assess and give perspective to their marketing overseas; and *enlist* the marketing people in the field in a reporting process that provides feedback and enhances their commitment to the process.

In the important watershed period of the 1980s, when the major economies were expanding and political risk analysis was beginning to emerge as a defined component of international strategic planning, corporate leaders never proceeded far beyond the introduction of the innovation. Maybe the line executives at the top just did not fully understand it or trust its value. Or else, it served as a plaything that embellished the corporate image, making the corporation look more like a government—a more sophisticated organism. Senior management often did not know whether to place the political risk assessment mechanism within "strategic planning" or "public affairs." The advantage of using the public affairs department was that "public affairs," so often thought of in terms of its propaganda function, could farm out the substantive political risk work to consultants (sometimes as far away from a corporate headquarters in the United States as Oxford University in England). As an outsider report, it would not be as binding psychologically on the potential end-user, who at a minimum could treat it as window dressing. The coordinator in charge of political risk assessment would assign and receive the weighty written report from the outside consultant, cover it with his own one-page memorandum and summary, and pass it to the requesting department and other interested parties. The uppermost echelon of management failed to help the analysts, inside and outside the corporate structure, develop a resonance with the varying needs of the planners at the corporate center and the marketing executives in the field. These individuals, the potential beneficiaries of such analytical work, often ignored it or gave up on it.

Glaring examples of bad, internal corporate flow concerning the political risk mechanism surfaced. In one instance, a subsidiary of a very large corporation contacted its people in the Washington, D.C., office of its parent to coordinate a meeting. A newly promoted staff officer, who just had visited the Washington office of the parent company, read an article in *Fortune Magazine* about political risk analysis. He liked the idea and hired one of the consultants whose picture was in the article. Phoning the Washington office to ask for meeting space, he was chagrined to be reminded that the major role of the international side of Washington operations was the implementation of *in-house* political risk analysis. He was abashed to find regular reports on his country of interest neatly filed not far from his desk in Houston and unopened!

And perhaps the greatest shortcoming of political risk analysis itself in the 1980s was its pretense of attempting to predict the future rather than getting down to the business of educating and sensitizing.

As international corporations and commercial banks were affected by events in Iran in 1978 and 1979, the need for a dimension of international strategic planning to cover political intelligence and analysis seemed urgent. Those banks concerned with default on their financing as well as with providing advice to their corporate clients took new stock of their planning apparatus. Several corporations with long gestation projects in third-world countries, such as oil companies and large-scale construction and engineering firms, found themselves hurt by the Iranian situation in particular. They could not even respond properly to the crisis at hand.

For example, one petroleum-related company with some ownership of equity interests in the Persian Gulf was actually in a quandary at its highest planning level about whether to withdraw while it had a chance to cut its losses. Pahlavi had fled at this stage of the revolutionary process, but this one company actually wondered how it might look if the shah were able to return through some magical intervention.

It did not trust the intelligence mechanism that it had in place.

Corporations were generally unprepared for such extreme political contingencies. Those with no involvement in the Persian Gulf region at that critical time suddenly realized that they had cause to be alarmed about exposures in apparently less predictable areas elsewhere in the third world.

What was to be done? Many of these international business organizations—particularly the banks—already had economists or entire economics departments studying the international business investment climate. Lending institutions, concerned with default on financing or servicing their clients properly already had kept a watchful eye on financial indicators. But by this time, economists who had been operating *in vacuo* or whose command of political and social conditions in a given country was limited to a quick phone call to a Washington office (normally simply a public affairs and lobbying operation) increasingly had come to realize that political or social factors were inseparable from macroeconomic and even nuts-and-bolts, commercial questions. The social upheaval in Iran now provided an impetus for more sophisticated intelligence gathering on the political side and for the recruitment of political scientists, usually with backgrounds in specific geographical areas.

But such attempts at restructuring at bottom were *reactive* and not properly integrated into the whole corporate strategic planning and marketing thrust. In one large manufacturing company, the economist, an "old hand" working out of headquarters in Ohio, now had a political scientist–counterpart working *alongside* him (if one considered "alongside" being in a Washington, D.C., office). The choice of locating the political analyst in the nation's capital is arguably correct in terms of closer access to certain sources of information. Nevertheless, being situated in a Washington office is not the same as being positioned at headquarters. The economist logically served as the fulcrum of the program, and yet he never became properly educated in international affairs. The political analyst was perceived to be out in left field. Contact between the two analysts was largely restricted to the use of a telephone, still a barrier in the age of communications. The operation failed within a few years.

One major bank, already heavily committed internationally before the events in Iran, proceeded to construct a full-scale political risk apparatus at its New York headquarters. Nevertheless, the economists and political analysts remained separate animals—in a somewhat happier state of cooperation than peaceful coexistence but distanced from one another both by the "traditional" parameters of their disciplines and their physical situations in the corporation. And if such a thing as cross-fertilization between the disciplines ever developed, the offspring appear to have been stillborn.

By the mid-1980s, in a recession that took a particular toll among developing countries in the third world, the international debt crisis emerged. Maxidevaluations, currency controls, import restrictions, delays in payment, expropriations of banks and bank-owned companies, and failure to meet repayments on private debt became commonplace from Latin America to Africa.

High-level management seemed inclined to swing back in the opposite direction. Some made statements to this effect: "What's needed these days is proper financial planning to alert us to the risks against which a corporation or bank really can protect itself!"

Some corporations actually fired their political analysts or cut back generally on their staffs of geographic area specialists. The rationale might have been as follows: What good are they anyway? Even if they can identify a political problem, there is little that we can do about it. The people in the field say that what we consider political problems are no worse than the ones that we face back in the United States. And, besides, how often do social revolutions like the one in Iran occur?

AN INTEGRATED APPROACH TO BUSINESS ENVIRONMENT ANALYSIS

The reality is that the disruptiveness of political and social problems is as persistent as the more identifiable financial clouds that we can sight on the horizon. (For example, there was a Russian-American businessman who smugly set up an office in Leningrad for his export-import business with the new "Soviet Union" after Gorbachev's fall. He supposed that he would continue to have the unobstructed opportunity of a pioneer to do business. A year later, the Commonwealth of Independent States [CIS] was reconstituted, and many of the rules of the larger political and foreign investment game were rewritten.)

If the corporate planner is wise enough to use the social sciences as a tool, he might also be well outfitted and know what to do with them. This facility can aid a corporation beyond the phase of planning to enter an unfamiliar market. These tools can extend beyond the initial plan to enter a new market and serve the enterprise as it positions itself in the host country and integrates it-self into the new environment.

At the early stage of planning, one might think it simpler to forecast major economic adjustments in a third-world country than to become entangled in a seemingly complex web of political and social factors that may or may not have direct bearing on a business enterprise. The potential economic risks are reasonably clear-cut and the statistical indicators are there for those who know where and how to look.

The less developed countries of the third world and the nascent free mar-ket systems in the former Soviet bloc of eastern and central Europe do emit easy-to-read economic warning signals. They are operating under the measur-able parameters of their own less developed economies and often under the constraints of the multilateral lending institutions.

Knowing with greater certainty that we might expect currency controls or major devaluations in a host country forces us to make choices, to keep options open in the negotiating process, and to leverage ourselves appropriately.

But the apparently greater predictability of macroeconomic outcomes within a defined time frame in a host country is not always free of significant political complications. Moreover, the relative precision of such forecasts provides real comfort only if one has yet to make a decision to enter that market. If a company is already is well entrenched, political resources and cultural-specific, political maneuvers—namely, political analysis carried to a more sophisticated level of adaptation to the environment—can once again be the only recourse for mini-mizing any negative ramifications of one's presence in the host country and set-ting the stage for future expansion.

In actuality, a balance must be struck in international strategic planning and country risk management; economics and politics comprise an integrated equa-tion for measuring the host country environmental risk and disincentives to for eign direct investment, sales, or extending loans. Political/social analysis, a re-view of business climate or commercial conditions, and financial/economic analysis all have their own sets of variables. *But they are interrelated.* (Some of the ways in which the three categories affect one another will be demonstrated later.)

An integrated approach protects against the cyclical emphasis that the tide of world events seems to cast on one set of factors over another. It reflects an un-derstanding of the persisting complexity of world conditions. We see that even as political uncertainties in the third world seem to diminish and economic risk be-comes more homogenized, challenges arise in the second world. From the devel-oping free market in eastern and central Europe to the politics of a fully emergent European Union (EU), new sorts of uncertainty are surfacing that demand an in-tertwined analytical approach.

It is important also to remember that the economic and political/social cate-gories each are inherently relevant to the bottom line.

In the political category, for example, it is not just a revolution or surge of nationalism that can threaten a company's assets. Terrorism, civil disorder of one sort or another, labor agitation, anti-Western scapegoating and foreign policy initiatives, populist trends, a breach in communications between the local level and the center, conflicts arising from tensions between parochial and modern institutions and attitudes, and now even how nations redefine their borders and institutional relationships—all these factors and more can have negative, and sometimes disastrous, consequences for a foreign business deal.

On the economic side of a good planning perspective, one must expect that hard currency reserves, debt service performance, inflation, growth in the gross domestic product, subsidized prices, and (now more than ever) the whole question of the interface between the public and private sectors are among a host of variables that can lead to outcomes that could swallow an investment.

Any of these conditions—political or economic—can have a direct impact on the personnel, installations, remittance of profits, and effective operations of an enterprise overseas. The very survival of a foreign company's investment in a host country can be in question. And some misjudgments can even leave a trail of legal and public relations troubles behind the actual surcease of the business enterprise.

Even if a political factor (such as erosion of middle-class support for the government) or an economic variable (such as pervasive subsidies) does not have an immediate or direct impact on doing a specific type of business in country X, an analysis of all the relevant conditions and a discussion of various ways in which they might combine to produce a worst-case scenario will influence the content and style of negotiation and will educate the operations and marketing executive in the field.

For current and future use, the operations executive will have in hand not just a set of possible "outcomes" for his or her country of responsibility, but a framework for unraveling events as they occur on the spot. The analysis will serve not just as a background study replete with projections but as a set of signposts and a game plan—a map for careful observation and planning. And taken a step or two farther, as the company settles into a new market, this early research can become a building block for the enterprise's becoming an integral part of the host country's broader business environment.

ENVIRONMENT ASSESSMENT: AN APPROACH TO WEIGHING POLITICAL AND ECONOMIC RISK AGAINST OPPORTUNITY

We take it as a matter of course in our home country that new business opportunities carry concomitant risks or drawbacks. In our business expansion domestically, we look for attendant risks in the nature of the deal itself or in circumstances directly related to the business at hand. They are usually visible or easily identifiable to us. We live with such risks or cope with them, usually as part of the transaction itself.

In strange cultural, legal, and institutional environments overseas, the astute businessperson can take much less for granted. Time and money can be lost in great measure just in pursuing and negotiating a given overseas opportunity. Before a company rushes headlong into what the pressured marketing executive perceives to be a golden opportunity, one must weigh this opportunity against the potential business environment problems in a host country and compare it to opportunities elsewhere.

This aspect of international strategic planning can be called "country environment assessment." What might hitherto have been cloaked in a veil of secrecy and dubbed "political risk analysis" can be explicated systematically and understood. If there is an art to relating political and economic variables to the impact on business, it is not a free-form art. Our analytical approach is offered as a way to cut through the headlines to the bottom line.

All new environments—from Tuscaloosa to Tanzania—have singular characteristics that might be problematic for a business deal. Of course, the developing countries are stranger to us. They have procedures for doing business that are either less formalized or less in conformance with our own customs and seem to be *less predictable*. Some of the administrative mechanisms that have evolved in third-world countries result directly from the lessons learned from dealing with the previously rapacious practices of foreign countries and corporations. When the foreign investor is poised to position himself in a new host country, he encounters logic of national self-interest in the web of apparent "obstacles" and regulations that appear at first glance. He will have to learn and live with them. But, more important, he will have to sensitize himself to the *underlying cultural, political and economic roots* in order to find acceptable ways to cut through them.

Given the target markets of foreign investors as they enter the twenty-first century, the variables discussed in this book have a distinct orientation toward the third world. We are inclined to agree, with Thabo Mbeke, the new president of a democratic South Africa, that this century may well "belong to the African nations." Economically, the developed world must expand in less developed markets since it will be playing a more level game worldwide.

This revised edition also considers the ways in which certain variables will apply to the changes of the 1990s in Europe, especially in the newly democratic countries. In the advanced markets of western Europe, the recent close cooperation among countries as an economic bloc would have astounded the idealists and integration theorists earlier in the twentieth century. U.S. and other corporations will have to alter business practices in the EU member states, logistically and otherwise. In central and eastern Europe, where formerly planned economies are giving way to free market adjustments and whole maps are being redrawn, political risk analysis will be as crucial as in some of the less developed areas of sub-Saharan Africa.

Some additional variables of political and social risk have been added to this new edition, notably, human rights conditions and rule of law. Pressures in a postindustrial world and the flow of global communications make it increasingly difficult for governments to abuse the human and physical landscapes with impunity. A new set of overarching values and norms of conduct for humanity, a human-centered ecology, and the ways in which mankind will be governed seems to be evolving. The information revolution subjects a nascent government, no matter how authoritarian and inward looking, to pressure from its people and from critical political factions as well as from the global community. The foreign enterprise must not only learn to neutralize itself against domestic and international pressures for the welfare of human beings and the environment, but also must develop *locally sensitive* plans for proactively harnessing the political forces that would move them in a progressive direction. It should consider working with activist political groups and influential members of the local elites to preempt the mounting of pressures against the enterprise and to create a positive role and image for itself.

When we talk about political risk in the environment of a relatively new and unfamiliar international market, we are referring generally to countries that are developing an institutionalized social and political infrastructure — nations in the making. Not all of these are emerging countries. The last decade of the twentieth century had an eerily mystical tone. The world moved forward while it concomitantly, sometimes in the course of the same transformation, resurrected nineteenth-century national entities and aspiring ethnopolitical local areas, from Chechnya in the Caucasus to Yugoslavia and the fledglings Bosnia and Kosovo, all with different territorial and economic visions of themselves. Some areas might be in the process of advancing even as they are engaged in a backward-looking process. The former communist and socialist systems that have remained intact, such as Poland and Hungary, have been struggling to build economies and political institutions based on the free market and democracy. And still other former bastions of Marxism-Leninism are threatened by a centripetal pull from local strongholds even as they seek to privatize much of their economic systems in the postmodern world.

Our discussion is not really directed at relatively stable areas like Australia or Canada. But if the very same variables were taken as a total inventory of environmental risks and disincentives in foreign host countries, some would be applicable in the more stable, developed world. Even in the United States, in times of uncertainty, we can see shadows of our less developed past when our industrial base was small and needed protection, when regions and states emotionally contested the federal governments, when regulations varied in a patently conflictual way from state to state, and when a trend toward secession threatened national unity. For the more developed and culturally familiar markets, the business planner will find our inventory useful and can selectively identify problems with a minimum of reinterpretation.

The factors in our analysis should be considered from two standpoints. First, does the problem exist or what is the *probability* that it will occur? Second, what would be the *impact* of such a problem or turn of events on foreign business in general or on a particular project? No matter how serious a problem, if it does not have a markedly negative impact on a particular business deal, the matter is not insurmountable.

Consciously or unconsciously, one necessarily ascribes weights to the problems in a given environment. Although the quantification of cross-cultural scenarios can lead to oversimplification and can block the way to substantive understanding of what is going on in a country, the use of numbers as a means of manipulating the user's attention is not discouraged.

If a country environment analysis is done in a comprehensive and structured manner, it can be useful to attach numerical ratings to *probability* and *impact* and then add a further weighting to each of the variables under consideration. This is not really a quantitative adaptation of the variables, but rather a deliberate manipulation to reflect the analyst's subjective judgment. It might help the user and decision maker at different levels to sharpen his or her focus and to generate questions of his or her own.

In the pages that follow, the reader will be guided through a host of factors—social and cultural, political, economic, and financial—that historically have affected the environment for international investment and trade. Included are myriad examples and case illustrations that can provide a framework for analysis—a prism through which the reader will be able to view events and situations as they unfold with the undertaking of fresh explorations of unfamiliar markets.

I

Assessing Domestic Conditions in the Host Country: Political, Social, and Economic

Assessing Domestic Political Conditions: An Inventory of Variables

LEADERSHIP SUCCESSION

In all countries, but particularly those with authoritarian political systems, leadership succession can be a critical political problem. It becomes a political risk to the foreign business entity when procedures for a smooth transition of political leadership have not been constitutionally established or have not gained legitimacy among the elite (particularly in some third-world countries where the masses are relatively naive politically) or among the people at large.

A leadership succession crisis, generated by an uncharted change in leaders, causes uncertainty and turbulence at different levels of society and can be disruptive to business as usual. In countries where military governments actually have overturned an established civilian political process through a coercive takeover and maintain their rule by means of top-down controls, it becomes imperative that a normal electoral process be restored in a reasonable amount of time. Some systems do not evolve through this process in a unilinear manner.

Look, for example, at Pakistan's return from military dictatorship to democracy and its cycle back to military government. In its development, Pakistan has been fraught with ideological extremes and fears that it must not veer from a pragmatic path. As the projected elections of 1985 approached, the question then was whether President Zia ul-Haq, who had seized power from a socialist-populist government in a military coup, would be able to manage local and national elections on a nonparty basis (the intention being to exclude the PPP, the left-leaning followers of former president Zulfikar Ali Bhutto who had been executed) and to integrate an indirect military control into grassroots civilian government. If after seven years Zia could not bring off the promised election successfully, his own staying power might be jeopardized. And if he did succeed, lesser followers still could be swept away!

As it happened, the reemergence of the electoral process in Pakistan broke the unsteady grip of the military. The horse got away from the soldier, and a decade passed before the military returned in full force in 1999.

This pattern of military intervention demonstrates a lack of trust in civil government to withstand violent disorder and crisis. By the late 1990s, the military had come to reassert itself over the Kargil bus ride meeting between India's Atal Behari Vajpayjee and Pakistan's Mian Mohammad Nawaz Sharif. Pakistan had been infiltrating troops disguised as civilians into Kashmir, and a dangerous conflagration broke out between troops of the both countries. India was on the verge of real war, and Sharif withdrew the troops. The military dissolved parliament and had him removed. In 1999, under circumstances of a deteriorating economy and troubled by the host of parties intruding into the electoral process, the moderate, highly professional General Pervaiz Musharraf moved against Sharif a second time in a direct coup.

The bloodless removal and house arrest of Prime Minister Sharif in part fits a trend in postindependence Pakistan of looking to military authority as a viable temporary alternative to extremism, factionalism, and social disorder. Military government has tended to arise in recent times as a vaccine against anticipated ideological government or the onslaught of political disorder that comes from mismanagement and abuses of power by the elected government. As the democratic process began to open after General Zia's attempt in the early 1980s to become the legitimately elected leader, a fear lingered over the disorder that political parties and competing ideologies might create. Amendment Eight, the product of Zia's last days, allowed the president to dissolve parliament and to ban political parties; the military could not be penalized for actions carried out during a state of emergency. The military, fundamentally pragmatic and a vanguard of technological modernization, entered the scene as a bulwark against Islamist ascendancy, protecting against extremism, instability, and unpredictability in the political process and dealing with a mismanaged and sluggish bureaucracy in key departments like Water Conservancy. But simultaneously its setting aside of civilian government has jeopardized the credibility of democratic institutions. However justifiable in terms of the economic situation or maintaining security against India, this usurpation of civilian power throws the whole political system into question.

In the longer term, an unimpeded evolution of participatory democracy in Pakistan could offer an institutionalized stability that promises to be more enduring than the concentration of power in the most competent autocratic leader. The reality is that civilian successors to an undemocratic, business-like military government might fall short of the idealized picture of acting swiftly in the national interest, but they have been *elected by the people through constitutional means*. Continued reliance on the intervention of the military—even in dire economic crisis—to ensure government action and social order introduces an uncertainty into the equation that jeopardizes the flow of business as usual. Even the foreign enterprise can suffer if such military intervention puts Western democratic governments on edge.

If fractious and unyielding political parties are to survive in an institutionalized civilian electoral process, future civilian leadership must strive for some consensus. It is a matter of self-interest. Extreme ideologies and points of view will be buffeted in the course of political debate over time by other interests and diluted by the practical need to rule. Through increasing consensus, the Pakistanis will achieve a more viable democratic process and a successful output in coping with the exigencies of ruling a modern country. A shared commitment to the system (particularly from the interest groups and political parties of the middle class) contributes to the prospect of social stability and ensures certain continuity at the level of government where doing business usually matters.

After the Departure of a Charismatic Leader

In cases where the departed leader has established himself as a result of his leadership in a movement or national liberation, and when his appeal to the people is founded on personal charisma, the lack of institutionalized procedures for succession assumes an even greater importance. In parts of Africa or Asia, the death of an individual who guided a country through independence and into modernity would leave a leadership vacuum in its wake. With the leader of independence removed from the scene, who could possibly measure up as a successor even if designated by the preeminent predecessor? Institutional procedures for selecting a successor would be too new and untried to be trusted easily by the factions and groups with power and influence.

People who have identified closely with a bigger-than-life national leader often have been susceptible to a disorienting identity crisis. The death knell of a magically potent leader can resound at the local levels of control and administration. Inhabitants of a newly emerging nation often tend to lose their focus on modern administrative structures and personnel and fall back on tribal or traditional identities. They stop trusting modern ways and revert to the traditional. Or they might become so psychologically disoriented and confused about the direction of things as to resort to anarchic behavior or emigration. In Kenya, Jomo Kenyatta's successor, Daniel Arap Moi, was threatened in his first years with a raft of assassination attempts. He managed to hold onto power through the exercise of increasingly conspicuous repression (so much repression that it became a signature of his regime). Ghana's civilian rule has been unsuccessful since the death of Kwame Nkrumah. It has been followed by one coup after another.

In Africa today, old independence leaders like the social democrat Julius Nyerere of Tanzania and Marxist-Leninist one-party leader Robert Mugabe of Zimbabwe, are among the few "fathers of the revolution" still to be in power. When

such leaders depart, their symbols and doctrinal writings alone are often insuffi-
cient to see the country through the transitional period in an orderly manner. In
Indonesia, the late President Sukarno's "Five People's Principles" (Pantja Cila)
rang hollow when sounded by an elitist soldier republic; in Burma (now called
Myanmar), the departed independence leader U Nu, once out of the way, elicited
a contemptuous response from a new generation of intellectuals and students; and
today in Turkey Kemal Atatürk's principles of secularism, nationalism, and modernization exist in tension with traditional institutional resistances in society and
the resurgence of Islam. For the thinkers and would-be civilian leaders of today,
Nu's "Burmese Way to Socialism" seems not only outmoded but also hypocritical when it is invoked by a seemingly ruthless, corrupt, and unreasoning military
regime. In Myanmar (Burma), a nascent popular rebellion has been simmering
while a newly emergent articulator of the people's interest—a woman and a poet,
a new charismatic force and a democrat—agitates quietly under the eye of the
military and the police.

A corollary to the question of a succession after the death or departure of an
important leader (one who has a broad following and either a mesmerizing effect
or a terrorizing hold on his people) is the *power vacuum* that his absence creates.
What other leader has the strength and can seem to tower high enough to take his
place and to command the loyalty of a broad constituency?

For example, the mere withdrawal of Burma's powerful postindependence
leader Ne Win to a behind-the-scenes role left the chairman of the ruling committee to face the 1990s with tenuous last resort to bribery and coercion. Ne Win
had shunted aside his more able successors. The new leadership's power base in
an international era of democratizing trends is the military alone, and political
power in that camp most certainly will grow out of the biggest gun! When excluding from an arbitrary demonetarization even the military elite (removing and
not replacing certain denominations of currency without notice, as in the early
1990s), the man on the platform easily can lose his footing.

The power vacuum created by the absence of strong and viable leadership can
lead to one military takeover after another in the fashion of musical chairs. And
even with the onset of civilian rule, if an election is won by a weak compromise
candidate who is unable to reverse an economic decline or build a base of lasting
support, the military conceivably will intervene again. Worse still for an investor,
a sustained power vacuum can reinforce the generativity of an antisystemic,
grassroots movement that might entirely rewrite the rules of the game. Of course,
such an outcome is not necessarily undesirable unless a foreign investor already
is in the game!

In very hierarchical social systems from Asia to Mexico, even *local leadership*
becomes a factor in stability and can be of concern to a foreign investor. In such
cases, the people's real interaction with formal government occurs at a village
or county level, and their perception of formal state authority and the political
system's intervention is shaped at the bottom of a pyramid. The foreign busi-

nessperson too must deal with these local-level leaders, whether for special permits or licenses or for the negotiation and implementation of a contract.

During the early Cultural Revolution in the People's Republic of China in the late 1960s, the Western business presence was minimal. But let us look at what happened when local party leaders were discredited in China at the height of the Great Proletarian Cultural Revolution. People were thrown into a state of chaos. With social uncertainty, a potential for disorder, and no certain locus of decision making at the grassroots, business undertakings of any sort became paralyzed. The social trauma in China was so great that in the south the Cultural Revolution precipitated a wave of illegal emigration to Hong Kong. Such migrations traditionally had been more symptomatic of economic disaster and famine. The apotheosis during the Cultural Revolution period of Chairman Mao Zedong (alternative spelling Mao Tse-tung) might have been an attempt to steady and unify society by lifting the locus of all authority to the heavens. (Staring at a god-like statue of himself in Tiananmen Square, Mao told American journalist Edgar Snow that he felt like a Buddhist monk in the rain without an umbrella.)

The Bottom Line

Change of any sort naturally elicits anxiety, but leadership change in a less developed country is not necessarily cause for alarm. *On the contrary, some types of radical change in leadership at the top do not represent crises at all.* In some Latin American countries, for example, a coup d'état, or golpe, against an apparently legitimate government is not necessarily a departure from normality in the context of the country's historical political culture. *In such cases, there can be stability in instability!*

The international planner must focus on impact. What effect would a succession crisis have on the type of foreign business in question? Perhaps none if the project is not closely linked to the person of a departed leader. But consider that major construction projects undertaken in Ghana to enhance Nkrumah's prestige were particularly vulnerable after his ouster. In Indonesia, the pet developmental projects of Suharto's cabinet ministers could also be shelved with the advent of a new government. Interim President B. J. Habibie's Batam Island project, which the former minister of science and technology once promoted to foreign investors as a "possible alternative to Singapore," might even give way to other island options once considered—along with Batam—as good ground for a foreign development zone.

Uncertainty in Thailand

The impact on foreign investment can be more generalized if an uncertain, incoming regime defends itself against international criticism by overreacting nationalistically or blames an economic decline on the nature of the foreign business presence. In Thailand in 1992, a quasi-military government with civilian trappings uncomfortably tried to fill an immediate power vacuum by displacing a popularly elected, if truly questionable, president-elect with a senior military person. A longer-term power vacuum in the real sense had existed since well before the military's coup against the elected government in February 1991.

The existence of a government, five of whose parties in parliament are promilitary and whose ultimate authority rests with the military, might not have appeared to have major repercussions for foreign investment. After all, most military-backed governments tend to be rather conservative and favor private enterprise, and Thailand's military is no exception.

But in 1992, the military came out from behind the scenes. The duly elected, civilian prime minister with an apparently drug-tainted background, was pushed aside for a military candidate, General Suchinda Krapayoon. The George Bush administration supported his selection over the duly elected candidate. Discouraged by the illegitimacy of the government and so many years of de facto military government, the students within months took to the streets. Thailand has a long history of student protest. The draconian suppression of this mass unrest by the military has not necessarily put out the fire. Students in Thailand want more, and they want revenge for the brutality of the military.

The foreign investment community must now ask itself: Will business proceed as normal with the government's resignation and a "political cease fire" negotiated by the king? Will the students and intellectual elite accept a compromise government in which the pivotal locus of real power is still the military and promilitary parties in parliament? Is the king enough of a living legitimating symbol to see Thailand through to a sort of compromise civilian government? Will an accommodation truly satisfy the parties who would take to the street and those who would bash their heads? As the King of Siam declared in the celebrated musical, *The King and I*: 'Tis a puzzlement!

The major consideration for all businesspersons now, Thai and American, witnessing a possible strengthening of parliamentary government, is whether the rules of the game for doing business might change. Nothing so radical would be either likely or in anyone's best interests. Be careful, however, of a latent tendency even among the military (Suchinda Krapayoon took a rhetorical swipe at the Bush administration) to scapegoat U.S. investors in the face of continued domestic economic and social frustrations. All other things being equal, a military-civilian condominium of interests could be expected to tow the line, that is to say, the bottom line.

Venezuela and Peru: Populist Elements of the Military

It should not be taken for granted that the military as an interest group will *always* be favorably inclined toward an unfettered free market and will encourage foreign investment. In some cases, a movement within the military can react nationalistically against what it perceives to be a civilian government's betrayal of the expectations of the people. A subjective frustration of upward mobility in the ranks can combine with populist sentiment to propel a segment of the armed forces against an elected government.

The attempted coup against President Carlos Andres Pérez of Venezuela in 1992 is a good example. Comprised of middle-rank and second-rung officers and led by a thirty-seven-year-old lieutenant colonel who previously had been an instructor at Venezuela's military academy, the uprising in the army hoped to win the support of students, intellectuals, workers, and the "progressive" church. Among its apparent objectives: the reversal of the Pérez government's removal of restrictions on the free market and Pérez's introduction of austerity measures that had left more than half the population with less than one daily meal.

A relatively anonymous army officer perhaps had jumped the gun by surrounding the president's residence early one morning in 1990 and had elicited incredulous grins from foreign political advisors who supposed that Pérez was the candidate of, and for, the people.

When Pérez was later impeached for misappropriation of funds and other charges of corruption, Colonel Hugo Chavez entered the limelight and became the new people's choice. By 1998, Chavez was moved from imprisonment for his role in the coup to the presidency and Casa Rosada, the Venezuelan counterpart of our White House. Freely elected on a platform of waging a "peaceful revolution," Chavez continued to be committed to a populist orientation. He certainly did not seem to be the political chameleon that Pérez had become. From a relatively poor middle-class background, he railed persuasively against the old oligarchy and elites, referring to them as "squealing pigs." The leader of a new political force, he made a constitutionally unprecedented bid for reelection when his term expired, thereby broadening the base of the political system beyond the predictable alternation of the two major traditional political parties in power. The extension of his tenure beyond this term, as well as some adjustments in his constitutional reform, has been intended to strengthen the presidency.

As a former soldier, will Chavez proceed too far in restoring an authoritarian quality to the civilian process? Already his popularly approved Constitutional Charter, allowing the president to succeed himself (not permitted in the 1961 constitution), strengthens the central executive against the states and municipalities and permits military intervention in "emergency" situations. This explicit revision, which invites more top-down control and intervention, arguably conforms more closely to the underlying Venezuelan political culture. After Chavez, Venezuelan voters should have a broader range of choices because an "outsider" has jostled the political system and the political base has been broadened.

Usually, the military acts as a modernizing force in developing countries. But some elements of the military inherently can be prejudiced against industrialization and the foreign investment that has provided its impetus. The foreign businessperson should make a distinction between Chavez's "peaceful revolution" (an assault yet to occur against the domestic concentration of Venezuela's wealth in an elite) and any efforts to impede the progress of foreign investment. The Chavez administration has been in office a while, has developed a consensus for governing, and has made its compromises. Thus far, it has succeeded on the strength of its cries against corruption. The combination of zealous rhetoric and pragmatic compromise does not forebode the irrational rejection of industrialization and modernization, but rather suggests a more considered and balanced one! This is not a real revolution. Not using force, it has to bend! The populist orientation of the regime—mostly talk until now—might be expected to be further tempered by compromise to maintain a certain economic stability and avoid undermining international confidence and broadening a political constituency for reelection. Even Chavez's own military seems to be chafing against budgetary cuts in military spending and the colonel's proclivity to make the army more of a political instrument for social services than a professional instrument of defense.

However, as the next term advances and Chavez's "honeymoon" comes to an end, the president will need to leave his imprint and will not want too many detractors. The foreign investor might have to reposition himself, develop new political ties, and undertake a more people-oriented development strategy. A precipitate panic reaction at this time—joining the stampede of the many investors who might run away or stay away—is unwarranted and could be self-destructive.

In Peru, to take another example, a sizable portion of the armed forces have poor and rural backgrounds and have risen through the ranks while retaining their ties to their roots. They have also been positioned against a Marxist-Leninist guerrilla opposition to the status quo. If this segment of the armed forces (particularly the navy) were to assume power, prejudice might be translated into policy and further complicate an already troublesome situation for foreign investors in that country.

Burma: When the Military Government Hangs on by Its Teeth

When the military eschews the political process as in Burma and rules unreasonably through a combination of bark, bite, and bribery, it is not likely to hold together a country that is fraught with ethnic divisions and liberation struggles. A central government can stay in place for a time if it has the wherewithal to intimidate and run its small domain like a prison. But absent a stable social environment, how can business be carried on as usual?

In all cases involving leadership succession problems, the strategic planner must ask: Are efforts being made in a potential host country to groom successors? Autocratic rulers might seem to want to cultivate protégés, but they also apparently have singular difficulty in reconciling themselves to their own political mortality and in delegating power to others. It often happens that if an emerging figure in the political elite becomes too popular or appears to be developing his own constituency, he is consigned to obscurity. Former president Suharto of Indonesia fashioned a pattern of demoting ministers of state who become too popular. Former president Ahmadou Ahidjo of Cameroon and Ne Win of Burma each have found it difficult to release the grip of power once a successor has assumed office. Ahidjo actually attempted coups against his overly assertive successor Paul Biya and brought the country to the brink of civil war.

Another question to ask: If there is a succession struggle, are some factions better positioned than others? In Indonesia, for example, where interpersonal relations and cross-cutting alliances are so important, it is crucial to tie into the right political group, directly or indirectly, through an informal network of friends and acquaintances. If the Indonesians with whom one worked closely were linked to a high-profile group that was identified with the corrupt Suharto leadership, such a position, once advantageous in the short term, might turn out to be a liability under the Islamist Abdulrahhman Wahid and his coalition. At least it is likely to leave the foreign business entity subject to new political manipulations. An alignment with Indonesians whose political linkages have been middle-of-the-road or adaptable would continue to be more sensible, especially if reform leads to further erosion of the military's behind-the-scenes influence. The well-placed investor is advised to study the connections interpersonally of his Indonesian business associates and attempt an educated balancing act, perhaps adding new elements to his local company leadership composition.

A final problem for the corporate strategist is to examine the evolving attitudes and policies of the key political protagonists as they pertain to foreign investment and trade in the appropriate product or service area. The planning group in a corporation must also gauge the extent to which a consensus has developed for that particular perspective. In other words, after the factions that are apt to come to power are identified and their positions with regard to foreign investment in general and the enterprise in question are considered, the support of their power base must be assayed. (What cannot be learned through published materials can often be obtained through personal interviews and the gossipy inquiries of local executives.)

Turkey As a Case of Successful Transition

In Turkey, the military (which had come to power during the violence of the 1970s) approved and supported the reconstruction of a constitutional civilian government through the election of November 6, 1983. It was anticipated that the well-positioned Motherland Party's candidate Turgut Ozal would be chosen prime minister. The military junta, or National Security Council, resigned their commissions and remained as a governing advisory council under President (formerly general) Kenan Evren.

The potential for a tug of war between the two ruling bodies still exists. The military is more bureaucratic and interventionist, yet never evidenced a firm commitment to induce foreign businesspeople to invest. The paucity of investment before the new political system was returned to civilian rule reflects an enduring suspicion on the part of foreign investors that they would encounter the same bureaucratic hostility as in the past toward foreign capital. Foreign businesspeople too have had a memory of the ability of political forces to arouse an apparently natural antagonism toward outsiders among the people.

But in 1983, Turgut Özal, who already was recognized for his open-door economic policy and his creation of a Foreign Investment Department when he was serving as deputy prime minister under the military, initiated policies favorable to Western business and worked toward privatization and building a consensus among his constituency for liberal policies toward foreign investment. The key question was not whether the former International Monetary Fund (IMF) officer would approve of investment but whether he would encounter resistances along the way. At bottom, would he be able to survive the rocky road of leadership transition and be able to build legitimacy for the new government without watering down his policies? He and Evren had long political lives, but their reformist policies soon ran afoul of conservative forces. Özal capitulated. Legitimacy was constructed at the expense of much improvement in foreign investment and the structure of the economy.

In the next few years, the Turkish nation-state is poised for some further progress. Civilian government has remained intact and withstood the assault of militant Islam and a virulent nationwide upsurge in the Kurdish movement to secede. In 1994, a military-supported coalition government kept an Islamist party's rule at bay. In the late 1990s, an effective military and police apparatus, perhaps receiving international support, was able to capture the dynamic Kurdish militant leader Ocalan and at least temporarily decapitate a movement that threatened the nation. A series of cataclysmic earthquakes rocked the country in 1999 and left a wake of devastation so horrible that many superstitious Turks saw them as a heavenly sign of the decline in the legitimacy of the system. But the international reaction was so sympathetic that Turkey's economy, already ailing, could rebound somewhat and perhaps even benefit from the experience. On the diplomatic front, Greece and other neighboring countries have become friendlier, and Turkey is a little closer to being admitted to the European Union. The average Turk in the street seldom agrees with this optimistic appraisal, superstitiously commenting, "M'shallah" (loosely translated, "If it happens, it happens").

A leadership succession crisis that is politically and socially destabilizing often creates a mood of pervasive uncertainty. This dread and confusion also can presage such consequences as the undermining of one's enterprise. In the panicky effort to build some consensus, an emerging leadership might engage in nationalization and expropriation of certain companies, or during economic hardship, opt to default on private and public debts.

Such a political crisis often does not just mean the absence of successors but the failure to choose successors in an acceptable way. When local or national leadership fails to replace itself in a manner that is perceived as inclusive and procedurally proper, the popular reaction can impede business as usual and jeopardize company expatriate personnel living in the host country.

A company's own installations, operations, and personnel certainly are at risk of suffering the consequences of anomic civil disorder and chaos among a dissatisfied and frustrated people. Witness the case of mob violence in India by the Sikhs, who have been on the rise ever since the assassination of Indira Gandhi and, later, her son Rajiv. The fact that in recent years elections have turned into scenes of chaos and killing does not attest to confidence either in existing leadership (at the national level and in certain localities) or the method of renewal and election of the political elite.

The awareness that elite factions are competing for the control of the country can also lead to an unreasonable assertiveness on the part of interest groups, including the staging of widespread strikes.

And in a demonstration of the interrelatedness of politics and economics, a political leadership crisis can also cause a lack of confidence among the people that extends to a mass run on banks and capital flight. Concomitant currency controls would paralyze a foreign company's operations!

The question of leadership succession crisis usually has applied to third-world countries where real leadership has been embodied in one person with whom the people have come to identify closely, where there are no established procedures for leadership transition, or where such procedures have not obtained sufficient legitimacy to ward off an interloper. Now, the emergence of a new political complexion and the creation of new nation-states in the former Soviet Union and Eastern Europe, poses an even greater challenge to the business planner as institutions are changed and rules are rewritten.

Applied to the More or Less Developed World: Spain as a Case of Political Modernization

In a still more general sense, the "leadership succession" problem also can be applied to analysis of the more routine processes of change in leadership or party administration in relatively developed countries. Spain is an interesting case study.

Since the death of Francisco Franco in November 1975, Spain has developed into a democracy—in form, a constitutional monarchy. Although Spain has withstood coup attempts by two groups within the military and security forces, the country's democratic institutions are still fragile and have not really gained grounding *in history*. It may be too early to be sure about the steadfastness of democratic institutions in Spain and its peoples' (particularly the military's) commitment to them. Felipe González's socialist party (PSOE) had a strong popular base in the 1980s and the Cortes (parliament) has been fundamentally centrist. The fascists per se have a constituency of only about one percent of the voting public; the communists (PCE) have only a handful of seats in the Cortes. Therefore, the threat from either the left or the extreme far right has been negligible.

A critical problem is that the earlier, and almost charismatic, appeal of González wore thin as a result of economic hardship and an austerity program, the party's veering to a more economically conservative hue, and conspicuous corruption—scandal after scandal—in the upper echelon of party and government. Given González's aloofness when confronted with apparent stagnation and despair, the socialists lost their majority the end of the 1980s.

At that time, the situation looked this way to us. If an economically desperate situation had called for an immediate proactive agenda for the people, or if the government were to become bogged down in inertia with right-center or left-center parties unable to form a coalition to unseat González, the military might intervene "for the sake of the country." In another scenario, if Prime Minister González were to have been assassinated, the military certainly might have taken over. González's persona had come to symbolize post-Franco democracy in Spain.

The actual outcome, the election of a right-wing candidate by a narrow margin who was forced to align his party with the regional Catalan Party, did not look promising but at least represented electoral change. What happened was that the government had an opportunity to build a consensus, renew itself, and actually increase its legitimacy. The Jose Marie Aznar government put the economy on a sounder footing and created two million jobs. In elections in 2000, Prime Minister Aznar's party was reelected by a large margin and his now centrist policies have a popular mandate. The era of the military intervention and the charismatic dictator would seem to have passed in Spain but it still needs to be considered as a possible scenario.

A short time ago, before the experience of the threat to Pérez in Venezuela in 1992, such scenarios as the military's return from their barracks would have been considered unlikely even in a young democracy like Spain. Yet, in reality, if no coalition had developed between left center or right center or between the remnants of the old centrist UCD and the right-wing Popular Alliance, the system would have atrophied and left a vacuum.

Thus, in Spain a matter of constitutional transition could have become constitutional crisis if no real transition had taken place. And this sort of crisis in the best of circumstances, where all viable factions favor foreign investment to a greater or lesser extent, still would have had an indirect bearing on the psychological environment for the foreign business entity.

CRISIS OF LEGITIMACY OF A REGIME

A regime's legitimacy is as important symbolically as the gold at Fort Knox. It represents the trust or social contract between a political system and the people under its administration.

The previously discussed leadership succession question revolves about the uncertainty of the process of change from one leadership to another. But a legitimacy crisis will last longer and metastasize like a cancer. It occurs when the very form, procedures, and institutions of government fail to establish credibility among the people or lose that trust after protracted failure to perform the functions expected of them.

Underlying the regime's *raison d'être* is frequently a constitution or an ideology or set of national principles—a promise to deliver. These must stand the test of time and serve as the framework for concrete development. In a simple metaphor, to maintain itself effectively over time, a political system must build up a reserve of credit. This is accomplished through outputs (policy and legislation) that serve the aggregate needs of society and justify the continued existence of a regime even in the face of adversity. When the regime discredits itself, it draws down on the reserve. If the process of erosion continues unredeemed, the whole system falls into jeopardy and is vulnerable to challenge.

The legitimacy of a system is difficult to gauge because the limits of tolerance of leadership abuse vary from country to country. Given the difficulty in measuring the erosion of a political regime's legitimacy (sometimes, in making a concrete case for it cross-culturally), it is extremely difficult to convince senior management to limit or withdraw an investment from a host country or even to pay attention to what is happening. This was the author's experience when a professional colleague tried to convince his own company to pull out of Iran even as Mohammad Reza Pahlavi's regime was teetering on the front pages.

Tunisia as a Case

Tunisia illustrates how legitimacy can come to constitute a problem. Although the December 1983–January 1984 bread riots raised the question of leadership succession in that country and indeed served as one catalyst for change, it was really the ongoing erosion of legitimacy of the Bourguiba government that led to an intervention. Habib Bourguiba, the nation's independence leader since 1957, had enjoyed a nearly charismatic hold on his people in earlier days. As he became progressively more senile with illness and began to lose credibility before his people, the grace he enjoyed began to lose its gloss. Mme. Bourguiba's meddling in "palace politics" with the prime minister, other cabinet ministers, and the head of the ruling Destourian Party shamed the office and the image of the republic; the government's ineptness in economic management and in implementing equitable, or at least politically clever, austerity measures had triggered riots; the largest trade union increasingly was becoming the handmaiden of the Bourguiba regime; and the nation's party system had been undermined by the apparent rigging of the election of 1981. By 1986, when I first examined political risk in Tunisia, I predicted either a grassroots upheaval led by some militant Islamic movement or, more likely, a top-down military coup.

What happened was that Bourguiba sought to deal with a severe challenge from Islamic militants who were critical of the regime by making martyrs out of their leaders. He opted not to heed advice that he ought to use alternate methods to control the Islamic clergy. Instead of handling them with adroitness, he was obdurately heavy-handed. Pending the threat of an upheaval, State Minister of the Interior Ben Ali took the helm.

The 1987 takeover was constitutional; the cabinet was exercising its right to intercede should the president's health prevent him from competent leadership. But what happened never could have occurred during the first few decades of Bourguiba's charmed, authoritarian presidency.

Peru: The Military as an Interim Stabilizer

Particularly in an era of trumpeting "democratizing" trends worldwide, the legitimacy of a so-called civil government can be tricky to define. Constitutional democrats in more developed societies often hasten with ideological fervor to apply norms and value judgments that might not fit some political cultures or societies at their particular stages of modernization. When President Alberto Keinya Fujimori of Peru dissolved parliament with the backing of the military, his avowed purpose was to cope with a host of paralyzing problems. These included corruption, a system of courts that had been intimidated and bribed not to mete justice to drug traffickers, and the challenge of an ominous guerrilla organization Sendero Luminoso (Shining Path). The latter had grown in size, and the scope of its terrorist activities now extended to the deliberate taking of lives, including those of foreign businesspersons.

The U.S. government and others were quick to condemn as a coup an executive action that exercised the power of the military. International democrats to the north argued that "dictatorial" intervention in parliamentary government would be self-defeating and would undermine the legitimate civilian process of rule and transition of power. The foreign investor found himself with as much to fear from international pressures and sanctions as from the obvious edginess in the host country (already in a state of crisis).

Arguably, a system's legitimacy ought to be culturally determined. Seventy percent of Peruvians surveyed approved of Fujimori's suspension of rules and freedoms as an alternative to uncontrollable social violence, lack of security, and hampered domestic travel. Peru's regional neighbors, like Colombia and Argentina, had experienced an intolerable sort of chaos in earlier times.

Since Fujimori's seemingly precipitate, military-backed action in 1992, Peru's Sendero Luminoso has largely been incapacitated, its remnants driven to isolated areas of the countryside; the economic infrastructure has been strengthened; and the political system is moving forward and *incrementally* establishing legitimacy for the civilian parliamentary process.

Turkey: Military as Cushion for Sustaining Legitimacy

Military intervention can be brazen in disrupting the civil process to suppress social disorder, and yet it also is capable in certain political cultures of resisting the giddy temptation to grasp political power. Moreover, it can go a distance farther by encouraging the country's evolution into a sounder, institutionalized democracy. In southern Europe, a successful democracy in Turkey reemerged gradually and steadily from naked military intervention. The founder of the modern Turkish state, Kemal Atatürk, had imposed in the 1920s an ideology of nationalism, secularism, and democracy that by the 1970s and 1980s ran up against the resistance of traditional institutions and attitudes, ethnic loyalties, and customs and militant Islam. For a time, the general consensus seemed to favor military suppression of the uncontrollable social and political violence in the streets. The extreme left and right parties got people out in the streets to create disorder, and the civilian government demonstrated its ineptness. It was paralyzed when it came to policing mob violence or enacting appropriate measures in economic crisis.

The military leadership's reaction was first to assume the mantle of the presidency, while allowing the civilian prime minister to rule under their aegis and to prepare a new constitution. The man who acceded to the prime ministership was a trusted official from the last government and well respected.

The Turkish military consistently has been highly professional and secular, and committed to the concept of Atatürk's revolution to produce a modern state. It effectively orchestrated the return to civilian rule. In the face of economic crisis and the threat of Islamic rule undermining the state's secular orientation, the military wielded its influence again in 1994 but avoided a coup and put in place a coalition civilian government.

The military can intervene in crisis, but it is not disposed to construct a new polity. The Turkish civilian government's major failure since the first quarter of the twentieth century has been its lack of sustained ability fully to develop Atatürk's promise of national unity and a modern political and economic state. Nationalism is a dangerous ideological appeal. Culturally, the people seem to long for the authority that a parliamentary system rarely provides. Economically, parliamentary government has made little headway since the military encouraged Prime Minister Turgut Özal in 1982 to proceed with a program of privatization and thereby attract more foreign investment. Investment from overseas slowed incrementally until Özal's death in 1993. With only $12 million in foreign investment as it entered the millennium, Turkey must meet the challenge to modernize or get washed over like its bygone cities.

Time and tide are some justification for civilian democratic government to persist in Turkey. Perhaps, Turkey now sees an opportunity to turn its earth-moving natural disasters to an advantage and rally international support to propel it forward. The challenge to the legitimacy of the government lies in incorporating key strains of the Turkish political culture—respect for authority and devout belief in Islam—into its political process and spiritual ethos.

Colombia: A Case of Questionable Legitimacy

In Colombia, the key issue in past years has seemed to be the political system's legitimacy. American businesspeople, whom the author interviewed in summer 1984, were sure that they understood the situation because they had been posted in the capital city and could observe daily events. A representative of the U.S. Chamber of Commerce there argued that investment conditions could not be better because the economy seemed to be on a slight upswing (he had been charting long-term trends), an *anticipated* maxidevaluation had not taken place and did not seem imminent, and the recently elected government seemed to be resolving a long-standing and widespread problem of guerrilla terrorism.

During the years that followed, these American expatriate commentators from Bogotá could not have been proved more mistaken. Their perspective was based on their proximity to separate events (they looked at the parts rather than the whole) and a natural bias that stemmed from the vested interests of the marketing executive. Guerrilla violence in Colombia increased, and the country's president announced that the treasury was on the verge of bankruptcy. For the shorter-term businessperson, the psychological uncertainty alone of working in a state of crisis was unnerving.

The erosion of the government's legitimacy increased. The country continued to be ruled by a tight oligarchy and the guerrillas and bandits remained unbeaten in spite of the best efforts of the military. Voter turnout for intervening presidential elections has been at about the 50 percent level and possibly lower. This apathy has been compounded by the system's incapacity for some time to deal with worsening general economic and social conditions. It has seemed to reflect alienation and has gnawed away at the legitimacy of political institutions. Pervasiveness of political and social corruption from an illegal drug trade (narcotics are Colombia's biggest export), as well as the government's ambivalence over suppressing it, have served to discredit the political parties, state bureaucracy, legislature, and the judicial branch. The possibility of a creeping military, or military-backed takeover looms in the foreground if the soldiers are not kept happy.

Foreign business interests suffer in the process, but the worst political scenarios for outsiders concerned with the country's stability have never unraveled. Instead, the ubiquity of the drug influence has led to the evolution of a strange mutation, a new sort of outlaw republic or narcocracy. The infusion of hard currency from narcotics into the Colombian economy appeared to be almost regenerative. The assassination of a dynamic and popular candidate for the presidency, a vital democrat, in a tragic way seemed to give the system a reprieve and mark a new decline in social morality. The newfound cocaine wealth was properly distributed among the elite and the "trickle down" effect from drug sales for a time made popular resistance more manageable.

But such a system, patently hypocritical and an embarrassment to its citizens, has scarcely any legitimacy. The trade-off in using a drug-export-based economy to stabilize the political system in the short term was the utter contamination of every part of the administration. Even the courts have been hostage to, or in collusion with, the drug infrastructure. The only due process in Columbia can be found in the factories for treating the coca for market. The oligarchic and intermediary economic elites have grown farther apart from the masses, the development of the middle class has withered in a limited economy, and once again large-scale social rebellion exists in the cities and in the countryside.

Every new political system accumulates legitimacy, or credibility, only gradually over time. Similarly, failures of the system to perform such as our own Watergate scandal or an inability to set right a foundering economy, tend to diminish, or at least call into question, this legitimacy. Once a regime loses its "creditworthiness"—and this happens only after many failures to carry out the essential mandate of its constituency (sometimes the base is only the articulate elite and does not include a politically inactive majority of the people)—it may have to resort to force of arms. The more the regime has to resort to police or military suppression to quell riots or protests, quash an attempted coup, or suppress guerrilla activity, the more it demonstrates its weakness. And sooner or later it is replaced. It is up to the international environment analyst, whether he or she works for a bank or multinational corporation (MNC), to be aware of a political system's creeping political bankruptcy, to identify those groups prepared to mount a challenge to the ruling order, to gauge their relative strengths, and then to try to anticipate the timing.

FRUSTRATIONS OF RISING EXPECTATIONS AND HOPES FOR SOCIAL MOBILITY

As members of a capitalist society, most of us want and strive to better ourselves. Even members of societies that theoretically are more equitable want to be better than equal. What is at first an economic question of survival and comfort also assumes a psychologically competitive animus. Less privileged people want to escape the dreariness of their lives. In third-world countries, a peasant's fantasies often embrace visions of the modern sector and the promise it might hold him. In a world in which a radio, television, or computer can be found in almost every village and in which transportation networks make travel to the city a possibility, peasants are less inclined to stay on the traditional farm and eke out an uncertain living. Instead, they move to the cities, often to discover that they are not easily employable. There they endure crowded neighborhoods of slums and hovels because they hope to become regularly employed workers. In many developing agrarian societies, a gainfully employed worker is indeed considered part of the broader middle class. Once an individual has attained middle-class status, he moves to a better neighborhood and continues to look upward.

Frustration can occur at any point in the upward mobility of members of a developing society. It stems from the promise of economic and social rewards, or even the fleeting taste of those rewards, and then the failure to attain and hold onto them. Never to experience "progress" is less disturbing psychologically than to experience it and then undergo a setback. In the cities of developing countries, frustration of upward mobility is often compounded by such phenomena as psychological uprootedness, poor housing conditions, population density, and growing political awareness in the crowded urban slums and barrios. At bottom, it springs from inflation, layoffs, and denial of opportunity for advancement. When similar frustrations are shared by many, they can become political. The collective frustrations can be manifested through the legitimate utilization of the electoral process, or they can be expressed more explosively through bread riots, work stoppages, isolated strikes, or general strikes. The more compelling the sense of personal frustration and the less receptive the authorities are to considering articulated grievances, the more likely seems to be the possibility of some sort of civil disorder.

What types of developments in a given country could alert the analyst to possible trouble? First, an example of a political act that could have been destabilizing was the promise of new housing that Belisario Betancur offered the Colombian people when he ran for the presidency in the early 1980s. Over one million people submitted applications for a total of fifty thousand available units. Similarly, Venezuela's Carlos Andres Pérez promised in the imagery of his campaign in 1990 a better life—more food and free education for the poor, working people. Instead, he implemented austerity measures and was impeached on allegations of personally stealing from the coffers. If his popular successor, Hugo Chavez, is to renew legitimacy for the democratic process in his country, he will ultimately have to address concretely some sort of retrenchment and relieve the pressure on the poor.

In developing countries, as in the United States and the rest of the developed world, the middle class is particularly vulnerable to inflation and economic recession. In Nigeria, the firing of many government workers within months of the Buhari coup in December 1983 contributed to the erosion of middle-class support for the new government. (In earlier years, it had become apparent how dependent an earlier military regime had been for its support on the middle class).

In recent years, "middle class" has come to represent a newfound status for a large proportion of people. In Southeast Asia in the 1990s before the "crash," factories were teeming with unionized workers, and white collar workers in government were either unhappy about the uneven increase in wages or beginning to enjoy a latitude in their lives that made them crave new nonmaterialistic goals such as greater political participation. They were on their way to becoming a new middle class or at least showing some of the values often associated with it in the West. In sum, when people have something, it is not just a question of holding on to what they have got but getting something more! In the 1992 riots in Bangkok, students, government workers, and unionized workers were in the streets putting their lives on the line for a greater say in the political process.

With the depression in Asian economies in the late 1990s, political stability really hung in the balance. The newly upwardly mobile from the 1980s were pushed down the slope. Students in Indonesia, who had hopes about professional jobs, grouped with the worker-middle class (organized as a pressure group during the more prosperous years), who found themselves unemployed and thwarted by the crimp in their spending power. Using rallying cries like "elite corruption" and "ethnic discrimination," they mobilized violent crowds in the streets and ultimately demanded the resignation of a president who had held power since a bloody coup in the 1960s.

Rising expectations therefore pick up momentum as new goals are met. They are particularly felt most acutely among the educated in secondary schools and universities. Many of these young people represent the first generation in their families to obtain an education, usually at considerable sacrifice to their parents. Their families share the expectation that they will enter the technocracy. In Cameroon, university graduates in large numbers search for appropriate positions in their homeland, but neither the bureaucracy nor the industrial base can accommodate them. Could they not constitute a source of antisocial or political instability in the system? In Turkey, barring the impact of the 1999 earthquakes, the economy has been stable. The irony is that because of the promise of greater prosperity with international assistance and a boost from future entry into the European Union, Turkey will have a large pool of educated people who will be seeking an important role for themselves in the adult world. If they are frustrated in their search, they could become a real source of political pressure on the system.

DISAFFECTION OF MIDDLE CLASS, PROFESSIONAL SUPPORT FROM THE REGIME

In developing countries suffering from economic and social deterioration, the middle class can be pivotal. And the question of rising expectations, just discussed, is closely wedded to the development of this class in a modernizing society.

Historically, in any prerevolutionary situation, this class has been comprised of waverers. Let the government overreact to mass violence with violence of its own, and these equivocal supporters can become radicalized. Any one of our readers who has ever stood on the edge of a political demonstration as a neutral observer probably is aware of the effect of a bullying and billying squad of police appearing on the scene with the explicit mandate to break up the crowd; one's head can be easily turned with a few swings of the stick.

If this class can serve as the swing group in a politically confrontive situation, it also is the pool from which will emerge any dissatisfied "counter-elite." Educated, young members of the middle class are most susceptible when they attempt to carve a niche for themselves in the adult world and improve the economic lot of their families of origin. As revolutionists in China, Mao Zedong, Zhou Enlai, and Deng Xiaoping, if not strictly middle class in origin, all belonged to the group of newly educated in their country. A student counter-elite in today's China, tinder for the likes of the 1989 Tiananmen Square massacre, also persist as a spark for igniting protest at critical moments throughout urban China. Among the disaffected in the younger generation of Chinese must surely be individuals who, bereft of the ideological symbols of a previous generation, have not yet economically benefited from the new dawn or crave a more participatory political role. If the economic situation in China were to take a downward spiral, energies that are now for the most part channeled into job mobility could be directed in a traditional political direction that resonates with the historic role of students as a political vanguard in China.

The urban M-19 guerrilla organization and even the rural guerrilla forces in Colombia historically have been comprised of educated, middle-class students who felt excluded by age *and* class from the political process. These people hold great expectations both about advancement in economic status and participation in the political process; in many instances, able to look over their shoulders and see their own family's poor origins, they want to be part of a process of social change that will ensure a future for themselves and their children.

Just as a middle-class loss of confidence can indicate an erosion of a system's legitimacy, its forbearance can shore up an established order. In some Latin American countries, a conservative, Roman Catholic middle class might put up with infringements of human rights to avoid a period of extreme disorder and chaos. The majority of the Argentine middle class was apparently willing to endure the anti-Peronist police terror of the military junta for some time in the 1970s because the military seemed to be a preferable alternative at first to the tyranny of guerrillas and Peronist terrorists in the streets. Only very slowly, and under changed social and economic circumstances, did sympathies turn significantly in the direction of the families that had suffered seemingly unjustifiable and deplorable "disappearances" of their close relatives. For the Argentine middle class to abandon the military government, it took not only the experience of being touched in some personal way by the regime's reign of terror, but also the crunch of economic chaos and the humiliation of defeat in a war with the British over the Falkland Islands.

Because the movements of a third-world country's middle class can be like shifting sands, they should not be overinterpreted. Nevertheless, the appropriate bank officers or operations executives of a corporation should try to gauge their sentiments, particularly at a time of significant social or economic change. Similarly, one should observe how well the regime is attempting to develop a consensus for major policy innovations among this ever-broadening social stratum. The untroubled implementation, for example, of an IMF–induced economic austerity program can hinge on the limits of tolerance of the middle class. Even if violence erupts in the streets, a more reflective middle class can serve as the mainstay of the regime and support the argument for giving short-term hardship a chance to work.

It is not so difficult to gain an impressionistic sense of the support of the middle class for the political system. Intelligence information can be garnered from the newspapers targeted at this class, from conversations with university professors and informal chats with shopkeepers and, second-hand, from local journalists and other knowledgeable sources in the community. Even cab drivers now in third-world urban centers can serve as the same sort of barometer of middle-class alienation that New York cabbies once personified. Sometimes this shadowy information can suggest positive evolutionary trends within the political-social system. In Turkey, middle-class enthusiasm for the civilian system bodes well for its future. In economically strained Latin American countries like Venezuela, where the wealth has become still more inequitably distributed, middle-class and student disaffection with official corruption and skewed social and economic policies have given impetus to the consideration of more radical alternatives.

ISSUE OF AN UNDERLYING INCLINATION TO DEFAULT, NATIONALIZE, OR EXPROPRIATE GRADUALLY THROUGH INCREASED REGULATIONS

The strength and viability of a political system matter little if there are underlying factors that would encourage nationalization or default on debt. As we analyze a new society and how its characteristics might influence our bottom line, we should also be aware of the importance of *historical attitudes*, particularly with regard to default on debt or nationalization without fair compensation—the gravest risks to international business. The MNC fears the outright expropriation of its equity and assets by a foreign country or the host government's takeover of the local company under the pressure of mounting regulations and restrictions.

Such unfavorable outcomes for MNCs can be influenced by a host of variables: the nature of the industry (e.g., is it considered strategic?), the ideology of the ruling political elite (e.g., has a certain type of social revolution just taken place?), economic conditions and domestic and international political issues (e.g., could a regional political maneuver by a foreign company's home government serve as pretext for threatening the company's local assets?).

Generally speaking, the international sweep of finance and investment has helped considerably to define the parameters for doing business and has been making bandit-like expropriation more of an anachronism. It is far more likely now that new enterprises considered by the host country to be of critical strategic importance are established from the start as joint local/foreign companies with a formula for gradual nationalization built into the agreement in a way that affords the foreign investor a profitable tenure as the business develops.

But the *exceptions* to this assumption make it important to look at the host country's history of performance with regard to expropriation and default, or more specifically, the attitudes of the host country's differing political groups concerning these matters. Of course, one should be sufficiently flexible to recognize that the positions of certain political groups have evolved—in some cases 180 degrees—with the passage of time and such changing circumstances as the increased popularity of monetarist theory and the increasing tendency to recognize relatively unfettered foreign investment as a stimulus to economic growth. President Carlos Andres Pérez of Venezuela, for example, who in 1974 had nationalized the country's oil industry, had become a champion of the private sector by the time of his second bid for his country's presidency in the late 1980s. Many foreign businesspeople who had witnessed the earlier expropriation of the oil industry or whose perception of Pérez's early persona remained frozen in history were slow to grasp the radical shift in Venezuela's foreign investment orientation, but they were wiser to play it safe for a while.

A look at each country's history of intervention in the private sector can provide additional insights and often reassurance about the paradoxical advantage and/or leverage a foreign firm might now enjoy in a specific cultural context.

Many nations, particularly in Latin America, have learned that excess expropriations have led to a monstrous, unproductive public sector that saps the country's reserves. Mexico is in a curious position. In September 1982, because of critical economic circumstances involving a run on the banks, the Jose Lopez Portillo government nationalized the banks and, with them, 45 percent of bank-owned private companies. That administration's realization of the negative effects of government ownership would tend to prevent nationalization in the future. Any political proclivity henceforth to appease a bellicose domestic left with rhetoric about a greater role for the state in economic operations must be offset by this harsh memory of statism gone awry.

A still more clear-cut case of a country's having developed an aversion to nationalization from its own historical experience is Peru. Between 1968 and 1975, General Juan Velasco Alvarado's junta redistributed the country's wealth. Several large MNCs were expropriated and foreign mining companies were forced to expand their investments at contractual disadvantage to themselves. The result was ruination for Peru. From the tenure of President Fernando Belaúnde Terry onward, the economy has become increasingly liberalized. Even if there were another military coup, it is unlikely that the next junta would be as radical as its precursor in the 1970s. On the contrary, foreign enterprises now constitute a critical interest group and can use their position for leverage with the new administration. Not only are they a bulwark of the economy, but the message they transmit to the outer world can also give credibility to the new regime.

A country also might try to compensate for its historical image with regard to expropriation. The People's Republic of China wants to repatriate both Taiwan as much as Hong Kong, yet it must show the free world that this is *repatriation without expropriation*. The foreign community wants to feel as politically and socially unrestricted as in colonial Hong Kong. Immediately after the revolution, China granted "autonomous" status to its largest external trading zone of Shanghai; many Shanghainese capitalists stayed behind to manage their enterprises. However, within five years, Shanghai's enterprises had been integrated into the socialist economy through harassments ranging from punitive taxation to regulations and personal political pressures. But the China of today is much different! It has begun to recapture its prerevolutionary entrepreneurial spirit, to open up to foreign banks and service industries, and to delineate sectors of the economy in Shanghai and Shenzhen that seem to be unburdened by socialist strictures. These internal developments bode well for the secure future of an economically unbridled Hong Kong and laissez-faire in Taiwan if it should rejoin the mainland in years to come. China's willingness to give the former colony the breathing space it requires in the years following reintegration is an encouragement to the already active foreign investors and a positive signal to Taiwan concerning the promise of political rapprochement.

Thus, even given the apparently protective cocoon of globalization, we should examine the history of nationalization/expropriation and default as a political act in a given country. Such things still happen. A review of the historical situation should be an integral part of investment planning in a new host country. The review will ascertain the level of expropriation risk for investments and in some cases might well guide the investor to seek risk insurance coverage. We can also learn whether there might be ways to structure a contract in terms of technology transfer as well as joint ownership to put us in the best possible position to control our own outcomes.

Because expropriation "in the nation's interest" is a tradition that has not quite died in some places, and such decisions are always political, we must be certain to investigate the attitudes of the whole spectrum of the political elite. (Observe, if relevant, the way they react to their own past history of nationalization or how they have adjusted to the foreign economic presence currently in their midst.) Even in Peru where there is an almost overwhelming horror at the economic disaster of the 1970s, not long ago elements of the younger military officer corps might have allowed their populist leanings to cloud their judgment if they had come to power. And in China, if old ideologues ever were to resurface or new ideologues were to emerge to challenge the materialist modernizers, China could regress to an extreme version of "self-reliance" (admittedly a less likely scenario) and at least a selective targeting of "imperialist" investments. This shift in orientation could lead to repudiation of contract and expropriation, with or without compensation.

Indeed, xenophobia, or resentment of foreigners, is still a popular sentiment in a number of areas of the developing world. Beware of a desperate political elite that is in a position to manipulate such feelings during difficult economic times in order to scapegoat foreign enterprise. If China, for example, were to trip over its own interim ideology of nationalism and suffer a setback in maneuvers over the Taiwan Strait or Tibet, even the present government might retaliate against foreign enterprises of particular national origin. Or, it might make an example of those where anger over a national issue serves as a pretext for ulterior motives. A common argument in post-Soviet Russia is that certain industries were never supposed to be privatized, and given over to foreign nationals in the first place (See Michael Newcity's case study on Russia in chapter 5). This is not an acceptable rationale to the foreign investors several hundreds of million dollars after the fact.

The previous discussion, sometimes contradictory in referring to the proclivities of a given host country, only serves to underscore the need to be sensitive to the relevant variables and possible contingencies for each country and to monitor events from this baseline of knowledge.

Finally, a word about default on debt. A country's decision to default on external debt can reflect a fundamental attitudinal problem in the historical memory of the people. Officials and local businesspeople alike may seem to feel that they should be compensated for injustices suffered at the hand of the powerful nations a century ago. The foreign creditor, big and small, and the trader who expects to be paid are held accountable for their forbears. This resentment is rife in Latin America. A Venezuelan or a Mexican, for example, is not uncommonly disposed to justify not paying his debt by rationalizing that he has been unfairly gouged by the predatory enterprise from the north. Almost at the other extreme, the Chinese government has demonstrated its creditworthiness and aversion to default when it first repaid its loans from the Soviet Union after the Sino-Soviet dispute erupted in 1960. Like the adolescent child seeking to demonstrate its autonomy to its parent, China proved its independence and integrity to its erstwhile benefactor. And since the start of China's modernization program in cooperation with Western investors and commercial and multilateral lending institutions, it has been very judicious about drawing down on the credit lines made available to it.

CORRUPTION

Corruption is a critical—and yet tricky—issue for the foreign businessperson. The businessperson from a Western country really has to approach the question of corruption in a host country from at least two perspectives. A moralistic strain in the American culture in particular, reflected in the Jimmy Carter administration's promulgation of the Foreign Corrupt Practices Act, sometimes carries over into the U.S. businessperson's worldview and behavior overseas. Therefore, it is important to make an analytical distinction between the sort of institutionalized corruption in host countries that serves as a traditionally acceptable income supplement and the other category of special payoffs, bribes, and kickbacks to officials that in sheer enormity exceed the acceptable bounds of propriety in that country and jeopardize the legitimacy of the existing political system.

In many societies, corruption *in a manner of speaking* (usually informal payoffs, direct and indirect) has been institutionalized, sometimes over a span of centuries. Informal practices took root for redistributing wealth or compensating for the low salaries of government employees. In premodern China, scholar-gentry who ascended to official positions were given prebends (state-gained properties) as compensation for their service to the Confucian state. In turn, they theoretically took care of even the poorest in their large, extended families. In more recent decades in Indonesia, active military officers have been permitted to hold positions in business, in part to ensure their loyalty but also to supplement their low salaries and militate against the possibility of excessive corruption. Only if we arrogantly project our own Calvinist values on other cultures can we regard any of these practices as reprehensible. Even bribes and "facilitators" theoretically ought to be treated as the way some societies work. *However, when the intensity and breadth of official corruption surpass the threshold of tolerance of a country's own people, venality must be regarded as a threat to the stability of the political system.* Indeed, it can pose a very direct hazard to those foreign businesses that have become personally involved in projects developed under the aegis of highly profiled members of the political inner circle whose future is uncertain.

As people become more politically aware, they become more critical of unbounded corruption. Where the level of corruption among a narrow elite has risen in direct proportion to newly found oil wealth and has exacerbated already existing social inequities, the middle class becomes more disgruntled and begins to identify more with the poor and disenfranchised, thereby placing the system in a state of disequilibrium. In Thailand, corruption increasingly over the years has become a popular issue of attention and is now attracting a broader cross-section of organized labor and the middle class. In China and Indonesia, to take just two examples, when the national leaderships declare a war against corruption, they focus on a long-festering, deeply rooted political disease. An apocryphal story is that President Suharto once approached his statesman-like, outgoing Vice President Adam Malik and said: "You served your people well, but my regret is that you didn't take sufficient care of your family." In the Indonesian case, the spotlight in the next couple years will be on the Suharto family and other top, former officials who have taken the gravy and some of the beef for their families. The judicial proceedings may or may not serve as a lesson to present and future leaders and as an outlet for the frustration of the populace. But the outcome is unlikely to cure the deeper problem!

In China, at the Ninth Plenary Session of the National People's Congress in March 2000, President Jiang Zemin launched a crusade against official corruption. This campaign, like other previous housecleaning campaigns that often had been used as pretext to oust rivals in the party leadership, can also take people's minds off deeper sources of economic grievance and appease ideological critics. As in Indonesia, such an anticorruption sweep will try to drive home a lesson to officials at all levels. Moreover, corruption is easy for the masses to understand, and they can be worked up emotionally over the subject. In the interim, the key question in China and in Indonesia is whether the regime will undertake badly needed structural changes in the economy in order to alleviate problems like unemployment, parallel economy, and fiscal confusion.

Can a system survive if boundless corruption becomes endemic to officialdom at multiple levels? In Colombia, narcotics-related corruption pervades the political system down to the grassroots and is prevalent in the legislature, judiciary, and political parties. The phenomenon is as widespread as a malignant cancer. The question becomes one of whether the loss in legitimacy of political institutions and the attrition of the support of the educated middle class can be offset by the trickle-down effect on the whole economy from drug-related revenues. Will selectively scattered material payoffs allow the system to "muddle through?"

In countries with a historical pattern of military coups, corruption seems to have had a special appeal as a rallying point for the military. Official misbehavior, compounded by other social and economic problems, can be an invitation for the troops to file out of the barracks.

SECULAR AND SACRED IDEOLOGIES

When either a secular ideology or a religion takes on the characteristics of a political force, it can become an organizing ethos for challenging the system—a sort of cement that can hold a revolutionary entity together. The very political and structured organization of the Shia Muslim sect and its eschatological appeal provided a cause, a goal, and a psychological identity for the Iranian revolution.

Political religion (both secular and church-related) can perform similar functions for smaller-scale social protests and civil disobedience, both of which at worst can target business installations and/or disrupt operations, and at best can be alarming to the members of families of expatriate employees of a given country. It is truly uncomfortable to have to take shelter from a hysterical mob driven by a sense of moral self-righteousness.

Such movements can have a traumatic effect on the existing political system. In the 1960s in South Vietnam, militant Cao Dai Buddhists organized demonstrations that had a negative and psychologically destabilizing impact on the political mood and indirectly increased the effectiveness of communist activities. In Algeria in January 1992, the military had to intercede to prevent an Islamic government from legitimately coming to power through parliamentary election. In what is still very much a garrison state, the military annulled the vote in the runoff elections just as the fundamentalist Islamic Salvation Front (FIS) was on the verge of winning a majority. Later, the court banned the FIS from the political process. The fear then was that a reckless and unpredictable government would replace a weakened and scandal-racked National Liberation Front, the one party in power since 1962. Such an Islamic government might have grown in power with the stature of a grip on the presidency, imposed Islamic strictures on secular behavior, and perhaps would have discouraged foreign investment as part of a general condemnation of Westernization. As John P. Entelis points out in his case study on Algeria (see chapter 6), the constellation of power that has evolved until now consists of the military, statist bureaucracy, and Islam. The Islamic party really reflects the will of the vast majority of people, but it has been held in check by a self-interested and gargantuan bureaucracy and a military concerned with pragmatic stability.

Even in Indonesia, which the average Westerner in the past has tended to link with the East Asian and oriental mystique, Islamic militants have posed a problem by staging riots from time to time. Indonesia has the largest Muslim population in the world, and increasing numbers of young Indonesians have been turning to fundamentalist Islam in search of meaningful values as an alternative to a materialist life style and the hollow spiritual symbols of the military-associated government. With the turn of the new millennium, as Suharto resigned the presidency under popular pressure after thirty-five years of rule and handed over interim power to Vice President B. J. Habibie, Indonesians elected an Islamic president. It is appropriate that the new President Abdulrahhman Wahid should oversee a widespread prosecution of the flagrantly corrupt in the outgoing administration. The Indonesians, faced with a system of moral and fiscal bankruptcy, have given stature politically to their Islamic parties and co-opted a new source of spiritual strength and appeal to replace now-decayed revolutionary principles. The unsighted leader is foresighted enough to steer a pragmatic course and wisely compromise with members of the old government and the military.

In the past century, Marxism-Leninism has been the most common revolutionary ideology in the developing world. In the formation of many third-world nation-states, democracy *cum* capitalism did not provide a cogent thought system that could easily be communicated to lower echelons of leadership or to the masses. Marxism, the natural panacea, offered a centrally planned program of postrevolutionary economic development for the deprived. As many scholars have noted, it also served as a stick with which to beat the Western world and therefore was well suited to national liberation movements of various kinds. With the shattering of the Marxist-Leninist system in the former Soviet Union itself and the discrediting of centrally planned economies, only a few countries cling to its tenets. But China's adherence to Marxism-Leninism still looms large internationally; at the other end of the size spectrum, Zimbabwe struggles to make it work against old power structures, and Cuba, the subject of a path-breaking case study in this book (see chapter 7), still languishes with its revolutionary-period ideology on our perimeter. The vocabulary of communism is still used to cudgel the West and foreign enterprises when convenient. And many so-called Marxist-Leninist movements continue to exist in the backwater areas of still-divided countries from Africa to Southeast Asia, posing a threat to foreign oil installations and other types of infrastructure and endangering expatriate workers and lines of supply. Both Marxism-Leninism and the more militant forms of Islam have been the two ideologies that have most frequently served as focal points for political unrest in developing countries. It is probably fair to say that as Marxism-Leninism ceases to offer any long-term functional appeal, or is simply retained in name by certain states just to define the revolutionary origins of the country, the specter of the Islamic jihad will continue to move forward in stops and starts. Fundamentalist Islam can pose a real threat to some critical aspects of modernization if it is pushed to the periphery of the political arena and must mobilize as an *outsider* force.

Sometimes, curious hybrids can emerge. In Burma, the religion is Buddhism and the antiestablishment ideology is secular communism. The Buddhists show signs of increasing dissatisfaction under state jurisdiction. The Burmese Communist Party (BCP) and the monks could join forces, particularly if encouraged by social action in other circles. The acclaimed intellectual and student group, now the National League for Democracy, that surrounds the Burmese poet and charismatic social leader Aung San Suu Kyi in Rangoon could form a nucleus for drawing together such scattered fringe groups. Under an umbrella of loose theoretical constructs, it would remain poised against the overbearing military dictatorship that it in principle defeated electorally.

An ideology—a denunciation of the political economic status quo, a set of goals and objectives, a presentation of the means to achieve those ends, and the promise of a utopia at the end of the rainbow—is an essential force for binding together an antiestablishment movement bent on either revolution or demonstrations of militant social protest. In societies where the economically disenfranchised and most politically frustrated people have been displaced from their villages and are leading isolated and psychologically dislocated lives in dense urban slum areas, or where traditional ethnic and religious differences have made persons naturally mistrustful of one another, political religion is an indispensable tool for organizing against the existing political order and social hierarchy. Too often, however, foreigners and specifically foreign investors can become targeted in theory and/or practice as spoilers, agents of corruption, and scapegoats for a panoply of domestic problems.

DEMOGRAPHIC PATTERNS

At a deeper level than focussing on the expressions of discontent with a particular political system, the strategic planner can look at population growth and distribution trends in order to pinpoint undercurrents of tension within a social system. A good example of the burdensome effect of population growth on the economic complexion of a country is Kenya. Exceeding its own yearly increase in gross domestic product, Kenya's annual population growth rate has been among the highest in the world. In the 1980s, population growth was higher than 4.1 percent; as we enter the new century, it is estimated at between 2.5 and 2.7 percent. Eighty percent of the country's people are for the most part concentrated on the 20 percent of the land considered arable. Four hundred thousand young adults leave school and enter the job market every year. Kenya's population, as of a census in early 2000, was about twenty-eight million—about a million less than expected. Procreation in numbers is a sacred testament to masculinity in Kenyan society, but values are changing and the U.S. Agency for International Development's (USAID) policies have been effective. Politicians who were timid about pressing the issue of population control have become more flexible. As we observe this problem being tempered, we have to determine whether the change is adequate in the context of slow structural reform.

Unemployment and Rural to Urban Migration

Land subdivision, drought, the pressures of subsistence living in the countryside, and the appeal of what seems from afar to be a more comfortable life in the cities have led to a constant stream of refugees from the countryside to the urban centers. This problem is shared by most developing countries to a greater or lesser extent, and it is important to assess the various pressures brought to bear on the system and how well the system seems to be withstanding them. First, an extreme rural to urban imbalance can make inroads on the country's agricultural productivity, sometimes transforming a net exporter of food into a country that is no longer self-sufficient in feeding itself. Even people who are driven from the countryside by a temporary natural calamity like drought or flooding are unlikely to return to the land. A key question for the massive number of Mozambicans displaced from their lands by tragically devastating floods in the spring of 2000 was whether they could face the challenges of reconstruction and recultivation in their home villages or would become a burden on the hitherto smoothly modernizing urban sector.

Second, migration into the cities is socially and psychologically dislocating. If, as in Algeria, whole families tend to migrate together, the social problem is not as grave. But more often it happens that family members are separated from one another and the newcomers to the big cities feel isolated, alien, and emotionally disoriented. The floating rural populations that seek meager jobs in cities in China do so without proper government permission and have to hide from police as they try to find an existence. So many of the word's migrants from the countryside become frustrated by urban living conditions that do not measure up to their earlier fantasies. They can easily become hooligans and/or fall prey to antisystemic groups that offer friendship and identity through an appropriate ideology that reflects the cleavage between the haves and have nots.

Third, the population flow from the outlying areas to the high-density cities puts pressure on the more modern sector of the economy to provide adequate housing and social services (most often it simply fails to cope with the problem) and to absorb the new manpower into the employment force. Some unique countries like South Korea, with successful social health care plans and a continually expanding industrial base, have been able to absorb the flow. But even Korea has found it useful to establish special economic zones in some of the outlying towns in order to forestall an even greater shift of the population to the major cities than the current proportion of 75 percent.

Throughout the developing world, unemployment and underemployment in the cities are on the ascendant because of the phenomenon of unrelenting waves of hopeful migrants descending on the cities and industrializing economies that have not yet restructured properly. In some areas of Africa, unemployment and underemployment in the urban areas approach 30 percent of the workforce. At the same time, the government cannot afford to increase its public spending, and industry cannot expand at a rate fast enough to absorb this manpower. The disbanding of failed state enterprises in several countries has left large numbers of desperate people struggling to eke out a living by holding several jobs at once; others comprise a pool of idle, unemployed men who gripe on street corners and find damaging ways to deal with their humiliation. These frustrated unemployed and underemployed can easily erupt in civil violence.

Migration from Beyond the Borders

Some countries have the added problem of immigration from neighboring countries, where either economic and social conditions are worse or internal civil war has made life insecure and unstable. A heavy flow of migrant workers exists in the Middle East between the poorer countries and the oil-rich states, posing a problem of different cultures intermingling in an uncertain manner and perhaps even infusing a new element of more militant Islam into the host country. In Mexico—already suffering from a serious population problem—the influx of Guatemalan Indian refugees has put enormous pressure on an economic system already sapped by its own population. If social violence in Central America ever were to escalate again, this problem would be compounded. (This was one very practical reason why Mexico worked so hard to persuade the U.S. government to decrease its involvement in Central America and permit the civil war to ebb in Nicaragua and El Salvador).

Age Demographics: Youth and Politics

Many countries in the developing world experienced a big bulge in the rate of population growth in the 1960s. Even if the rate of population growth has decreased since that time as a result of the world campaign concerning birth control and unilateral efforts on the part of governments to educate their people and make contraceptives available, a large proportion of the total populations already is of working age. In Colombia, although the population growth rate had declined from 3 percent in the 1960s to 2.4 percent by the end of the 1980s, more and more young people have flooded the workforce as we entered the 1990s. Still other countries that have been slow to limit population growth have an even more disproportionate number of youth and young adults who have been hard pressed to find a place in the active workforce. In the "more advanced," less developed countries (LDCs), where the secondary and higher educational system is now well developed, young graduates are looking for positions commensurate with their training. In many cases, the bureaucracies are already swollen and the industrial base has not developed at a sufficient pace to absorb these young people, particularly the better educated among them. Although these new candidates for the workforce have the option of expressing themselves through the vote, participation in the actual "moving and shaking" of the political process and selection of programmatic priorities is usually not open to them. In so many societies, a gerontocracy actually prevails in the formal and informal political structures of society down to the grassroots level. Adults who have been involved in the struggle for a while can become inured to the system. But members of the younger generation are exposed to modern ideas and are full of adolescent expectations about autonomy and proving themselves in adult workforce roles to their families of origin. These young adults often chafe at the ineluctable encounter with the market's impenetrability.

In the decades following the Cultural Revolution in China, educated youths were politically frustrated from their earlier experiences and were wary of the risks of making too great a political commitment. Many reportedly chose to rechannel their efforts into economic pursuits when they had the opportunity. Educated youth in China who come of age in the decade ahead could conceivably revert to a pattern of protest if thwarted in their pursuit of economic opportunity or if political modernization does not proceed at a fast enough pace. Under such circumstances, they might find *some common ground* with the increasing pool of unemployed workers who have been laid off for being insufficiently productive.

In so many countries, young adults in effect are both economically and politically disenfranchised. Armed with an education and an ability to communicate, and susceptible to new ideals ranging from communism to the Koran, they are both potential leaders and recruits *for dissident movements*. Large numbers of bitter youth (educated and uneducated alike) who hang out idle and unemployed in the cities are positioned to spark broader outbursts of civil unrest. This is a very real political risk that can be monitored by operations executives on site.

MANPOWER, LABOR AGITATION, AND WORKER PARTICIPATION IN MANAGEMENT

Over the years, the local manpower question has been one of the greatest problems for the foreign investor. Is the manpower force as a whole reliable, adequately trained or sufficiently well educated to absorb special training for the tasks at hand? Will a new enterprise have to cope with absenteeism or various expressions of ineffective productivity by poorly motivated workers and lower-level managers? Will the foreign investor be put in the situation of negotiating for more expatriates on the job against a host country disposition to have new job opportunities for its own people? Will this version of technology transfer be feasible, and at what cost to the foreign investor? Is it not possible that in the end many of the local personnel, particularly executives, will be hired for *appearance* rather than *performance*? In Indonesia, for example, we have observed that in many cases the real enterprise, comprised of expatriate managers, acts as "consultant" to a dummy operating company.

Yet in this new era of globalization, the pools of educated youth who could not be absorbed by their countries' growth-stunted economic infrastructures now might be more adaptable to new technologies with proper conditions of cooperation in technology transfer between foreign and host countries. And in some countries in the less developed world, the manpower force—increasingly well-trained and less expensive than their counterparts in the most developed areas—can be a critical determinant of choosing a new manufacturing or marketing location. Some countries, like Israel, with the national security imperative of having to remain to some extent on a war footing, have made great strides in training their young people in higher technology. This country makes an excellent location for members of the electronics and high technology industries.

An Activist Labor Force

Viewed from a more negative perspective, the workforce can sometimes not only be unproductive, but it can also act as a potential source of dissonance and disruption—a dagger in the side of any enterprise established in a strange overseas host country. The threat to the integrity and smooth operation of a newly established company that could be posed by excessive agitation on the part of locally organized labor is almost self-evident. Work stoppages and strikes are capable of paralyzing local operations; moreover, if such actions have political overtones, they might become part of a much larger, nationwide social movement that could have an impact on international business or even the private sector as a whole. It is important to become informed about national confederations of unions in a host country, their links with the major political parties or the governing elite, and how effectively they can control their member unions at the grassroots level. Like our own AFL–CIO or Teamsters, some of the federations are not equally effective at gathering input at the lower level of the rank and file and aggregating and articulating those demands before the political policymakers. Their work might focus solely on manipulating and controlling their members. Only a decade ago in Tunisia, the Union Generale de Travoilleurs Tunisiennes (UGTT) was a militant movement whose leaders were jailed. By the mid-1980s, it was evolving into an apparent ally—

if not instrument—of the government. In Venezuela, where once the powerful Confederation de Trabajo de Venezuela (CTV) had considerable influence over the Accion Democratica (AD) Party, presidents from Jaime Lusinchi to Carlos Andres Pérez and the AD itself no longer seem to ascribe as much priority to organized labor interests. As a result, either the union could ossify or there could be a resurgence of strikes. In any case, the advantage of one large labor confederation is that it is usually either controllable or already part of the established system.

Still another factor that might invite further analysis of the dynamics of organized labor is the extent to which multiple labor federations might be utilized by competing parties and politicians, or the extent to which unions themselves might compete for power and support. As in the early Peronist movement in Argentina in the 1950s, such labor federations occasionally could be manipulated by dissident, fringe political parties to throw their massive weight against the established order. Demonstrations and general strikes could ensue that disrupt operations by paralyzing urban services. When politics and rivalry within the labor union become interwoven, the effect of the contest can have a direct impact on business operations. An example was the contest in Spain under the Felipé González presidency between the communist-led union, Comisiones Obreras, and the socialist-controlled UGT. As González maneuvered to bolster his own socialist union's standing vis-à-vis the communists, management was put under perhaps greater pressure to make concessions.

Much less predictable is a situation in which the larger federations have become inactive or where there are no national unions at all. Under such circumstances, local unions can develop more autonomy; they are less hierarchical, more informal, and more united in purpose. In Morocco, the large UMT is government-controlled, and the more militant opposition union seems to have been coerced into passivity. In such an atmosphere, scattered and localized wildcat strikes have occurred among taxi drivers, teachers, and some other groups. Under conditions of austerity and economic squeeze, local unions on both the left and right of the political spectrum are apt to become more aggressive. However, it is important to note that workers' strikes at mines and other extractive and infrastructural projects can be isolated and policed fairly easily.

A final factor to consider is that Western-style trade unions are now taking root among more skilled workers in countries like South Korea and Thailand. For these new middle-class Asians and for the governments, Western trade unions were at first uncomfortably foreign and have only been integrated into the organism of the host country after some disruption. South Korea, for example, experienced some serious work stoppages during the 1980s and early 1990s. The government will have to continue to be responsive to this new activist pressure group, and it remains to be seen what effect the severe depression in Asia at the end of the 1990s will have had on the movement.

Worker Participation in Management

A trend is taking place among the political elites of both developed and developing countries that has been variously motivated. In some cases, it has represented a gesture to forestall greater wage demands through inviting worker participation in decision making or actually is a genuine effort to complement the redistribution of wealth with a blurring of the distinction between management and labor. Still another consideration, probably in the minds of all advocates, is the notion that worker participation would increase the *esprit de corps* of a company and would spur productivity.

The European Community (EC), or European Union (EU), now based in Lisbon, is currently considering a series of directives that, if passed into law, will not only expand mandatory consultations between management and employees but will also set new guidelines regarding parent companies and subsidiaries in MNCs. Such guidelines would substantially increase the amount of information that companies would have to disclose about their operations.

The Vredeling Proposal has attracted much public attention in recent years. Under such a directive, companies would be required to provide employees with information regarding local and worldwide plans. Reporting would be statutory and penalties would be enforced for noncompliance.

Among the market economies of the developing countries, the staunchest proponent of worker participation in the management process seems to have been the Venezuelan CTV. MNCs must closely monitor any universalized comanagement schemes in countries with powerful labor unions.

CULTURAL, REGIONAL, AND TRADITIONAL/MODERN DIFFERENCES

In the developing world and the reemerging nations of eastern and central Europe, the strategic planner and operations executive must be mindful of tensions stemming from the heterogeneity of a country. Clashes between regions, cultures, and the traditional and modern sectors of societies are often interrelated and ought to be incorporated into planning, negotiating strategy, and consideration of the protection of installations and personnel. To MNCs and international banks, they pose such difficulties as a lack of coordination between center and regional institutions (e.g., between central and regional banks), the potential for disputes over jurisdiction, the inability of the center to enforce law and order over a region, regional separatist movements, and even civil war. A further threat to foreign business installations exists in the potential for violent explosiveness of the contradiction between the traditional and modern sectors of a society and the festering rivalries of unassimilated cultural and ethnic groups. The foreign businessperson might have to adapt to different styles of doing business or brace himself for social disturbances that develop as people feel that the dominant culture, or even modernity itself, is overtaking them or threatening their identities.

The problems involving cultural, regional, and traditional/modern divisions that are prevalent in some of the central and eastern European countries of the former Soviet bloc and in Africa, the Middle East, and South and Southeast Asia are caused by: (a) the artificial borders and linguistic/cultural overlays imposed by a dominant group or an earlier colonizing power; (b) the efforts of newly emergent (or reemergent in Europe) countries to create strong nation-states from a tapestry of ethnic groups; (c) the attempt of these diverse groups to cling to their solidarity and to preserve their traditional ethnic or religious identities in the face of modern institutions and laws; and (d) the efforts of old chauvinistic ethnic groups to reassert themselves against a weak central government in newly constituted states. Such rivalries within one nation's borders, whether in the Middle East or the Balkans, often represent a resistance to more generalized process of nation-building and national integration.

Regionalism

In dealing with the broad topic of regionalism, we must appreciate both its critical importance for operations planning in the earmarked host country and its far-reaching ramifications for doing business in the relatively developed world. In the more developed world, the distinction is that the obstacles are not usually life threatening. However, bureaucracy and conflicting red tape between one locality and another in areas as familiar as Canada and Newfoundland can seem as troublesome as the threat of ethnic rivalry elsewhere.

One of the first steps in actually getting operations underway in a new host country often involves regional politics. The foreign businessperson must obtain approval for a range of things from licenses to location site. (The manager of an oil company wishing to spud an oil well in the onshore Jiangxi Basin in China might find himself more directly impeded than would an oil man operating in the Cabinda enclave in Angola; the latter might be surrounded by Cabinda Liberation guerrillas, but the former might have to deal with cutting through layers of bureaucracy at several levels, from Jiangxi Province to the Central Ministry of Petroleum Industry in Beijing.) If the central government offers commercial incentives to invest in outlying areas for manufacturing purposes, the operations executive must weigh such incentives against the possible inconveniences of poor infrastructure, poor living conditions, and potential sources of regional unrest.

In other cases, a conflict might erupt between the central authority, provincial or state authority, and the local-level jurisdiction. Sometimes, as in the case of a developed country like Australia, disagreements are based on a legal or regulatory pretext. In Australia, a hydroelectric company being built for Tasmania was blocked by the central Australian government. The central government used provisions of an international convention on protecting wilderness areas as grounds for halting the project; the country's high court upheld that action. In post-Soviet Russia, foreign investors have been robbed of their enterprises in legal actions that alleged particular industries still belong in the public (state) domain. In Nigeria, because the state governments often stray too far from the central government's development plan, it is advisable for a foreign business enterprise to obtain *payment guarantees* from the Central Bank.

This sort of intense business planning leads to important precautions. The close-in study of idiosyncratic regional conditions or conflicts with the center, like the analysis of basic market conditions itself, is as important as the broadbrush judgments about political and economic trends. The marketing and field operations officers of the company should acquire this refined analytical perspective for this sort of approach, and at an early stage should consider retaining the services of local legal counsel.

The astute international businessperson ought to be aware that the differences between center and region might involve a range of complex and inconsistent procedures that will even impinge on the viability of the contract itself. In the People's Republic of China, for example, as many as three layers of bureaucracy may be involved, as well as the Party, which is the key decision-making locus at every level. In this case, proper planning at country headquarters will guide the operations officers through a snag by identifying an appropriate local agent or co-opting a well-connected person who can instruct his new employer on a course that will bypass such bureaucratic hurdles. In Chinese society, cultivating personal relationships (*Guanxi*) with the right individuals at the highest possible level (even above the relevant ministry itself) may do wonders! The process of developing relationships should not be left to local personnel; rather, it is appropriate for key company executives to reinforce through personal contact the higher-level relationships that are developed.

If a central government cannot easily communicate its directives to the state level and then to the grassroots, the ensuing political paralysis is apt to affect business operations. In precoup Nigeria, in spite of the fact that power had been diffused among nineteen states rather than the four old regional divisions that had permitted the major tribes to form political blocs, the lack of coordination between the president and state governors still had a crippling effect.

In some countries in the Middle East and Africa, nation-states are still so fragmented into their traditional, regional, or tribal units that the central government is limited in its power to exercise law and order. This factor is an important consideration for foreign businesses contemplating a project in such a "frontier" milieu. In southeast Turkey, for example, where the oil fields and many large-scale infrastructure projects are located, the Kurdish population makes its own law and order. Banditry and killings are common, and the local police arrest whomever they please and treat them as they like. The central government can do little to intervene in this Turkish version of the "Wild West."

Finally, regionalism in its extreme form can lead to wide-scale violence and civil war. The Ibo secessionist movement in eastern Nigeria in 1969–1970 fused a drive for tribal autonomy with economically motivated regional separation. The latent conflict in recent times in Nigeria between the Hausa-Fulani in the north and the Yoruba in the south represents a mix of regional economic imperatives, religious differences (Muslim and Christian), and tribalism. In a sense, the creation of the Bosnian state, with three generations of people loyal to that geographic entity, suggests the possibility once more of quelling antiquated rivalries.

Cultural and Traditional/Parochial Sources of Tension

Cultural heterogeneity remains a source of tension in many countries seeking to forge an almost contrived unity from a diversity of languages and customs. These old subcultures in the third world might have predated colonialism or semicolonialism; in eastern Europe and the former Soviet Union, some managed to survive (perhaps even as a psychological defense) the tyranny of central control and the imposition of a dominant ideology. Colonialism itself created artificial boundaries and entities. In Nigeria, the Ibo tribal structure, which spearheaded the Biafran secessionist movement of the 1960s, had been a product of the colonial era. Yet, comprised of many smaller communities with similar cultures, the Ibo perceived themselves as a culturally interrelated organization deserving autonomy and separate recognition from the Hausa-Fulani–controlled central government. In the Cameroon in the 1980s, former president Ahmadou Ahidjo adroitly deflected a potential conflict between the northern and southern regions onto the "colonial" rivalry between the anglophones (English-speaking people) and the majority francophones (French-speaking people). However, the new tensions increased, including disputes involving university curriculum and riots over the shooting by a francophone police officer of an anglophone citizen. These lines of friction, suggestive of problems in our own inner cities, can become serious against a backdrop of deteriorating economic conditions. In Burma, twenty-six armed, dissident ethnic groups vie for autonomous control of their slices of territory and absorb the energies of the central government in the fighting.

Some countries have found ways to cope with such diversity, and the astute businessperson ought to ascertain just how well the central government manages such tensions. One approach is simply the exercise of a modicum of tolerance. With the exception of periodic clampdowns on organized protest in Tibet, the People's Republic of China generally has been tolerant of the cultures and customs of its minorities until more recent years. A different approach is the utilization of coercion against ethnic assertiveness or employing a "carrot and stick" approach. The careful businessperson will examine how effective such postures have been in preserving social order and making it possible for the visitor to feel reasonably assured of safe passage around the country. One good test, for example, of the cleavage between Arabs and Berbers in Algeria in the early 1980s (this example is now outdated because of the development in recent years of a more imposing threat from the militant Muslims) was the 1981 uprising of the Berbers in the Kabyle (eastern Algeria) against a trend toward Arabization of the educational system. The prospect of the government's substituting Arabic for the French language in the schools threatened the Berbers' economic mobility through a pattern of pursuing jobs in France. The government reacted quickly to the unrest by suppressing it and then by instituting a faculty of language and culture at the local university. A volatile situation was successfully defused.

Where the idea of the nation-state is still new, the conflict between central government and the modern elements of society, on the one hand, and the local ethnic or tribal political structures and practices, on the other, can lead to problems of control and paralysis of the decision-making function. In this author's opinion, Nigeria has been particularly vulnerable in this regard. The creation of about twenty states that cut across the former tribal boundaries has militated against the recurrence of civil war along tribal lines. Yet the strength of some two hundred traditional cultural groups persists and makes the absorption of the groups into larger political bodies a long and difficult process. The recurrence of local riots, brought on by local Emirs, Muslim militants and other groups over the years has led to the crippling of government at lower levels, particularly in the north, and might hurt or slow down business operations that happened to locate in one of these areas. One also cannot discount the possibility of an immobilizing impact on business throughout the country of multiple localized outbreaks that seem to undermine the central authority.

HUMAN RIGHTS AND THE RULE OF LAW

In the postmodern era, the issue of violating human rights has become a sensitive social and political issue, with ramifications for the corporation at its home base and internationally. Host countries can no longer resort easily to unfair patterns of coercion against its people with impunity. Too many international organizations—often issuing their censure from Washington, D.C., or New York—monitor individual cases of harassment, arrest, and circumstances of detainment and internment across the world. The flagrant and illegitimate use of coercion in a host country creates an uncomfortable working environment for American and other foreign businesspeople, as will any major differential in practice. The threat of international sanctions against a country for its human rights violations not only might impinge on the routine of business but also might cast a particular foreign national—an American businessperson or engineer, for instance—in a role in which he is targeted for his government's behavior. The host country often sees sanctions as politically motivated, at best imperialistic or culturally self-righteous, and retaliates in any way it is able.

On a given day in 2000, as the U.S. Congress was debating the foreign trade bill for China, the lobby and lounge of the Shanghai Hilton was teeming with "practical-minded" foreign businesspeople who did not think human rights should be an issue. A more seasoned man argued: "This is China, not the United States. Chinese people respect an iron hand. People here worry more about instability and chaos. When are we ever going to stop being 'ugly Americans' and pushing our way of life on other peoples." A businesswoman beside him said, "When in Rome, do as the Romans do!"

The irony is that now as we approach the millenium, foreign businesspeople — and Americans in particular — *cannot afford to be nonjudgmental*. Tolerance is good if it is founded on mutual agreement about certain basic values. Foreign businesspeople must be mindful of constituencies in a host country that are just becoming articulate. Even if foreign investors and traders are not directly involved themselves in human rights violations or have no complicity in the breach of individual rights, foreign-owned business enterprises in a host market can be vulnerable. They may take no explicit stand on an issue so controversial, but they may be held liable for passively acquiescing. Neutrality is not good public relations back at home where violations of such values still stir people. Nor is it necessarily acceptable conduct in the host country once a trend for reform has gained momentum among the people.

When American and other Western business enterprises run afoul of human rights protests, trade sanctions, and the complicity of their people with a host government's repression, it is inexorably because they have deprecated the importance they attach to certain absolute values of human rights and cynically convinced themselves that they have adapted to the prevailing local culture. In some cases, corporations have been sucked into cooperating with the local system of political repression. They have developed a myopia that has blinded them to the legitimate interests of oppressed communities and their latent capacity in the longer term to affect political outcomes.

As foreign entities, international corporations must be on their best behavior. But it is important that they consider the cooperation of every segment of the broader community with which they interact or on which their operations have an impact. And they should have a standard — even an implicit one — to uphold. A policy of tolerant laissez-faire must be tempered by the realization that increasingly local citizens see them as adhering to a double standard: one for themselves and one for the "poor unfortunate common men" of the developing host country.

The historical irony is that in order to protect its interests — and its profits — foreign enterprise in the third world was at the outset of its overseas adventures a purveyor of values associated with human rights. The onslaught of modern imperialism on the third world in the nineteenth and twentieth centuries comprised a partnership of state, Western Christianity, and capitalist enterprise. The transmission of Western values in many cases became an excuse for worse abuses overseas. And businesspeople often turned a blind eye to real abuses in the local culture that furthered their own interests and were cost-effective.

By the end of the Second World War, when Eleanor Roosevelt and so many others made the "right of man" explicit, politicians increasingly manipulated the issue of human rights to provide a veil of legitimacy for other motives and the furtherance of other interests. American and international groups have used freedom of religion and freedom of movement in their fight to protect the parochial interest of primarily Jews to emigrate from the Soviet Union without interference or persecution. The human rights issue has validated great power status and has provided leverage against antagonists on the more tangible strategic and economic aspects of international affairs. Up through the Carter administration in the United States, it was an instrument for cudgeling the Soviet Union for inappropriate aggression or punishing other countries for less obvious abuses. It has served as currency for political candidates and as an animus for political rhetoric and partisan mobilization.

In the postmodern era, when rival eschatological ideologies have waned, and democracy is increasingly equated with modernization, human rights are taken more seriously. Along with the issue of preserving the environment, it seems that in actual practice human rights have been redefined to fit a shrinking world. For once, we can realistically expect that certain skeletal universal principles will be treated with as much respect as national sovereignty. The concept of human rights has taken on independent momentum as an ideology. Defined in a minimalist way, these rights involve due process in a system of even-handed, institutionalized justice. Due cause and fair treatment must precede the act of the state's depriving a citizen of his or her personal freedom or meting out punishment. More concretely and eloquently, these rights are set forth in the UN Charter and Geneva Conventions. Human Rights Watch, an organization that investigates civil rights abuses throughout the world, enumerates—succinctly but loosely and subject to interpretation—the conditions it monitors as "murders, disappearances, tortures, arbitrary imprisonment, discrimination, and other abuse of internationally recognized human rights." Based in New York, this advocacy organization's "goal" is "to hold governments accountable if they transgress the rights of other people."[1]

In the third world and newly privatizing countries of eastern Europe and the former Soviet Union, foreign investors become partners in the nation's domestic advancement. Economic progress becomes interwoven with the social and political process. Sometimes, the foreign subsidiaries of corporations—operating in areas known to be unsafe—have the local security forces at their disposal to protect them. But this protection is not a shield from responsibility to understand the local environment, relate to it in a positive way, and ascertain that the security forces are aware of the constraints under which they should operate in protecting a guest of the country. When the corporation refuses to find ways to channel environmental and other types of protest into constructive negotiations with the local people and relies on police suppression, it makes itself a collaborator in the abuses of the political system.

Dabhol Power Corporation was a case of such corporate local people's rights in a host country in the mid-1990s. The Houston-based multinational Enron Corporation operated this $3 billion project in the Maharashtra state of India. Even with one suspension of the enterprise after the nationalist BJP won the local election, the project continued on a fast track. Social scientists, unions, and politicians criticized Dabhol amid charges of corruption. But Enron and the Maharashtra government were determined to proceed; the Maharashtra government even bought a 30 percent interest loan from Enron. Leading environmental activists and leaders of villagers' organizations (whose complaints ranged from the need for transparency to the demand for Enron's contribution to development infrastructure, to the environmental impact, and to more jobs) staged a mass demonstration around the work site. State security forces beat people on the scene, detained them for further physical abuse, and made mass arrests, usually arbitrarily; except for a couple of minor pieces of sabotage, such demonstrations were believed to be peaceful. The forces denied them their right of free assembly and acted in a draconian fashion. In some cases, suspected protesters were even rounded up in advance of an anticipated demonstration.[2]

Enron was not simply a victim of circumstance, forced to defer to the supremacy of the authorities. If it was an impassive victim, it had let itself become one. Its subsidiary, the Dabhol Power Corporation had paid the state security forces for providing guards. It should have had some control over them. On the contrary, local management would not hear the appeals of demonstrators about violations and sometimes had those who questioned them arrested. Contractors at the projects were reported to have organized systematic harassment of activist villagers. Meanwhile, the Dabhol Power Corporation stood on the sideline.

Enron could have avoided this complicity in the misuse of law against local people if it had implemented an effective public relations strategy from the start, particularly at the grassroots level. Perhaps it was the pressure to complete this project on a fast track that made the heavy-handed approach more appealing. But it was incumbent on Enron as a public corporation to have responded to the *first* mass protest with systematic *crisis management.*

A crisis management team ideally would have comprised a senior management representative from the United States or the international point man in Washington, D.C., legal counsel, a representative for media relations, and a director of the local enterprise.

No public statements or media smooth talk would be as effective as dealing with the crisis by establishing a committee framework with government and people to sort out the problems. Such a committee or committees was long overdue by the first outbreak of mass outrage. Enron either did not have a proactive strategy for promoting its interest among the people, or management had put it aside.

A lesson might have been learned a few years earlier at Bhopal in India when chemical contamination locally sparked a furor, but it was not.

So many other foreign corporations enter a market relying on the cooperation of a government and do little to provoke local antagonism themselves, but find themselves wedged in a battle between local protestors upset with development policies and practices and the government authorities who would resist them. One such conflict between government and people involved the communities in the oil regions of Nigeria. This dispute that had been simmering because authorities had failed to use any oil income for benefits to the local people. Instead, oil income had seemed to disappear into foreign bank accounts. The authorities allegedly had not used even a portion of the revenue to develop the region and to provide new enterprises that might create a trickle-down effect.

In the 1990s, five major oil companies, including Shell, Mobil, and Chevron, got caught up in a situation that began with relatively unorganized protest in the oil regions of Nigeria to demand compensation for damage done to land and livelihood. When Ken Saro-Kiwa organized MOSOP (the first ethnic group to protest on behalf of the Ogoni people in this region), it did not take long for the military government to intercede. The military arrested and executed Saro-Kiwa and eight others in the mid-1990s and stepped up a brutal and often illegal repression of mostly peaceful protests throughout the region. In some cases, people protested for reasons only remotely related to oil. Many participants, probably not necessarily the ones who had cut a pipeline, were youths who simply felt excluded from the political systems but were nonetheless brutalized.[3] Paramilitary mobile police, regular police, or the army beat and illegally detained petitioners or group protesters gathered in a peaceful way. Protesters at Chevron's Parabe Platform in Ondo state, who had come to ask for compensation for the environmental damage that Chevron had done by digging canals, were given an unexpected response. Chevron called the cops, and two youths consequently died at the hands of security forces.[4]

Oil companies are not unsophisticated about political risk and risk management. But often profits are so attractive that they proceed anyway and hope to get their work done and money out quickly. As bystanders to an essentially domestic conflict, they are only slightly less culpable than if they had actively engaged the protesters in violent confrontation. The fact is that in complex crisis situations some wrong calls are made, and an oil company foreman—or perhaps a higher authority—precipitately summons security forces that can not be restrained. Unjustifiable killings are whose fault then? In a way, the oil companies play into the host government's hands by making themselves the easier targets for nationwide dissent and creating bad publicity for themselves that hurts their standing at home and in the "civilized world." And, of course, home country sanctions against the host country will not improve the corporation's lot!

In a host country where values and practices might lead to compromising situations, it is not always easy for a corporation to have an explicit standard of ethics. Corporations do not like to think on this plane. At least, in South Africa, just a few years before a black African government was installed and apartheid ended, corporations that adhered to the Sullivan Principles or some similar standard could find white political allies in the country and could also joke to the "locals" (the white people) that they were under political pressure. The situation in most counties is not so black and white, clear-cut. But it is important that a corporation, like an individual, be true to itself. If it can espouse free market capitalism, it need make no apologies for having democratic convictions.

If a political risk analysis points to volatility in the community in which an enterprise is being located, the best way for the parent company not to compromise itself in security-related situations is to develop a system for the exchange of information and ideas in a positive way with the community. Look for the most politically articulate activists, traditional leaders, and representatives of women and youth.

Rule of Law

If one could dismiss human rights as a matter of "to each his own," one still would have to face the fact that the flagrant breaches of civil and human rights in certain countries often correspond to a disregard for the rule of law. In so many countries where people are tortured or arrested unjustly, the circumstances involve capriciousness and either the absence of protective laws or the disregard of them. Due process is not always followed and arrests often are more like disappearances.

Without a respect for law, the sovereign state and its security personnel are free to act as they please and to mete out punishment in an unfair, arbitrary way without issuing an explanation.

Foreign businesspeople cannot trust such a society and can even become its victims. For example, if Chinese authorities become too anxious about a Western individual's contacts with a particular publication or individual, they can first accuse him of obtaining wrongful information and then describe the information as "state secrets." The consequences could be interrogation, detainment in prison, or deportation.

Rule of law does not exist in the same degree in all countries and is virtually absent in some local areas like southeastern Turkey. It is, however, critically important to Westerners, as much as a framework for organization and guarantee of consistency and orderliness in conducting affairs as a cultural manifestation of our civilization. For the businessperson, this means the impersonal codification of regulations for rationally conducting business and arbitrating disputes. But it is also implies much more.

The rule of law is the hallmark of social stability. The post-Suharto reformist president of Indonesia, the moderate Islamist Abdulrahhman Wahid, has a mandate to democratize the whole system. But for political reasons, when he seeks to deal with the powerful Army Chief of Staff general Wiranto, he appeals to the national interest. In order to justify his struggle with the military and to advance the investigation of the army's involvement in the killings in East Timor, he cites the importance of demonstrating that the rule of law and that national institutions are being respected. In other words, without a credible legal system, chaos might follow and international opinion would turn.

Closer to the bottom line, the businessperson must be assured that contracts will be honored and that the laws governing his operations will be consistent. Michael Newcity demonstrates in his case study of Russia that the state judicial system must honor its commitments. The transition from a command economy to a privatized one can be fraught with twists and turns as the state strives for balance and resolves which areas are more strategic than others. However, the foreign businessperson who invested early and signed agreements under certain private enterprise assumptions should not have to risk being penalized because the government has changed its mind. Worse still, he should not be penalized by capricious decisions concerning his case in which a contrived rationale based on a sudden change in state policy is an excuse for expropriation.

In many developing countries that have yet to integrate their regulatory systems, the foreign investor might have to deal with conflicts between central and local statutes or differing statutes that contradict one another. Knowing the right people and officials helps, but one can never be sure of oneself in unclearly charted territory subject to the vagaries of policy interpretation and the subjective whims of officials.

CIVIL DISORDER: VIOLENCE AND TERRORISM

Many of the issues that we have discussed can culminate in organized mass violence. This social violence can indirectly affect us by upsetting the political system and the routine of business as usual. It occasionally directly explodes at our bottom line when our own installations, personnel, and flow of commerce are at risk.

When a businessperson evaluates a new market or host country, he or she must consider the prospects for organized mass violence (through unions, associations, political parties, or student vanguard organizations), anomic outbursts of social violence (such as the spontaneous crowd hysteria of overturning trains and buses or beating up a scapegoated minority person or foreigner), or a general state of lawlessness. If a society is given to organized violence, which under certain circumstances might escalate and spread, executives should be aware of the fact.

Even if it falls far short of a social revolution, civil disorder, particularly when it spreads like wildfire from city to city, can disrupt international business operations and pose obvious hazards for expatriate personnel. Many countries in the third world have histories of civil unrest. In Yugoslavia and some non-Russian areas of the former Soviet Union, one can expect ethnic conflict, compounded by other variables like economic inequities, to persist even after major squabbles over borders and cultural autonomy seem to have been resolved.

The threat of social violence should not be a deterrent to investing in a country or even expanding operations there, but the astute businessperson who evaluates the situation for his company should consider five factors that will help show him what to expect. A strategy can then be formulated on the basis of considering risk against opportunity in a fully informed way.

Look into these conditions:

1. The history of civil violence in a given country (frequency, causes, and pattern of locations).
2. The extent of the deterioration of economic, social, and human rights conditions, and whether a boiling point seems to be approaching.
3. Organizations (religious, political, student, and/or labor) that might spearhead or manipulate demonstrations or riots.
4. The likelihood of an outbreak's being easily contained by the police or military through the effective threat or utilization of coercion.
5. The focus of acts of civil disorder: Would they deliberately target foreigners and foreign business installations, and why?

Outbreaks of civil unrest are so numerous and in many ways so redundant that it is unnecessary to go through a litany of them. The situation in Egypt provides a historic lesson through its cost-of-living riots in 1977 and the economic disaster that preceded them. Similar outbreaks were avoided in the 1980s because austerity programs were not implemented precipitously. It was not just the foreign investor who learned from the experience. One buffeting force against future mass demonstrations protesting the Mubarak government is the Egyptian cultural proclivity toward deference in the face of credible authority. In the 1980s, Mohammed Hosni Mubarak consolidated his power vis-à-vis the military, strengthened his position before the Egyptian people, and learned to manipulate the Egyptian people's penchant for obeisance to authority. With a stronger domestic position, enhanced by a very positive international image, he now stands before a relatively compliant nationwide constituency. In the event of any social eruption, it is likely that President Mubarak would have little difficulty in bringing the disturbance under control. *An understanding of the mechanisms of control and their efficacy in a country is as important as the ability to identify potential sources of civil disorder and to predict volatility.*

Not only is the possibility of a given type of civil disorder predictable, but careful observation can also sometimes anticipate the timing of the event. In the months preceding the food riots in January 1984 in the Rif Mountains in Morocco, a reduction in food price subsidies was undertaken. On December 17, King Hassan II appeared on television ostensibly to talk about a new census that would lead to a more equitable distribution of wealth among rich and poor; he implicitly was letting the people know that they were in for harder times under a draft budget that was then under consideration. At the same time, an exit tax was introduced that penalized the migrant workers in the north; a crackdown on contraband upset the small-scale smuggling operations among the poorer people of the region; the nucleus of the nation's police force was called up to provide security for the Islamic Conference meeting that the king was proudly hosting in Marrakech, thereby limiting their dispersal throughout the country; and the king declared a national holiday and let the restless young people out of school. Any well-coordinated monitoring of the situation between the strategic-planning complement at corporate headquarters and an astute on-site field manager (observing, contacting corporate headquarters with an inquiry, and then further interpreting events) should have been able to forecast what was to be a limited period of popular unrest.

We should emphasize again that the excessive use of state violence to deal with social unrest could be the undoing of the political system. Indeed, the frequent use of harsh force to beat down popular protest can be perceived as evidence of the government's weakness; the very act of using brutal force can radicalize citizens who would otherwise be waverers or settle for the status quo. The successful exercise of control, a sort of manipulation of popular opinion and cultural disposition, is not the same as the resort to repetitive coercion.

Finally, in many vast countries from Nigeria to China, violent civil outbreaks can be isolated. In China, acts of labor demonstrations and violence occur every year by the hundreds throughout the country. When the Tiananmen students' and workers' demonstration simmered in the hot sun of Beijing in May–June 1989, countless counterpart demonstrations and repressive violence took place in cities as far west as Chengdu, Sichuan. In more rural and inland areas, the spread of what Mao Zedong described as the "prairie fire" of rebellious activity could be contained. In 1989, university students communicated by fax machine at the universities; nowadays, the Internet is available to them. Even China's pervasive police network will be stymied in the suppression of information flow through computer networks. But the levers of control are effective in China when a plainclothes policeman is already on the scene, poised to act as soon as someone clenches a fist. The internal security system is so structured that it can control outbreaks of social violence and presumably isolate them physically from spreading geographically and among the different classes of people.

TERRORISM

Still another variant of social/political violence is terrorism. Private consultants in the United States and Europe specialize in monitoring acts of terrorism that range from blowing up installations to kidnapping businesspeople, murders, and political executions. Statistics on terrorist incidents are available to companies via on-line computer services. Often, as in Colombia, crime or banditry, kidnapping for ransom, and violence connected with the illicit drug traffic and political protest are interwoven. The purpose of political kidnapping can be (a) to gain the release of colleagues from prison, domestically and internationally (b) to obtain a material ransom, and (c) simply to make a political statement by the harassment and/or execution of the victim.

If we live in a world of increasing globalization of standards and practices, violence closes in on us from all sides as well. Often earmarked as its primary targets, businesspeople certainly cannot hide from terrorism. Nor can they create an effective image for themselves and their companies by going to work in a host country each day with gun turrets on the top of their vehicles. Since governments increasingly will refuse to meet political demands to rescue kidnap victims, and since host governments often forbid foreign corporations to make a transfer of money in kidnapping cases, an international bank or MNC can best protect its expatriate personnel by monitoring terrorism in countries of exposure and by developing crisis contingency plans for such emergencies overseas. Concrete preparations can provide guidance to personnel and their families about being properly circumspect, traveling to work by different routes, defensive driving, and other means of evading would-be perpetrators on site. Comprehensive plans would also establish a crisis action communications network; that is, a systematic program of response to a crisis between the local level and corporate headquarters.

In positioning themselves in questionable areas, strategic planners and field marketing executives must look for patterns that indicate *type* of activities, *locations* of prevalent acts of terrorism, and the *nature of the targets.* In Peru, several years ago the Sendero Luminoso guerrillas for the most part carefully targeted infrastructure projects in the southern Andes and left the people—and foreigners—alone. In the closing years of the 1990s, as the movement escalated and then fell into desperate decline, the lives of civilian personnel have come to be at risk. Moreover, the Sendero Luminoso's activities spread from the outlying areas of the population centers before its remnants retreated to the countryside. Colombia is notorious for its kidnappings—particularly in rural areas from Caquetá to the Magdalena Medio. In the cities too, political elements are at work. Even if the M-19 guerrillas could be extirpated from the cities, widespread urban crime would continue to endanger foreigners living in Bogotá who worry about the walk from their apartments in the luxurious high ground above the center of the city to their cars in the parking lot.

MILITARY UNREST

Countries with frequent military coups are often considered unstable. In cultures where political change is routinely wrought by military takeover, trauma and violence might well be minimal. Moreover, military interventions often restore order by deterring or reducing social unrest that could hamper the foreign businessperson. The foreign enterprise need be concerned only with the question of whether a particular type of military changeover can affect business as usual. Does an unusual set of new military usurpers have a bone to pick with the private sector, or will it leave the rules of the game alone? Will it meet the previous government's external financial obligations? In general, as we have stated earlier, a military government will continue to follow a tradition of conservative politics in such situations. The businessperson need be concerned only about the uncertainty and temporary paralysis that such a regime change might incur and whether his particular project might be too controversial and too closely linked to the previous leadership.

Can a military coup be anticipated? Some years ago we questioned an Africa expert on the likelihood of a military coup in Ghana. At the time, the civilian government of Hilla Limann was facing severe economic problems. The expert, who had in fact inadvertently allowed himself to become an advocate for democratic government in Ghana, said he considered a coup highly unlikely because no consensus for such a takeover had developed. Of course, no polls were taken when Flight Lieutenant Jerry John Rawlings replaced Limann. A general rule is that where there is a history of military control, the military might be inclined to rise again given appropriate and inviting circumstances.

It is useful to know whether the military, or part of it, regards itself as having political responsibilities. What general political, social, and economic circumstances would arouse its indignation? Does it see itself as an enforcer of morality and, like Nigerian colonel Muhammad Buhari's New Year's Eve coup of 1983–1984 or the 1992 attempted coup in Venezuela (the oldest democracy in Latin America), would its mission be to cleanse the Augean stables and to wash away official corruption?

Further analysis of the military, even in societies like Tunisia where the military does not perceive itself as any more political than perhaps in France or the United States, takes on particular importance in a time of political instability when the legitimacy of the civilian government might be called into question. If the alternative to social chaos is military intervention, nuances in the military's self-perception are important. The Moroccan military has generational differences. The most senior, and increasingly retiring, officers never developed a sense of separate identity since Morocco's independence; the younger officers, gradually working their way up the ladder in recent years, are more inclined to question the political order. They are also more likely to come from urban and Arab backgrounds than the preceding generation, are better educated, and tend to come from coastal middle-class families. They have become politically aware and might someday crave a political identity.

In anticipating a coup, it is also important to ask some fairly obvious questions. Are the troops happy? Do they have enough prestige, mobility (particularly junior to senior levels), pay, and other benefits? In Indonesia, both active and retired military officers are encouraged to take civilian and even corporate jobs, but some talk is circulating under the new government of major reforms in this area. Moreover, President Abdulrahhman Wahid has already proposed that troops stationed across the expanse of the country (an archipelago of some seven thousand islands, half of which are inhabited), and enjoying privileged influence and control in those areas, would be withdrawn to more centralized bases. If General Wiranto, chief of staff, and other key military officers were to be punished by a tribunal for their human rights abuses in East Timor and elsewhere, or more concrete steps were taken to strip the senior military of the double-dipping jobs and their sinecures with private companies and foreign investors, the military might be disposed to prevent such "revolution" from above. However, it is important to observe how well Wahid is testing the limits of struggle with the military and compromising with them when necessary. Such a gradualist approach might chip away at the military's power before it can muster the momentum to intervene.

In China, the military—perhaps the major source of instability during the past years of modernization—has been courted and restored to prominence at the same time as it has been professionalized and equipped with more sophisticated weaponry. In Algeria (a highly militarized society), not only is the president a product of the military, but the army is also represented in the ruling party, state, and judiciary.

Finally, we must ask ourselves: If a coup, what then? In most cases, as we have previously discussed, the most likely disruption would derive from the atmosphere of uncertainty surrounding the military takeover. To prepare optimally for such a contingency, a more focused analysis of the military is required. Published information might exist on dissidence within the armed forces of an unpredictable host country. Other insights might be shared on a personal level by State Department specialists and analysts and observers in other organs of the executive branch. One might discover, for example, a rivalry between field command and headquarters about reconciliation with communist insurgents, or learn that a markedly large number of the younger officers have come to embrace a militant form of Islam. A most important factor to consider in examining the ranks of the military in third-world countries is that elements within the armed forces might have poor, rural origins and adhere to a populist orientation that could prejudice them against MNCs and international lending institutions if they came to power.

EXTERNAL TERRITORIAL DISPUTES

Territorial disputes have taken on some new importance since the Falkland Islands war in Argentina and Iraq's efforts to grab oil-rich areas in Kuwait. Notwithstanding the importance of greed as a motive for aggressively pursuing some territorial claims, often such incursions beyond one's own unquestioned borders represent a means of diverting the people's attention away from its own domestic economic ills. A close examination of the political rhetoric, the way it resonates with the people's emotions, and the nature of the domestic problems on both sides can help the corporate planner gauge the importance of this dimension of political risk to operations.

Most border disputes in the third world have their origin in colonial times when boundaries were imposed on them. What is the substance today of a nation's claims for territory against another and how salient is a country's commitment to regain or retain the territory in question? Have developments occurred to defuse the emotional content of the contest? For example, by 1984, Guinea and Guinea-Bissau had taken their dispute to The Hague for adjudication. Nigeria and Cameroon, which in the past had argued hotly over avowedly oil-rich border areas, were enjoying cordial relations because of a change of government in Nigeria. Post-Soviet Russia under Boris Yeltsin and Vladimir Putin has also made progress in appeasing the People's Republic of China on its northeastern perimeter. For years, during China's anti-Soviet and generally xenophobic Cultural Revolution, Chinese and Russian soldiers engaged in border clashes in Heilongjiang along the Ussuri River and elsewhere. Minor skirmishes took place in an emotionally charged atmosphere, involving Chinese brandishing guns and Russian soldiers urinating on posters of Mao Zedong throughout the 1960s and into the 1970s. Now, China is interested in consolidating its borders—all of them—and the Russians have met with the Chinese at the negotiating table. However, in the late 1990s, China created outposts in the contested Spratly and Paracel Islands in the South China Sea, a potentially oil-rich seabed. A number of foreign oil companies that would also like to do business with China now have to consider hedging their bets.

In regions where local wars frequently erupt (such as the cluster of states surrounding and including Israel), a foreign company must be careful about operating in contested areas, major cities, or strategic locations with concentrations of heavy infrastructure. The converse situation also obtains. Thus, although hostilities ranging from skirmishes to war seemed to be imminent between Syria and Israel for years, a foreign company did not necessarily have to be gun-shy. If an opportunity had presented itself to build a pipeline in remote western Syria, personnel and equipment would have been away from the line of fire.

External conflict can also be destabilizing to the domestic situation in a given country. Over the years, Moroccan king Hassan II's war in the Western Sahara won the applause of the people but drained the country's economic resources; yet, if the new king were to quit now and compromise with the Polisario, his own people might force him from his throne. If Syria reacted to what it perceived to be an inadequate resolution of the West Bank issue and went to war with Israel, the country could fall into political disarray. A less-than-successful war, or peace, with Israel could force Hafiz al-Assad or his weaker son out of power and leave a leadership vacuum that in the case of a failed peace could be filled by the Muslim Brotherhood or elements sympathetic to it. Such an outcome potentially could be more threatening to a Western business presence in Damascus than war itself.

Still another consideration for international corporate planners (particularly in the extractive industries) is the inadvisability of locating in an area disputed by two or more countries. In such contests, the U.S. government usually warns that it cannot be accountable for the safety of its citizens. In an area that was being offered as an oil concession in the 1980s off South Korea, sovereignty over the terrain was being asserted not only by South Korea, but by Taiwan, the People's Republic of China, and, of course, North Korea. In an earlier period in the East China Sea, China once shelled the boats of a concessionaire affiliated with another claimant country. Given the normalization of relations with Vietnam and the end of U.S. sanctions, the lower portion of the South China Sea including the Spratly and Paracel Islands will be a promising offshore oil area. To penetrate this new area of opportunity and avoid risking whatever footing they might have in China, corporate negotiators will have to be sensitive to the volatility of the border dispute; certainly the consummation of any concrete deals will have to be predicated on a possibly protracted process of negotiating international agreements between Vietnam and China. Other countries also feel they have stakes in this offshore area and in others in the region, which constitutes a legal problem that could take on graver importance in the future.

ELITES IN AN ELITIST COUNTRY: PICKING THE PLAYERS

In examining the political stability of a host country or the ways in which policies might evolve to the advantage or detriment of a particular foreign enterprise, both corporate planners and marketing executives in the field ought to identify the key actors or groups of actors within the political and social elites. Quite often they overlap. Although sometimes the importance of interpersonal networks (who knows whom and who is related to whom) is overriding, it is usually of critical value to ascertain where individuals stand on the issues of direct and indirect influence on your business dealings. (For a general discussion of the phenomenon with regard to the party elite groups in one country, China, see chapter 4.)

A still more refined planning approach would look more intensively at the less apparent divergences within one group of actors itself. Thus, within one country's military elite, it might simply not be enough to know that there is some sort of tension between junior and senior officers. Mix with them or talk to U.S. agencies that have looked into the question and try to determine how their origins and worldviews might differ and what the complaints are that might surface? Also, how well entrenched in the senior command are those officers who are less desirable from a foreign business standpoint? In the Thai army, and now in the parliament, General Chawalit Yongchayut, who encouraged the left-leaning, so-called "Democratic Soldiers' Coup" in April 1981, was still in the 1990s a major military/political figure in Thailand. Since the uncertain recovery of parliamentary democracy in Thailand in 1992, Chawalit could well represent the "opposition" and be a prime mover among the more idealistic soldiers in the future should economic and social/political circumstances warrant intervention.

Among the civilians in either developing countries or even more developed societies like Venezuela and Taiwan, we would look not just at the different political parties or interest (special interest) groups but at the cliques and factions within them as well. We might ask: (a) Are these factions divisive? (In Syria, one could try to assess how well organized or fragmented the political opposition is to the Muslim Brotherhood.) (b) Can all factions be identified? (Not all are represented by a formal group.) (c) Do not distinct and even conflicting groups comprise individuals whose allegiances within the same large group hinge as much on interpersonal relations as they do on the substance of the issues? (d) Do we find cross-cutting alliances among individuals who are linked to several groups, and do these alliances serve to ameliorate social and political tensions in general?

The latter two lines of questioning are particularly applicable to a country like Indonesia. Indeed, one can make the argument that Indonesia has been controlled by an interlocking directorate of elite groups, which have run the gamut from the president's inner circle to the more vociferous dissidents. In Indonesia, everyone seems to know everyone else personally, and the system appears to be virtually all-inclusive; in other words, even the "outsiders" are inside.

To prepare for a long-term stay in such a market, a company must learn who is who and who has "stabbed whom in the back." Foreign investors should know with what party and with what faction potential business associates should be affiliated, how might their particular group lend positive support to the enterprise, and, finally, how well situated this political faction would be in the event of a leadership succession crisis in the nation. Such information can probably be obtained on site in a very social way as one explores for partners and local allies. This sort of inquiry can be carried out openly as the logical and sophisticated extension of a corporation's normal check of local market conditions; it even can be integrated into a public relations effort to get to know one's local principals and associates more closely.

Making well-situated political friends for an enterprise and choosing local principals and associates with attention to their influence and standing is not only a critical safeguard for the welfare of the new enterprise but a clever way for the foreign businessman to position himself for a longer stay in the market. The initial advantage of painstakingly investigating the place of local associates in a host country's system of elites is that the process itself will constitute an education about how the social and political system functions. Later, if a foreign enterprise is victimized by the foul play of its local principals or comes up against attempts at official extortion, the well-positioned outsider can appeal to strategically well-placed friends in the political system. Even serious bureaucratic roadblocks can be cleared with the intervention of the right people. In societies like Indonesia or the Philippines, characterized by interpersonal networks, important relations have to be cultivated and massaged continuously. The apparent plan of Roger Daft,

Coca-Cola's newly appointed CEO in 2000, to move his headquarters from one important country location to another theoretically is an excellent (if extreme) idea for comingling with the local powers and making his company an integral part of the business environment.

It is never enough just to make the contact for your company; the contact must be developed. High-level, courtesy visits from the home corporation's upper-level executives and CEO will strengthen the bonding.

NATIONALISM AND NATIONAL GOALS

In the process of nation-building, it becomes necessary for a shared set of values, called national identity or nationalism, to be inculcated among all the people within a country's boundaries. Particularly at an early stage of nation-building, nationalism should not be perceived as a threat to the outside. On the contrary, it is useful in the long run because it contributes to the cohesiveness of entities often comprising many diverse ethnic groups. However, some of the permutations of this unifying national symbolism historically have proven to be dangerous and destabilizing to the international community (either regional, as in Iraq's incursions in the Persian Gulf area, or on a wider scale).

International business also must be wary of xenophobia, a historical hostility to foreigners among the people in some countries. Often, this nationalistic, ethnocentric, or perhaps just provincially naive resentment of outsiders takes the form of a proclivity to blame foreign business interests or Western materialist values for corroding or contaminating the traditional culture or, at the bottom line, exploiting the country and damaging the economy. Nationalistic fist-shaking leads also to the accusation that the IMF and multilaterals are bleeding the country by insisting on austerity plans as conditions for credit.

Whether it involves an adventurous military occupation by Argentina of the Falkland Islands or a politically explosive domestic economic crisis that is alienating the people's support for the political system, nationalism can often be effectively manipulated by the political leadership for the sake of self-preservation. If the leadership feels that its message will tap a xenophobic strain in the ingrained nationalism of the people, it might scapegoat foreign investors or blame the richer countries for the high-interest loans "forced upon them" by capitalist banks. In the early stage of China's transition to privatizing parts of the economy, the trauma of increased unemployment from state-run enterprises and the emerging differential in incomes in the urban sector led to open criticism of Western styles and materialist values. "Westernization is proceeding too fast," many Chinese intellectuals began to balk in the 1990s. "We're learning bad habits and losing our values." In this way, the Western "incursion" of investments and imports has been made a scapegoat for the government's failure to hold and develop a coherent ideological identity and post-Maoist ethos to meet the challenge of brazen

Western consumer materialism. The 1996 publication in China of *China Can Say No*, a collection of essays put together by former Cultural Revolution Red Guards, essentially said that the U.S. and Japanese imperialists had pushed China around long enough. China could say "No!" and make the outsider compensate this generation for the depredations that imperialism of a more brutal kind had wrought on previous generations. The problem for China in entering the global mainstream is that its nationalistic resistance is apt to be in direct proportion to the extent to which it must swallow—whether in the form of values or hairstyles—the once-denounced "sugar-coated bullets of the West."

The Mexican leadership, in the last phase of Jose Lopez Portillo's term in the early 1980s, tried to turn its back on its external debt problem by manipulating what it perceived to be a shared "Yanqui go home!" attitude on the part of two other debt-burdened Latin American countries. But the others refused to cooperate, and it was only then that Mexico began to seriously face its structural problems in negotiations with the IMF.

Mexico's desperate reaching out for a sort of extranational communalism, a regional cultural bond of south against north, suggests that in a shrinking world, strictly nationalistic sentiments can be stretched beyond borders in an effort to cast a net for regional loyalties. Thus, Mexico would not betray Fidel Castro rhetorically to the United States, and Nigeria in good economic times was able to put the squeeze on British Petroleum because of its interests through the 1980s in the then apartheid nation of South Africa. In the third world in general, however, this is the weakest form of emotionalism. It is perhaps least amenable to mobilization. The average villager in a nascent developing country finds it hard to identify with the concept of a nation-state, much less look beyond it. However, the villager in a more modern developing nation (e.g., Morocco) can become fired with fury over a squabble over precise national boundaries.

In the absence of a unifying ideological appeal, nationalism can be a rallying cry whenever the government demands a compelling need for unity. In China, the Taiwan issue has been a cornerstone of external policy since the revolution succeeded on the mainland. It is a manifestation of a territorial imperative in itself but also a means to an end. It invokes emotion from the people, and in 2000 even appeals to young people who appear to be moved by little beyond self-interest. Thus, when competing groups (including the military) jockey for power at a plenary session of the National People's Congress in Beijing, the saber and flag emerge and threats issue from the central government.

As nationalism continues to develop in the newly formed, or slowly integrated, states, emotional or ideological loyalties beyond the nation-state tend to be thinner. While U.S. businesspeople were treated badly throughout most of Latin America for the U.S. position during the Falkland Islands interlude in Argentina in the 1980s, no serious incidents occurred. Similarly, Nigeria's earlier militant position against companies doing business with the South Africa of apartheid in most low-profile cases was a matter of lip service; Nigeria could not afford to oust all MNCs and banks with interests in South Africa. National interest in reality came first!

The trend toward globalism indeed might encourage a shift in the long run away from parochial nationalism (although it is more easily discussed than accomplished) toward a greater investment in transnational economic and political cooperation. In the more developed countries, the phenomenon of finding commonalties beyond national borders was an animating force behind the early shaping of the EC. In the still-developing parts of the world, we see some concerted efforts to form a regional economic and political bond before country-specific nationalism becomes too overpowering. The former "frontline states" of southern Africa, for example, have been trying to implement an overarching union in the Southern African Development Coordinating Commission (SADCC). But consider that in this era of a truly globalized universe of communications and economic relations, regional groupings will be more apt to become anachronisms than the historically rooted nation-states.

The newly independent states of eastern Europe and the separate member states of the former Soviet Union (now the Confederation of Independent States [CIS]) have experienced a resurgence of nineteenth-century nationalism that first revived itself with a flourish during the Soviet transition (perestroika) under Mikhail Gorbachev. The result has led to some violent struggles over borders and efforts by ethnic entities, like Chechnya, to secede from the Russian Republic or the Confederation. Among conservative groups in the United States, some political strategists even encourage these old antagonisms, hoping to play one state off another and all against the "Russian bear."[5] The potential for "acting out" in the resource-rich Ukraine could lead to a conflagration that might escalate into nuclear conflict.

The increased proliferation of nuclear weapons and better delivery systems have "kicked up a notch" the potential damage of nationalistic conflicts. If North Korea's authoritarian Communist regime, now armed with limited missiles, were to seek national unity by force with the south, the whole region and more could be endangered. If India and Pakistan collide in full conflagration over their timeworn dispute concerning Kashmir, both sides could utilize their nuclear weapons capacity, and all of South Asia would experience the aftershock of catastrophe. Should China push its brinkmanship diplomacy too far vis-à-vis Taiwan, it might arrive at a point where in order to regain "face," it sees its best option as attack. Even limiting itself to the option of firing crippling ballistic missiles against industrial and military installations as a sort of coercive diplomacy, the end results would be unpredictable and potentially disastrous to the region. Nationalism in the twenty-first century, *perhaps on the increase as a means of offsetting the leavening effect of globalism*, will be much more heavily armed than in its earlier heyday in the nineteenth century and definitely more a threat to business as usual.

SOCIAL REVOLUTION AND LIVING WITH THE WINNERS

The seemingly ultimate question is whether a social upheaval looms in the foreground—a successful rebellion that would bring in a new set of elite groups and perhaps even alter the rules of the game altogether. Such revolutions depend for their success on just the right combination of some of the factors already discussed and others yet to be covered, sparked by a catalyst that will bring about combustion and the rise of a new elite.

We already have discussed rising economic expectations. But no force can deal more of a blow to the political system or constitute more of a catalyst to mob violence than the introduction of political and social reform measures and then the reversal of these concessions. The old hypothesis that Czar Alexander III's freeing the serfs might have set the Russian revolution in motion certainly seems to have withstood the critical predilections of countless social scientists. As the citizens' access to the political system improves, their level of self and political awareness usually increases. When individuals come to perceive that their horizons can be expanded and that common needs can be achieved by acting in concert with others, they will not readily be shoved back into "solitary confinement." If this catalyst triggers widespread civil disorder, the businessperson must be poised for a social explosion.

The threat of social violence should not be a deterrent to investing. The foreign investor must examine it in the context of his or her plan and the nature and location of the installation. Rebellion can abate, and it can be isolated.

At what point does a rebellion become a revolution? Only the best intelligence can predict that a rebellious movement is gathering enough momentum or forming coalitions with other antisystemic groups to topple a political or social system. Only the most objective analysis of the coordination between capital and villages can indicate whether the central government is decaying and its influence deteriorating. A simple paradigm, comprising the existence of a rebellious organization or coalition, a binding revolutionary ideology, and the delegitimation of the central government might not necessarily reflect a specific reality. External interference and unknowns can also affect the outcome. As we approach the culmination of a revolutionary movement, let us say, well after the theater was set ablaze in Iran in 1978, what at first might have seemed to be a rebellion becomes a more predictably successful revolution. But there is often very little a corporate or bank executive can do about recovering assets from the host country. Indeed, while the existing regime still has a chance, the investor/creditor is inclined to tie his fortunes to the government that welcomed him. *After all, many revolts are launched, but few succeed.* A survey of companies with investments or trade exposures in Iran prior to 1979 indicates that more than 75 percent lost all but a small percentage of their assets in the revolution.

A national liberation struggle, like the war for black rule in Zimbabwe (formerly Rhodesia), poses a particular problem for the corporate strategist. In revolution-torn Zimbabwe, only a radical would have been so bold as to support Robert Mugabe or pro-Soviet Joshua Nkomo, and only a blind conservative would have identified too closely with Ian Smith or Abel Muzorewa. According to political risk analyst Bill Overholt, the pragmatic and conservative businessperson had only one choice. He had to ascertain that his losses would not be too disastrous and that he was positioned to avail himself of opportunities if they occurred. "Because of the uncertainty, [the businessperson] would not align himself with any individual or party. But he would recognize that the old order was finished and would carefully but visibly cut any strong existing ties to the associates of Smith and Muzorewa, taking care to do so in a way that would not lead to government reaction in the short run."[6]

If a bank or MNC already has substantial interests at stake as an apparently revolutionary movement unravels, a concerted effort should be made to analyze the character of the movement and consider its options in the country. On-site operations executives often are politically myopic, or they just do not want to believe that they are witnessing the ground caving in beneath them. Key factors to observe in assessing the denouement of a revolutionary movement as it might affect future business interests are:

1. *The nature of the personality of the revolutionary leaders.* What is their social background—their socioeconomic class, schooling, and religious or ethnic affiliation? Are they likely to embrace a populist worldview because of their origins?
2. *Factionalism.* Are there cleavages within the revolutionary elite, and can one position oneself appropriately? Is it best to address the impending revolutionary government as a collective entity?
3. *The nature of the ideology.* Does the ideology promise the realization of some apocalyptic vision upon accession to political power? Is it an adaptation of some external ideology, like Shia Islam or Marxism-Leninism? Is it being used primarily to hold a broad-based revolutionary organization together? Is there room within its theoretical bounds for the sorts of tactical, or even strategic, flexibility that would permit private investment to continue after the revolution's victory?
4. *The question of external assistance.* In a complex revolution/civil war, as in Zimbabwe or Angola where different revolutionary groups have remained at odds with one another, does the struggle invite external interference from a superpower or jingoistic regional power? A given faction in any internal war should not be labeled "pro-American," "pro-Soviet," or a "Libyan ally" just for accepting donations. The recipient of aid may repay with rhetorical fealty, but in fact the manipulator may well be the one who is being manipulated. In the actual case of Zimbabwe, Robert Mugabe, called "pro-Chinese" and a "Maoist" in the 1960s and 1970s, still shares a cordial relationship with China, but then China's character has changed markedly;

Mugabe's ZANU party-dominated government, like the Chinese, now supports a mixed, private-public economy but in no real way is trying to emulate a Chinese model of any sort.

Given the likelihood that revolutionary movements from time to time will ascend to power, a foreign company or bank can roll with the punches. Gulf Oil is still ensconced in Angola nearly two decades after independence and civil war. And Marxist-Leninist revolutions do evolve—a basically foreign ideology that serves a revolutionary movement well as an organizing set of principles may have to be altered to cope with the harsh realities of restoring order in the aftermath of victory.

NOTES

1. *The ENRON Corporation: Corporate Complicity in Human Rights Violations* (New York–Washington, Human Rights Watch, January 1999), p. iv.

2. *The ENRON Corporation*, pp. 2–5.

3. *The Price of Oil* (New York–Washington, Human Rights Watch, January 1999), pp. 9–12.

4. *The Price of Oil.*

5. The author attended private meetings of the American Foreign Policy Council, a conservative think-tank in Washington, D.C., in the summer of 1996, with former Ukrainian leader Leonid Kravchuk (one of a triumvirate responsible for deposing Gorbachev). At this meeting, former officials under President Ronald Reagan stirred Kravchuk up against Russia and suggested that there were pro-Ukrainians and pro-Russians in the Executive Branch and on Capitol Hill.

6. William H. Overholt, *Political Risk* (London: Euromoney Publications, 1982), p. 20.

2

Cultural Factors, the Critical Threats to Foreign Investment, and the Trade Constraints We Impose on Ourselves

THE POLITICAL CULTURE SIDE OF INTERNATIONAL BUSINESS UNDERSTANDING

One very important facet of political risk, or international environment, analysis is the recognition that every country has its own unique cultural characteristics, the more salient of which can affect political attitudes and behavior and might even constitute constraints against social disorder and upheaval. For this analysis, the political science term "political culture" serves best to describe this dimension. Sidney Verba defines it this way: "The political culture of a society consists of the system of empirical beliefs, expressive symbols, and values which defines the situation in which a political action takes place."[1] Defining the term further, Lucian Pye states: "Each generation must receive its politics from the previous one [and] react against that process to find its own politics."[2] In other words, political culture can be a country's subjective orientation to politics that develops psychodynamically over several generations.

Often, an appreciation of special characteristics that influence one nation's particular political orientation can have a direct, positive impact on doing business there. The strategic planner or international business development executive can draw on these elements to formulate a marketing approach to that country or to position his or her organization comfortably for a long stay in that particular host country. Let us examine the ways in which a country's political culture might affect the stability of the broader political environment for international business operations.

Constraints against Upheavals

Any society has certain values, orientations, and organizational characteristics that lend themselves to top-down manipulation for the purpose of control. Often, these psychological levers of political and social control outweigh the apparent threats to political order, and the analyst should be as attentive to one side of the equation as to the other. Some societies have safety valves, such as a prevalent "ethnic minority," perhaps overseas Chinese who are resented for their entrepreneurial skills, against which the government can deflect hostilities that ought to be directed against the system itself.

In societies like Indonesia and Algeria, social control and manipulation by the political leadership seem to coincide with a deep attitude of deference toward authority on the part of the people. In Algeria, the regime will respond to a mass demonstration first by dispatching the military to the scene to knock heads and make arrests and then by taking steps to pacify the interest groups in question. The military barracks are omnipresent throughout Algiers and outlying towns, and create a peculiarly somber atmosphere. In Indonesia, the authoritarian approach of the Suharto government was fairly effective for a decade or two; however, ironically, because it compromised too much, it suddenly appeared weak. By succumbing to charges of corruption and treating Islamic fundamentalists mildly, it became vulnerable to other pressure, seemed to yield in economic crisis to the International Monetary Fund, and ultimately took a more tolerant official stance in East Timor. The end result was that it had to face a situation of opposition from all directions. Suharto, and then his former pragmatic and conciliatory cabinet member B. J. Habibie, stepped down from the presidency.

Other societies seem inclined to accept the oppressiveness of authoritarian regimes as a preferable alternative to earlier periods of political chaos, gang or guerrilla terrorism, or general social unrest. The Argentine and Chilean middle classes tolerated "disappearances" of friends and relatives, some kidnapped in daylight by thugs in plainclothes, because they might have been tainted by guilt of associating with leftists. Not until severe crises, like economic squeeze and national humiliation, converged and undermined the system's legitimacy did the mothers and other forces join hands to depose Argentina's generals and Chile's Augusto Pinochet Ugarte.

Oftentimes, a combination of political cultural orientation and social structure work against mass upheavals. For instance, a dense urban population comprising relatively educated people who are unable to find proper employment would be a constituency for organized social protest. Yet, though circumstances conform to this paradigm in Algeria, they are offset by the migration of whole extended families to the city at one time. The preservation of the rural family unit ameliorates the psychological trauma of leaving home, and of not finding a "better life in the city."

In Mexico, a plethora of complex social and political conditions exists that in another cultural milieu could portend a political cataclysm. These include the following: an extremely uneven distribution of wealth between the cities and countryside, a high debt burden coupled with near-zero economic growth, an adult work force only 50 percent of which is adequately employed, an acute population growth problem, an inordinate number of politically aware young people entering an overburdened job market, an outmoded land tenure system, extreme rural-to-urban migration, and a frightening density of population in the main cities. Add to these factors periodic economic jolts, which stem in part from worldwide conditions, and one can imagine hordes of political risk consultants clamoring at the doors of major corporations like Mexican jumping beans, offering a diagnostic workup pointing the way to terminal social revolution.

Mexico, however, is in little danger of either social revolution or military takeover for a number of sound political and economic reasons. The conditions on which we will focus here are social and political-cultural:

1. Mexico's social structure in general and its political system in particular are characterized by patron-client relationships through which political dissidents are co-opted into the system and which ensures top-down control. The people seem to respect power and central authority. Each person in a position of authority is limited by authoritative and paternalistic figures above him. The patron-client relationship is so well developed that in most instances local grievances involving everything from health clinics to sewerage are settled by appeal to the local political authority. More vocal critics of the system at the grassroots level of the system usually have been co-opted into it.
2. An apparently low level of interpersonal trust tends to militate against the formation of collective groupings that might pit themselves against the macrosystem.
3. Family consciousness is strong and normally will take precedence over other social and political obligations—a factor that also works against a person's taking the risk of joining or forming a political organization that is apt to get his family into trouble. Also, as in the case of Algeria, the existence of large, extended families in urban areas tends to dispel feelings of alienation and anomie that might otherwise contribute to antisocial behavior expressed through political channels.

Image of the World

A people's image of itself, its memory of events, fundamental attitudes, and unconscious fears can be relayed from one generation to another and can be reflected in its view of the outside world. This perception may be revealed in the speeches and writings of its preeminent personalities—past and present—and in the efforts of political leaders to manipulate certain sentiments among the people. Some insight concerning a country's cultural manipulations and gyrations and how it must represent itself to the outside world can help the foreign businessperson understand how and why he might be perceived a certain way. Can the American operations executive, for example, who is seeking to make headway in a francophone African country, adapt to the prejudices against him and exploit the weaknesses of competitors who are nationals of other countries? Can a businessperson trying to establish an enterprise in Zimbabwe cut through "anti-imperialist" allusions and "anti-Zionist" political rhetoric and realize that these are almost ritualistic incantations that have little to do with the realities of negotiating a sound deal?

From the standpoint of risk to foreign business, what is the propensity of a country to xenophobia or to more specifically directed hostility toward a foreign power whose nationals now work within its borders? At the outset of sanctions in the 1980s, Libyans taunted some expatriates who had remained behind to maintain a foreign company's installations.

Could a national leader, under adverse economic conditions, point a finger at a foreign country or company and evoke a special emotional, popular reaction that would divert attention away from the government in power? Could a third-world nation—at one time wedded to the West in a colonial or neocolonial relationship—have a national compensation neurosis? In China, to cite one possible example, there is an historical memory, perpetuated by political elites over generations, of unfair exploitation by the Western imperialist countries in the nineteenth century. Are the United States, Japan, and several European countries now being made to compensate for past misbehavior by being subjected to difficult negotiating terms and to an unusually demanding sort of technology transfer? Or, to go back in history even further, are the barbarians expected to pay tribute to the Middle Kingdom before receiving the gift of normal commerce? Westerners put themselves at a disadvantage with the Chinese by virtue of standing in awe of China. These questions are merely musings—but important musings nonetheless.

AN UNDERLYING INCLINATION TO DEFAULT, NATIONALIZE, OR EXPROPRIATE GRADUALLY AND BY ATTRITION

Let us consider an issue that is close to political culture considerations but is perhaps best considered in its own separate context. Expropriation or nationalization without preagreed compensation is a real hazard to foreign investment. Certainly the strength and viability of a political system matter little if there are underlying attitudinal factors that would encourage nationalization or default on debt. A formal guarantee against nationalization without fair compensation is only partial safeguard against the expropriated investor's sustaining tremendous losses. As we analyze a new society and how its characteristics might influence our bottom line, we should be aware of the importance of historical attitudes, particularly with regard to default on debt or nationalization without reasonable compensation—the gravest risks to international business. The multinational corporation (MNC) fears the outright expropriation of its equity and assets by a foreign country or the host government's takeover of the local company under the pressure of mounting regulations and restrictions.

Of course, such unfavorable outcomes for MNCs can be influenced by a host of variables:

1. The nature of the industry (e.g., is it considered strategic?).
2. The ideology of the ruling political elite (e.g., has a certain type of social revolution just taken place?).
3. Economic conditions and domestic and international political issues (e.g., could a regional political maneuver by a foreign company's home government serve as pretext for threatening the company's local assets?).

Generally speaking, the international sweep of finance and investment has helped considerably to define the parameters for doing business and has been making bandit-like expropriation more of an anachronism. It is far more likely now that new enterprises considered by the host country to be of critical strategic importance are established from the start as joint local/foreign companies, with a formula for gradual nationalization built into the agreement in a way that affords the foreign investor a profitable tenure as the business develops.

But the exceptions to this assumption make it important to look at the host country's history of performance with regard to expropriation and default, or more specifically, the attitudes of the host country's differing political groups concerning these matters. Of course, one should be sufficiently flexible to recognize that the positions of certain political groups have evolved with the passage of time and with such changing circumstances as the increased popularity of monetarist theory and the increasing tendency to recognize relatively unfettered foreign investment as a stimulus to economic growth. President Carlos Andres Pérez of Venezuela, for example, who in 1974 had nationalized the country's oil industry, had become a champion of the private sector by the time his second bid for his country's presidency came around in the late 1980s. Many foreign businesspersons who had witnessed the earlier expropriation of the oil industry, or whose perception of Pérez's early persona remained frozen in history, were slow to grasp the radical shift in Venezuela's foreign investment orientation. They were wiser to err on the conservative side and to play it safe for a while.

A look at each country's history of intervention in the private sector can provide additional insights and often reassurance about the paradoxical advantage and/or leverage a foreign firm might now enjoy in a specific cultural context.

Many nations, particularly in Latin America, have learned that excess expropriations have led to a monstrous, unproductive public sector that saps the country's reserves. Mexico is in a curious position. In September 1982, because of critical economic circumstances involving a run on the banks, the Jose Lopez Portillo government nationalized the banks and, with them, 45 percent of bank-owned private companies. That administration's realization of the negative effects of government ownership and the memory thereof now ought to prevent nationalization in the future. Any political proclivity henceforth to appease a bellicose domestic left with rhetoric about a greater role for the state in economic operations would have to be offset by this harsh recollection of statism gone awry.

A still more clear-cut case of a country's having developed an aversion to nationalization from its own historical experience is Peru. Between 1968 and 1975, General Juan Velasco's junta redistributed the country's wealth. Several large MNCs were expropriated, and foreign mining companies were forced to expand their investments at contractual disadvantage to themselves. The result was ruination for Peru. From the tenure of President Fernando Belaúnde Terry onward, the economy has become increasingly liberalized. Even if there were another military coup, it is unlikely that the next junta would be as radical as its precursor in the 1970s. It might flex its rhetorical muscle, but it would be unlikely to rape the private sector or toss out foreign interests. On the contrary, foreign enterprises now constitute a critical interest group and can use their position for leverage with the new administration. Not only are they a bulwark of the economy, but the message they transmit to the outer world can also give credibility to the new regime.

A country also might try to compensate for its historical image with regard to expropriation. The People's Republic of China wants to repatriate both Taiwan and Hong Kong, yet it must show the free world that this is *repatriation without expropriation*.

Even given the apparently protective cocoon of globalization, we should examine the history of nationalization/expropriation and default as a political act in a given country. These things still can happen. A review of the historical situation should be an integral part of investment planning in a new host country *but the specific dynamics of change must be considered equally as important*. A historical review will ascertain the level of expropriation risk for investments and in some cases might guide the investor to seek risk insurance coverage. Indications that the government will bend over backwards in contrition for past expropriations are no reason not to hedge bets. We can also educate ourselves as to whether there might be ways to structure a contract in terms of technology transfer and joint ownership to enable more effective control of our own outcomes.

Because expropriation "in the nation's interest" is a tradition that has not quite died in some places, and such decisions are always political, we must be certain to investigate the attitudes of the whole spectrum of the political elite, particularly (if relevant) the way they react to their own past history of nationalization or how they have adjusted to the foreign economic presence currently in their midst.

Even in Peru where there is an almost overwhelming horror at the economic disaster of the 1970s, some elements of the younger military officer corps might allow their populist leanings to cloud their judgment if they came to power. And in China at some time in the future, if old ideologues were to resurface or new ideologues were to emerge to challenge the materialist modernizers, the country could regress to an extreme version of "self-reliance" and rejection of Western capitalism. This outcome is certainly unlikely in the five to ten years ahead (see the case study on China, chapter 4). But in such an extreme situation, repudiation of contract and expropriation, with or without compensation, would be weapons to draw from a building arsenal. Indeed xenophobia, or resentment of foreigners, is still a popular sentiment in a number of areas of the developing world. Beware of a desperate political elite that is in a position to manipulate such feelings during difficult economic times in order to shift the blame to foreign enterprise.

Our ambiguity here about the predilections of a given host country, only serves to underscore the need to be aware of the relevant variables and possible contingencies for each country and to monitor events from this baseline of knowledge.

Finally, a word about default on debt. A country's decision to default on external debt can reflect a fundamental attitudinal problem in the historic memory of the people. Officials and local businesspeople alike may seem to feel that they should be compensated for past injustices. The foreign creditor, big or small, and the trader who expects to be paid are held accountable for their forbears.

GOVERNMENT CONSTRAINTS AGAINST DOING BUSINESS ABROAD

Heretofore, we have examined political problems for business undertakings that have derived from the environment of the host country. Often, the political relations between our government at a given time and that of the host country have a direct influence on opportunities and conditions for doing business there. A company that operates in a country where its home government cannot protect its nationals is taking on an added risk. The corporation should determine first whether opportunity outweighs risk and/or whether it has the leverage on its own to secure its position in the country in question.

A diplomatic reversal can constitute even more of a trauma than the absence of normalized relations in the first place. The opening or upgrading of diplomatic relations between the home country and country X can lead to an investment treaty, trade initiatives, and even a honeymoon period in bilateral business relations. But the deterioration of diplomatic relations can make all these advances disappear and severely impair business. A U.S. MNC is particularly vulnerable to hostility and abuse. Sometimes the hostility takes the form of the people's violent aggression against installations because they seem to stand symbolically for the politics and economic policy of the home government.

A former vice president of a multinational, notes: "Contracts cannot be equated with diplomatic relations, which can be turned on and off as circumstances dictate. A corporation cannot pull out, leaving behind an 'Interests Section' to look after matters. . . . A corporation either attempts to live up to the terms of a contract, or it leaves. Generally, a corporation will do what it can to protect its current and future income and will stay on unless forced out by threat of life."[3]

A corporation can ill afford the damages to its reputation, not to mention the loss of its investments or assets, of withdrawing from the country in question. At the same time, it stands naked in the chill of the host country's political climate and frequently suffers from the related punitive measures taken by its own government (such as the Ronald Reagan administration's refusal to grant visas for needed personnel to maintain existing American-owned facilities in Libya).

Trade Sanctions/Embargoes/East-West Trade

It is easy to understand that the climate of diplomatic relations between two countries might have an indirectly salutary or conversely dissonant impact on the tone and volume of bilateral commerce. But for international businesspersons, the most noisome aspect of international relations concerns the manipulation of trade to augment foreign policy objectives. Indeed, sometimes the political disincentives to doing business overseas derive not from the aspects of instability in the projected host country. Rather, they originate in our own government's manipulation of the flow of trade for political leverage.

The United States, in particular, has always controlled exports for purposes of national security and foreign policy and when certain resources have been in short supply. The United States is notorious for using embargoes or exercising restrictions on dual technology solely for punctuating a specific political policy message to the government of the country in question. When another country acts in a way that the United States finds threatening, or even takes a stand at counterpoint with our national policy, we frequently resort to trade sanctions against it. Sometimes, as in the case of the Jackson-Vanek Amendment, Congress will have mandated certain courses of action for certain types of abuses (e.g., preventing freedom of emigration in socialist bloc countries) and the president must act. But usually a given administration has a great deal of leeway and can forestall or instigate such initiatives. Thus, President Jimmy Carter responded to Russia's incursions against Afghanistan by promulgating sanctions against the export of grain to the former Soviet Union. Conversely, President George Bush resisted strong congressional efforts to enact binding sanctions against the People's Republic of China after the Tiananmen Square arrests.

Economic sanctions forged from political steel surely send a message to the targeted country, but the U.S. government also deals a blow to interested exporters from Iowa to New York and jeopardizes the financial commitments of corporations that have positioned themselves in that market. Our government hurts others that have invested time and money in imminent commitments. In effect, we attempt to punish a particular foreign government by not permitting it to purchase the goods and services we regard as important to it. Unfortunately, seldom is one country the sole source of supply available to the purchaser, and our corporations suffer in the process.

Short of actual embargoes but just as harmful to the U.S.–based corporation, export controls imposed for foreign policy purposes can be employed as sanctions over such issues as apartheid, human rights, nuclear nonproliferation, transnational aggression, terrorism, and, in earlier days, East-West tensions. Here again the U.S. private sector pays the price! Efforts also to influence the lending policies of the multilaterals in certain countries indirectly make credit and projects less available to the U.S. developer.

The proclivity of large, supplier nations—particularly the United States—to utilize trade controls against other countries makes it necessary for us to look for trends in our own government's foreign policy instead of merely casting our gaze toward the host country in which we contemplate an exposure. In strategic planning, we can do our best to ready ourselves for this sort of foreign policy device and the concomitant loss of business by looking closely at our own administration in power and then examining which countries might be most vulnerable to the administration's prioritized issues and ideological tenets.

The U.S. Foreign Corrupt Practices Act

In 1978, in the spirit of continuing to make the United States a standard bearer for the rest of the world, Congress passed the Carter administration's Foreign Corrupt Practices Act, which was designed to prohibit corporate bribery of foreign government officials or involve them in a conflict of interest. Putting aside the philosophical question of whether one nation should impose its values on another—and so overbearingly—the language of the act puts the American businessperson in jeopardy whenever he attempts to do business in many third world countries. Wherever some degree of what we call official corruption has become an institutionalized social and political practice, the American businessperson— groomed in a Puritanical moral culture and nurtured by private enterprise and competition—is forced to apply his standards of a separation between business enterprise and government. What we regard as corruption is often just "the way things are done" in country X, whether it is "tea money" for a bureaucrat in Hong Kong or payment of a blind commission to an agent in Saudi Arabia with ties to pivotal figures in the royal family. The language of the act perhaps places an undue burden on the U.S. businessperson to become enough of an insider both to understand and, if necessary, reform local business practices.

Let us focus on just one particular aspect of the act. Under the bribery provision, a corporation can be liable in accordance with the "reason to know" standard if an intermediary or agent pays a bribe from his own pocket, even if the company had no knowledge of the agent's actions or intent. Moreover, there are no concrete standards for what constitutes a "reason to know." Suppose a certain corporation is seeking an oil concession in the Persian Gulf area. To accomplish the objective, the corporate representative has no alternative but to hire an agent in the country in question. Through his connections, the agent makes it possible for the representative to meet with the appropriate officials to negotiate a concession. The agent then collects his commission from the outsider. It is known that payoffs are commonplace in this particular country. Does the foreign company representative have "reason to know" that this agent's fee will be shared with government officials? In effect, was he paying the appropriate officials for meeting with him and even determining the outcome, and did he have cause to know that this would be the case? If so, he might be charged with violating the act and could be subject to fine and imprisonment.

In effect, the act inhibits the American businessperson from seeking to penetrate certain markets. Many corporations have ignored opportunities in Indonesia or Nigeria for this reason; others have approached new international business too cautiously and inadvertently have yielded ground to their competitors. Should the corporate representative ask for a letter from a host country's local agents or principals in which they disavow the intention of using bribery, or will he be offending and alienating them in the asking?

In general, this piece of legislation is a real hindrance to American business overseas. Corporations invest in legal counsel to monitor conformance of divisions and subsidiaries with this law. Not only is the language of the law ambiguous, but its purpose is also questionable and even self-defeating. What we regard as venality is just a way in many societies of distributing wealth or compensating underpaid bureaucrats and officials.

Antiboycott Restrictions

In yet another way, the U.S. government obstructs business operations overseas. The Export Administration Act expressly prohibits U.S. entities from doing business with a boycotted firm or in a boycotted country in cases where that boycott is fostered or imposed by any country against a country that is friendly to the United States. Of course, the allusion is specifically to the Arab boycott of Israel. U.S. businesspersons, like the U.S. government itself, are now often caught on the horns of a dilemma in which Arab countries can yield only so much in order to attract business from the West. As long as the Arab-Israeli dispute persists, corporations must adhere to a panoply of statutes in the law that enumerate in exhaustive detail what U.S. firms can and cannot do under the boycott. All of these legal conditions are accompanied by very detailed reporting requirements. As an example, a company may be charged for failing even to report a boycott request, let alone for complying with such a request.

Suffice it to say that the reporting burden alone deters many smaller companies from entering the international marketplace, and for firms it means maintaining separate staff to follow boycott-related developments in order to ensure compliance.

The Act of State Doctrine

The Act of State Doctrine is largely unique to the United States. Conceived in more gentlemanly times more than two hundred years ago, it affirms in essence that the legality of any action by any foreign state committed within its own territory cannot be challenged in our courts. An aggrieved U.S. company may be offered sympathy but nothing else. The denial of legal recourse in situations in which a sovereign government is involved as adversary makes it specially important to understand a welcoming country's politics and political culture, not to mention its economic and commercial circumstances, for deals to which the government is party. Thus, if a business interest is selling a service like public affairs representation to the executive office of a foreign government, negotiating the architectural and engineering consulting work for a nuclear power plant, or seeking a petroleum exploration and production concession, it should be circumspect about its partner on the other side and recognize its singularly unshielded exposure.

It is ironically noteworthy in the end that the U.S. government can be the private sector's worst enemy in dealing with certain foreign countries. In a sense, in many areas of the world U.S. business and financial interests might be at counterpoint with our own government policy. The activities of several U.S. oil companies at the very outset in Angola served as an example of limited defiance of the U.S. government. And when our government fails to recognize a particular country, it makes operations in that country more unsheltered and frightening for U.S. corporations and personnel. Furthermore, because our government will always assume a neutral position in territorial disputes, the U.S. government will not protect certain operations in contested areas. And if a contract is repudiated in the middle of a deal, our own courts will refuse to consider the matter. Finally, if a U.S. administration wants to apply pressure on a given country in which U.S. corporations are doing business, it can implement economic sanctions and withhold the approval of licenses that effectively will disrupt their in-country operations and possibly put them out of business altogether in that market.

NOTES

1. Lucian W. Pye and Sidney Verba, eds., *Political Culture and Political Development* (Princeton, N.J.: Princeton University Press, 1965), p. 513.

2. Pye and Verba, *Political Culture and Political Development*, p. 7.

3. Robert E. Ebel, "The Magic of Political Risk Analysis," in Mark B. Winchester, ed., *The International Essays for Business Decision Makers*, vol. 5 (Houston: Center for International Business, Arnacorn, 1980), p. 300.

3

Taking a Country's Economic and Commercial Temperature

As has been stated, the risks involved in financial transactions, particularly in developing countries, are at once political and economic. Political and economic development are intertwined, and in reality should not be separated. We often ask the question of how political changes will affect the economy. But fundamental economic restructuring and new exposures to foreign direct investment can have an equal impact on political configurations and attitudes.

Yet when a corporation looks at its exposure and its bottom line, it sometimes seems more convenient to focus on certain indicators that will point to direct and imminent risk to profits rather than seek a more complex picture of the political and social terrain. Good strategic planning should encompass the whole tapestry. We have seen that the more apparent political threats to the financial well being of an enterprise stem from such government actions as expropriation or the imposition of crippling legal restrictions that will lead to expropriation; freezing a foreign company's assets or insistence on divestment; a government's failure or the sort of paralysis that can induce political uncertainty, restrictions on repatriation of profits, social confusion or chaos; and disruptions from various types of civil disorders including strikes, terrorism, and revolution.

INDICATORS OF GENERAL FINANCIAL RISK

Sometimes corporate strategic planners and international marketing executives can be satisfied with a "quick fix," something concrete into which they can sink their teeth. Numbers, especially numbers that seem likely to predict specific outcomes affecting profits and currency outflow, are appealing. Financial risks—currency inconvertibility, devaluation of the local currency, delays in payment, default or rescheduling of external debt, and deposit blockages—are easier to predict because the financial indicators are quantified and are in the public record. Still, one must never forget their interrelatedness with political and social variables, which can buffet them at every turn.

Historically, we know what margins to apply to macroeconomic parameters and can make our comparisons at an early stage when we are first prioritizing new markets for investment. Although the political-social and economic environments should not be regarded as separate, they can be treated as analytically discrete. For our purposes here, we will examine more closely the salient economic indicators that can provide at least a measure of the financial context in which we will be implementing a business deal.

Although it is impossible to foresee what risks are entailed by investment in a particular country, it is possible for the treasurer or finance departments, with the assistance of the political and economic support staff in international strategic planning, to develop an accurate, up-to-the-minute assessment of those factors—foreign exchange fluctuations and control, devaluation, and payment delays—that most closely affect investment. One can maintain and update these analyses at short intervals. This part of a country evaluation, if scrupulously researched and carefully organized, can be presented in a concise, comprehensible form that will make sense to all reading it. To demonstrate this approach, Colombia in the early 1980s will be used as a case study. (Afterward, perhaps the readers would care to do a bit of research and make their own forecasts for the first decade of the twenty-first century based on the actual denouement of circumstances.)

When an organization lends foreign exchange to an entity in another country or expects to earn foreign exchange from operations in that country, it must rely on the ability of that nation's economy to generate sufficient foreign exchange not only to carry out its day-to-day operations, but also to repay loans denominated in foreign currencies. Therefore, while it is important to consider the host country's overall economic performance in a longer term, more reflective analysis can be a luxury. What matters most at the initial investment stage are the international transactions of the economy. These have the most direct bearing on whether a multinational or an intermediate-size company doing business in that country will be able to realize a return on its outlay. For this reason, our financial evaluation of Colombia in the 1980s begins with an "overview" (not unlike the brief executive summary) that sets forth the primacy of this perspective in recent historical context and pinpoints the key factors involved:

> The general long-term deterioration of the current account since 1972 and the large amounts of maturing short-term debt are two of the more pressing problems that faced this economy. In general terms, the current account deficit can be attributed to the two-year slump in world commodity prices. Commodities in this country

constitute a key source of its revenues. The commodity price slump is a result both of the world recession and the historical overvaluation of this currency relative to the currencies of its major trading partners. Colombia needs to take corrective measures to improve its current account position. Failure to take positive steps in this direction would have an adverse effect on the country's long-term development plans. In essence, Colombia in the 1980s might be expected to have shortages of foreign exchange. In the next six months, the government would have to accelerate its efforts to devalue the currency and would have to maintain or increase foreign exchange restrictions in an effort to improve the economy and avoid payment delays to suppliers.

After presenting this sort of profile of the country's international economic standing, noting the urgent need for a devaluation and the likely effect of such a devaluation on foreign exchange restrictions and the capacity to repay debts, we then can focus on at least six key indicators that justify our analysis of the country's environment for international business. To chart a course with some certainty, we need only check the following signposts:

1. Current account
2. Debt service ratio
3. Reserves-to-imports ratio
4. Export composition
5. Currency competitiveness
6. Import incompressibility

These indicators reliably measure a country's ability to generate the foreign exchange necessary to service foreign investment, repatriate capital and profits, and repay international loans. All these factors produce a comprehensive and interrelated picture of the economy. These same indicators might be used as a concrete basis for assessing the risks and opportunities in one country over another and prioritizing locations for business expansion. It is imperative that the data used in calculating these parameters be current—as up to date as possible. The volatility of developing nations, as well as the international marketplace in general, requires that economic developments be followed closely. Economic reports on these countries at least must be updated quarterly or even more often, and special attention should be focused on the semiannual and quarterly trends of the previous two years. Stale data might not only be useless but it might mislead us and distort our image of the economy. Therefore, information from commonly available references such as the *World Bank Debt Tables* and *International Financial Statistics (IFS)* ought to be supplemented by the most current available data gathered from private, independent experts and especially from field representatives of divisions or subsidiaries. Furthermore, this information must be verified by other sources (perhaps two) to ensure that it is reliable and unbiased. Current data are useless if they are not objective.

Let us look closely at the definition, implications, and significance of each of our six international economic indicators and see how Colombia measures up to standards in each case.

Current Account

The current account position is the net balance (exports less imports) on all transactions of merchandise, services, and unilateral transfers with all other countries within a specified time period. Consequently, this figure constitutes a measure of the foreign exchange flow in and out of a country. Generally, in developing countries, a current account deficit of 10 to 20 percent is cautionary; above 20 percent, it is alarming. Persistent deficits affect exchange rates and can result in the imposition of currency controls and import restrictions, which could hamper the operations of foreign corporations. Our data show that Colombia's current account position has been undulating at an alarming level since 1981 (see table 3.1).

Debt Service Ratio

The debt service ratio is the percentage of total export (i.e., debt: exports) required to finance annual interest and principal payments on the country's external debt. It covers the portion of the country's foreign exchange earnings that

Table 3.1   Colombia's Current Account: 1977–1983 (In Millions of U.S. Dollars)

	Exports FOB	Imports FOB	Transfers Net S-T	Curr. Acct. Balance	Carr. Acct. Exports %
1977	3514.00	3133.00	59.00	440.00	12.5213
1978	4130.00	3881.00	73.00	322.00	7.7966
1979	4851.00	4461.00	109.00	490.00	10.1010
1980	5862.00	6186.00	165.00	−159.00	−2.7124
1981	5014.00	7152.00	243.00	−1895.00	−37.7942
1982 1 st half	2571.00	3712.00	124.00	−2034.00 (a)	−39.5566
1982 2nd half	2421.00	3795.00	124.00	−2500.00 (a)	−51.6316
1982	4992.00	7507.00	248.00	−2267.00	−45.4127
1983 1 st quarter	1204.00 (e)	1720.00 (e)	62.50 (e)	−1814.00 (a)	−37.6661
1983 2nd quarter	1355.00 (e)	1648.00 (e)	62.50 (e)	−922.00 (a)	−17.0111
1983 3rd quarter	1304.00 (e)	1863.00 (e)	62.50 (e)	−1986.00 (a)	−38.0752
1983 4th quarter	1154.00 (e)	1936.00 (e)	62.50 (e)	−2878.00 (a)	−62.3484
1983	5017-00 (e)	7167.00 (e)	250.00 (e)	−1900.00 (e)	−37.8712

(a) = annualized
(e) = estimate
Note: All 1977–1982 data are from International Financial Statistics (November 1983).

must go to pay loans. Under such circumstances, foreign exchange that must be used to repay debt becomes unavailable for expenditures in other areas of the economy.

Different analyses may use different figures for computing the debt service ratio. In general, ratios that are based on both public and private debt are more accurate and reflective of the reality of the economic condition. While short-term debt (less than a year) is not often included in debt service calculations, it must be ascertained that this category of debt per se does not rise too rapidly as a percentage of total borrowing. A debt service ratio of 20 to 30 percent is cautionary; above 30 percent, alarming. All other things being equal, an alarming debt service index indicates a need for a more restrictive foreign exchange policy. Our data demonstrate that Colombia's combined public and private debt service ratio reached a precarious level in 1983 (the culmination of this case study), while its public sector debt service ratio continued to move upward toward a cautionary level (see table 3.2).

Generally, in looking at the debt service ratio of a country, the corporate strategist or marketing officer should weigh other factors before assuming the worst about a country's impending need for currency controls or limits on the repatriation of a foreign company's profits. Apart from the magnitude of a country's hard-currency reserve, one might look for the existence of special sources of inflowing aid or low-interest loans that have political or strategic implications.

Examine also the government's political awareness of the need to take corrective action without scaring off foreign direct investment and the political climate (i.e., consensus among the active political constituencies) in the host country for such remediation as measured devaluations that will limit purchasing power and the outflow of currency.

Reserves-to-Import Ratio

International reserves consist of a country's holdings of gold, its special drawing rights (SDRs), and its foreign exchange and reserve position in the International Monetary Fund (IMF). The reserves are used to protect a country from fluctuations in foreign exchange earnings. International reserves divided by the imports of goods and services produce what we call the reserves-to-imports ratio. From a different perspective, this percentage can be expressed in terms of the number of months for which the reserves can cover the current influx of imports. A ratio of two to three months is considered cautionary; less than two months is considered alarming. This ratio measures a country's ability to endure temporary balance-of-payments difficulties. A country's foreign exchange reserves can be used to finance imports and debt payments during periods of reduced export earnings or high import demand. In general, an indicator that falls in the "alarming" range reflects a country's loss of flexibility to cope with foreign exchange fluctuations and a need for immediate action if conditions of

Table 3.2 Colombia's Debt Service Ratios: Public, and Public and Private

	Debt Service Ratio—Public Only (millions US $)					Debt Service Ratio—Public and Private (millions US $)				
	Principal payments	Interest payments	Total debt service	Exports	Debt service ratio	Principal payments	Interest payments	Total debt service	Exports	Debt service ratio
1977	175.50	137.10	312.60	3556.00	8.79	234.10	161.00	395.10	3556.00	11.11
1978	224.80	168.20	393.00	4174.00	9.42	287.30	198.80	486.10	4174.00	11.65
1979	430.10	227.10	657.20	4952.00	13.27	472.20	270.10	742.30	4952.00	14.99
1980	263.10	282.20	545.30	5655.00	9.64	316.20	296.70	612.90	5655.00	10.84
1981	308.70	416.90	725.60	4953.00	14.65	581.70	564.10	1145.80	4953.00	23.13
1982 1st half	164.55	263.20	427.75	2571.00	16.64	N.A.	N.A.	674.50	2571.00	26.23
1982 2nd half	164.55	263.20	427.75	2421.00	17.67	N.A.	N.A.	674.50	2421.00	27.86
1982	329.10	526.40	855.50	4992.00	17.14	N.A.	N.A.	1349.00	4992.00	27.02
1983 1st quarter	101.15	140.05	241.20	1204.00 (e)	20.03	N.A.	N.A.	477.00	1204.00 (e)	39.62
1983 2nd quarter	101.15	140.05	241.20	1355.00 (e)	17.80	N.A.	N.A.	477.00	1355.00 (e)	35.20
1983 3rd quarter	101.15	140.05	241.20	1304.00 (e)	18.50	N.A.	N.A.	477.00	1304.00 (e)	36.58
1983 4th quarter	101.15	140.05	241.20	1154.00 (e)	20.90	N.A.	N.A.	477.00	1154.00 (e)	41.33
1983	404.60	560.20	964.80	5017.00 (e)	19.23	N.A.	N.A.	1908.00	5017.00 (e)	38.03

N.A. = not available.
(e) = estimate.
Note: The 1977–1981 total debt service and exports information are from the World Bank Debt Tables. The 1982 and 1983 public debt service figures are World Bank Debt Table projections. The 1982 and 1983 public and private debt service figures are Morgan Guaranty projections adjusted for short-term rollover debt. Without this adjustment the debt service figures would be 95 percent for 1982 and 98 percent for 1983. The 1982 exports are from *International Financial Statistics* (November 1983).

cross-border flow continue to deteriorate. Because the diversity of export and import baskets affect the need for reserves, this factor must be considered when interpreting this ratio.

A worst case might be an economy whose exports are limited primarily to one or just a few agriculturally derived commodities. (We will look at this question as a separate indicator later in this chapter.) Such a country would be particularly vulnerable to fluctuations in the price of international commodities; and if it were in the position of still being a net importer of food for its people, its hard-currency reserves could be depleted in an unstable and frequently soft international market. Our data show that Colombia's reserves-to-imports ratio remained at the sat isfactory level by the last year of our study, still representing a relative decline from the last years of the 1970s (see table 3.3).

Export Composition

Export composition consists of the level of concentration of each commodity in the overall export picture of the country. We look for vulnerability due to dependence on one commodity or a narrow range of commodities. The export composition factor measures what percentage of a nation's export revenue is accounted for by the commodity (i.e., how dependent those items are per se on the commodities) market in general. Reliance in one narrow commodity group for 30 to 50 percent of the economy's foreign exchange earnings would be cautionary, while more than 50 percent would be alarming.

Currency Competitiveness

Currency competitiveness measures the extent to which local inflation has been offset by the exchange rate movements. It is computed by dividing the inflation index by the exchange index. A high domestic exchange rate, reflected in the Consumer Price Index, will eventually render a country's exports noncompetitive in the world market. And imports will damage local industry by being less costly than domestic goods. This situation augurs ill for the survival of domestic producers and causes large current account deficits. The customary remedy is to devalue the local currency and thereby reverse the trend. Politically unpopular with local populations, devaluations have become the thrust of the IMF's economic restructuring recommendations to third world countries and the former nonmarket economies of Europe.

The theoretical extent of devaluation needed to achieve currency competitiveness tentatively can be projected. An index of 1.3 to 1.5 is cautionary; if it exceeds 1.5, it is alarming. However, it really is difficult to project a completely reliable range for this factor. In the case of Colombia, our data show that the country's currency competitiveness hovered at the cautionary level during the four years preceding our study in the early 1980s (see table 3.4).

Table 3.3   Colombia's Reserves/Imports (In Millions of U.S. Dollars)

	Reserves less gold	Gold—market Gold—million troy ounces	Gold—market price edp London	Gold reserves	Total reserves incl. gold	Imports	Reserves in Reserves as % of imports	Reserves in months of imports
1977	1747.00	1.7310	160.60	278.00	2025.00	3133.00	64.63	7.76
1978	2366.00	1.9610	208.20	408.28	2774.28	3881.00	71.48	6.58
1979	3844.00	2.3170	455.20	1054.70	4898.70	4461.00	109.81	13.18
1980	4831.00	2.7870	595.20	1658.82	6489.82	6186.00	104.91	12.59
1981	4801.00	3.3550	410.70	1377.90	6178.90	7152.00	86.39	10.37
1982 1st half	4301.00	3.5790	314.90	1127.03	5428.03	7424.00 (a)	73.11	8.77
1982 2nd half	3861.00	3.8170	444.00	1694.75	5555.75	7590.00 (a)	73.20	8.78
1982	3861.00	3.8170	444.00	1694.75	5555.75	7507.00	74.01	8.88
1983 1st quarter	3157.00	3.9230	419.90	1651.05	4808.05	6880.00 (a)	69.88	8.39
1983 2nd quarter	2774.00	4.0250	413.00	1662.33	4436.33	6592.00 (a)	67.30	8.08
1983 3rd quarter	2015.00	4.1450	405.30	1679.97	3694.97	7542.00 (a)	49.58	5.95
1983 4th quarter	2000.00 (e)	4.2000 (e)	385.00 (e)	1617.00	3617.00	7744.00 (a)	46.71	5.60
1983	2000.00 (e)	4.2000 (e)	385.00 (e)	1617.00	3617.00	7167.00 (e)	50.47	6.06

(a) = annualized
(e) = estimate.
Note: All reserve data are from the *International Financial Statistics* (November 1983).

Table 3.4   Colombia's Currency Competitiveness: Change in Inflation/Exchange Rate

	Consumer Price Index—Colombia 1975 = /00	Exchange rate in pesos	Consumer Price Index—United States 1975 = 100	Ratio
1977	159.40	37.86	115.40	1.20
1978	189.40	41.00	125.90	1.21
1979	258.50	44.00	142.60	1.36
1980	327.70	50.92	160.30	1.32
1981	413.50	59.07	174.60	1.32
1982 1st half	473.90	63.84	180.30	1.36
1982 2nd half	512.96	70.29	181.42	1.33
1982	512.96	70.29	181.42	1.33
1983 1st quarter	536.38	74.19	182.04	1.31
1983 2nd quarter	570.87	78.51	184.94	1.30
1983 3rd quarter	607.97 (e)	83.40	188.22 (e)	1.28
1983 4th quarter	647.49 (e)	89.27 (e)	190.49 (e)	1.26
1983	647.49 (e)	89.27 (e)	190.49 (e)	1.26

(e) = estimate. *Note:* All data except estimates from IFS.
Note: The 1975 CPI (United States and Colombia) = 100. The 1975 exchange rate: 32.%P/dollar. The CPI and exchange rate are end of period figures.

Import Incompressibility

When a country is not self-sufficient in food and fuel, these commodities necessarily constitute its essential imports. They are the country's lifeblood and are vital to the functioning of the economy. From our perspective, the ratio of food and fuel to the total import of goods and services should determine what we call the import incompressibility of a country's economy. The ability of a country to discourage imports by manipulating the exchange rate depends in large part on the composition of its whole import package. Comparatively high dependency on essential imports reduces the feasibility of the devaluation option as a means of cutting down total imports to more manageable levels; the end result might be as desperate as the resort to foreign exchange controls. Further, external dependency in an area critical to the operation of the economy is subject to the vagaries of international politics. The cutting of an oil pipeline from a port country by terrorists or a war in the Persian Gulf to punish Saddam Hussein could throw this sort of vulnerable economy into a state of paralysis. An indicator between 25 and 35 percent suggests that the situation is cautionary; a ratio of above 35 percent should be considered precarious. Our data show that Colombia's import incompressibility rose steadily from a satisfactory level in 1970 to a possibly stable but cautionary level by 1983, the last year of our study (see table 3.5).

82   *David M. Raddock*

Table 3.5   Colombia's Import Incompressibility

	Fuel imports		Food imports		Food and fuel as % of total imports
	% of imports	U.S. $ in millions	% of imports	U.S. $ in millions	
1977	6.80	213.04	9.70	303.90	16.50
1978	7.30	283.31	8.50	329.89	15.80
1979	10.10	450.56	7.10	316.73	17.20
1980	12.20	754.69	9.30	575.30	21.50
1981	13.00	929.76	10.00	715.20	23.00 (e)
1982 1st half	14.00 (a)	1039.36	11.00 (a)	816.64	25.00 (a)
1982 2nd half	14.00 (a)	1062.60	11.00 (a)	834.90	25.00 (a)
1982	14.00 (e)	1050.98	11.00 (e)	825.77	25.00 (e)
1983 1st quarter	15.00 (a)	1032.00	12.00 (a)	825.60	27.00 (a)
1983 2nd quarter	15.00 (a)	988.80	12.00 (a)	791.04	27.00 (a)
1983 3rd quarter	15.00 (a)	1117.80	12.00 (a)	894.24	27.00 (a)
1983 4th quarter	15.00 (a)	1161.60	12.00 (a)	929.28	27.00 (a)
1983	15.00 (e)	1075.05	12.00 (e)	860.04	27.00 (e)

(a) = Annualized.
(e) = Estimate.
Note: All data except estimates from the International Monetary Fund's Supplement on Trade Statistics.

The data used in calculating the previous six indicators and the trends shown suggest that the indicators can be aggregated simply, allowing us to determine the soundness of our footing purely from a macroeconomic standpoint (political considerations, of course, always can intervene) in any country in which we might contemplate an exposure.

For an integrated understanding of the financial risks that bear on investment in a particular country, the user is encouraged to dig into the database and the tables and graphs. Grasping fully the basis for our interpretation should instill confidence and increase the user's sensitivity to the need to monitor longitudinally the data for certain critical indicators. In the case of Colombia in the early 1980s, the user has been pointed naturally in the direction of such negative possible outcomes as sudden maxidevaluations and foreign exchange controls; and he might also expect problems with debt repayment as a consequence of a worst-case downward spiral in current account position, debt service, currency competitiveness, and import incompressibility. The financial risk picture in a given country becomes clearer, but we make a deliberate effort to avoid oversimplifying our interpretation. We will show how politics might intervene as considerations, without confusing the issues too much or compromising the analytical distinctiveness of our analysis. Larger countervailing political and social trends are treated separately.

This kind of analysis—focusing on the problems themselves—is very useful to strategic planners and regional marketing executives as they order their priorities. However murky the economic situation of a country, it is important, indeed essential, that the delineation of its pivotal problems be as unambiguous and direct as possible. The commitment to a persistent analytical clarity should not produce simplistically blanket descriptions of a country's general economic situation, but rather an eyes-open and tough-minded interpretation of the current facts and the recent historical trends. No financial risk assessment is foolproof or capable of pointing a sure finger to actual outcomes, but in its precision it can instill confidence in the likelihood of certain scenarios. Correct numerical data and solid interpretation can deter even the most zealous marketing officer, who is anxious about meeting short-term pressures to deliver at the bottom line and who thinks that he is staring at what he thinks is a jewel of a business deal, from walking into a minefield.

The advantage of the financial/macroeconomic overview for countries under consideration either for foreign direct investment or long-term trade is that it permits the user at different levels to approach individual transactions in the context of a clearly defined topography of a less developed economy's critical financial characteristics and with a personal understanding that is supported by reliable, up-to-the-minute data.

For MNCs or smaller companies ensconced in an economically troubled country, panic is supplanted by the assurance of a foreknowledge of trends. The information based on an ongoing tracking of a country's economy facilitates certain expectations of problems associated with operations like the year-end translation of funds. Major devaluations, currency controls, significant debt rescheduling, and delays in payment all can be anticipated.

In addition, this use of risk indicators can provide the basis for a compromise between centralized and decentralized control of foreign exchange transfers in the case of MNCs. It provides the local manager with the leeway to borrow and lend as well as to cover exposed positions at corporate rates. At the same time, the central treasury of the corporation is able to assay the net local position of its subsidiaries in order to decide if it needs to obtain a forward exchange contract from a commercial bank. This system is particularly beneficial to the nonbank MNC because it encourages local initiative while leaving the management of foreign exchange controls to the centralized treasury. Service companies, which depend on the foreign exchange earnings of the country for their funding, will derive special benefits from this approach.

Finally, our suggested analysis of financial risk and planning for certain types of outcomes is meant to be particularly helpful to corporations whose local projects have longer gestation periods (e.g., nuclear power plants or coal mines). MNCs whose project financing depends on future local earnings either to repay a loan involved or to compensate the parent company will strategically benefit from our currency projections.

COMMERCIAL CONDITIONS AND DISINCENTIVES

Politics aside and in plain business terms, the macroeconomic environment should be only the second criterion for deciding whether to invest in a given overseas (particularly a third world or Russian/eastern European) market. In considering the underpinnings of a good overseas business deal, the paramount priority is the desirability of the undertaking itself: its contractual terms and capital, reliability of partners, credit arrangements, return of invested capital, time frame, and profitability.

But the merits of the deal and the soundness of the broader economic environment are not sufficient. Still another problematic facet of doing business overseas consists of the market conditions in a host country. Although some products and services have singular characteristics and ramifications, we do not refer here necessarily to their specific marketability. Rather, we are concerned with the *procedural and circumstantial context of doing business* in a particular country, particularly where economic development is at a different stage from our own and where cultural behavior can vary so widely. For example, when we identify a problem of a shortage of skilled labor in a given country, we are not throwing up a red flag and advising a certain type of investor to stay away. We are simply educating ourselves properly about the commercial environment. Indeed, skilled-labor shortages need not be a drawback for some types of business operations because they might serve as leverage at the negotiation table.

Similarly, when we *prepare ourselves* before negotiations in many countries for the host country to demand that the foreign enterprise provide certain types of peripherally related infrastructure, we already will have been able to estimate additional costs relative to profits. We then can decide judiciously what options, if any, would make the job feasible and approach the table properly informed.

A corporation should familiarize itself with the host country's business regulations. The U.S. Department of Commerce or the U.S. International Chamber of Commerce will provide a list of local legal firms. Punitive taxation is a critical factor to consider. For example, if we already are aware that taxation on foreign enterprise and expatriates is excessive, we can weigh this fact against the other variables and may choose to go elsewhere. In Colombia for many years, harsh taxes were keeping companies away, particularly in the petroleum industry where levies were discriminatory; the foreign oil companies that were producing in Colombia became increasingly alienated by rising taxes, whispers about nationalization, and the worsening social situation.

If the financial variables that we have discussed in this chapter must be considered *risks*, then commercial conditions must be regarded critically as *disincentives*. Although most commercial features of a host country are not usually as critical as political and economic risks, they do have the capacity to erode a business deal after it is underway.

An interrelationship also exists between the commercial environment and the political and social dimensions. Spain is an example. To appease the left wing of its socialist party (PSOE) and secure its support for joining NATO shortly after it was voted into office, the Felipe González administration canceled contracts for five of ten U.S. export-import bank-financed nuclear power facilities. In this case, political considerations clearly determined commercial circumstances. Politics are also a convenient rationalization. Companies in Indonesia have been subverted on the pretext of a need suddenly to heed environmentalists. In turn, commercial factors have influenced political moods. In Venezuela in the late 1970s, just as political attitudes were softening toward foreign intervention, an American construction company—with more than the usually permitted share of equity ownership—advertised its enterprise as its own, reactivated Venezuelan nationalism, and set off a chain reaction that reinforced the formalized Andean Commission (ANCOM) restraints on foreign ownership.

A HALL OF MIRRORS: NEVER LOSE SIGHT OF THE ANALYTICAL INTERFACE AMONG CATEGORIES

It is important to recognize the interdependence of macroeconomic-financial, political-social, and commercial criteria as part of the necessary education to gain a business footing in a strange country. If the business planner and marketing officers do not do their proper homework, they are apt to trip themselves up! International marketing executives certainly are capable of developing their own "feel" for the local terrain and can handle the "nuts and bolts" detailed analysis themselves. But it is important to enumerate here the broader aspects of commercial disincentives: drawbacks that can virtually be taken as risks and, under certain circumstances, could sabotage a business operation. These include the following: *restrictions on capital flows*, such as import controls and deliberately engineered problems in currency transfer in both directions through the central bank; *limitations on foreign investment*, including prescribed limits and guidelines for equity ownership, expansion, and divestment (these conditions might vary with a change in the host government's administration or with a modification of political atmosphere); *limits on the employment of expatriate personnel at varying levels* (a real impediment when a project requires skilled labor that is not readily available in the host country); *limits on the local availability of skilled or unskilled labor* (in some countries, like Tunisia or Pakistan, even the less-skilled workers customarily might migrate to other countries in the region for more lucrative jobs); *bureaucratic inefficiency and corruption,* which in some cases can bog down business deals and ongoing operations to such an extent that they make the Ethiopian government's management of the distribution of food and aid to the starving seem smooth; *contract repudiation*, for which even the best safeguards—personal political contacts in a country like Indonesia—do not always come through on your side; in the case of construction and infrastructure projects, a pattern of *arbitrary actions against performance guarantee bonds* by a state agency; the aforementioned *punitive corporate or personal income taxation* (in Tunisia, expatriates are taxed so highly that a company's use of its own managerial personnel is de facto restricted); *the official attitude toward contract arbitration* (keep tabs on post-Soviet Russia); and the not-to-be minimized drawback of confronting a weak and inadequate physical infrastructure to provide access to and from, and to support, the project at hand.

Often the local government will try to entice the investor to establish a presence in outlying areas by offering tax holidays and other incentives. The businessperson must weigh the infrastructural costs, as well as skilled-labor needs, against these inducements. In Guinea, with less than one thousand miles of paved roads, any undertaking would necessarily incur a heavy front-end cost just to create the proper environment, transportation, and communications to get underway. And in remote parts of China, onshore oil is so waxy and viscous that it would be unfeasible for a potential foreign joint-venture partner to construct a heated pipeline to transport the petroleum in liquid state to the coastline or any major urban center. In the past, the price of oil has been subsidized well below market value. Now the Chinese government is waging a campaign to persuade foreign service companies to come into these hardship areas and tough it out, build ancillary infrastructure, and develop innovative ways to transport and pipe the impossible dream—all in the guise of opportunity, China's "new frontier!"

Although analytical distinctions must be made, it takes little imagination to suppose that politics, political culture, macroeconomic circumstances, and commercial conditions all are interrelated. Nevertheless, how often do we hear, both in the home office and in the field, that because there is little one can do to control the uncertainties of a nation's politics, one ought to focus on financial variables alone. Yet to position itself for a long-term stay in a country, a company must not only know what is going on politically but perhaps become a player—an unobtrusive one—in the game. And to operate effectively, the foreign business entity must adapt to, as well as from time to time manipulate, the mechanics of the commercial system.

On the economic side, politics is often a crucial consideration. Many a decision not to introduce a maxidevaluation, when financial variables might have warranted such a radical step, was either deferred or carried out in dribbles for political reasons. The memory of riots in the streets, coups elicited by the more populist elements in the military, or the army's draconian suppression of social violence—all can deter a government from performing much-needed radical surgery.

The commercial environment too is intertwined with political considerations. Political influence from above can cut through the red tape and conflicting regulations of an obdurate commercial bureaucracy. Governments can be lobbied to streamline existing regulations and take further steps toward eliminating parastatal companies as well as rationalizing the public's oversight role in the commercial arena. Many governments, like Egypt's and Gabon's, muddy the business environment by dumping political friends into the commercial bureaucracy. Where public sector companies play an important role in the economic process, their utilization as receptacles for political patronage appointees does little to increase the efficiency of carrying on business.

A WORD BEFORE PROCEEDING

The reader now should have a certain grasp of the analytical variables that make an investment in Siberia more complex than one in Alaska, a trade agreement with an agency of the government of China more arcane and difficult to negotiate than with a major company in San Francisco's Chinatown. It is not just a question of strange faces and strange places—although that is indeed a psychological facet of the process. In spite of the fact that foreign environments increasingly are becoming part of the international legal and business mainstream, the differences that remain can determine the successful outcome of both the business deal in the making and a seminal operation that has reached a stage where it wants to secure and improve its position in a host country.

As much as we might continue to expect modernity to homogenize phenomena throughout the world, we will be startled from time to time by the reenactment of pre–World War I ethnic fights several generations after they had supposedly receded into the annals of history. We will continue to witness the undermining of the legitimacy of seemingly well-anchored governments, terrorism against foreign businesspeople and against all kinds of installations, and in all likelihood, nearly all the factors that we have attempted to present in this core section of the book as a prism for the businessperson to gain her or his bearings in a host country.

Whether or not a knowledge of these variables will help the businessperson entering the twenty-first century to navigate new markets and avoid the pitfalls in concrete ways, the perspective that has been presented here (replete with illustrations from over thirty countries) at least will sensitize him to the need for proceeding with a wide-angle lens at all times.

The country case studies to follow, all contributed by area specialists, and for the most part framed according to the variables outlined in our preceding discussion, will go a step farther. Each chapter stands as an essay in its own right. The authors, in creative ways, have emphasized those variables from the book's method and approach that most seem to apply to circumstances in the specific country under discussion. The lead chapter on China, which both Steven I. Levine and I wrote together, is based on our years of study of the Chinese—traditional and modern—polity, as well as a comparative perspective on the development of the Soviet Union. After discussing the risks in China (most of which are shared by other third-world countries but some of which have a unique mystique in Chinese culture), we analyze the constraints and state controls against widespread civil disorder or dismemberment. The road ahead for China may be rocky (and we point out all the markers), but China will expand the free market sector of its economy in the next years ahead in spite of a current deflationary trend. As it enters the World Trade Organization, it will be drawn irreversibly into the more predictable flow of the international mainstream. Liberalization of the economy will proceed. But at what cost to its 1.3 billion people, who still are largely dependent on job security and subsidies of basic needs? Will instability and social disturbances result? Will the Chinese people, still repressed by a security apparatus but lacking an ideology to embrace or a government of uncertain legitimacy, be able to ride out the transformation?

In his treatment of present-day, post-Soviet Russia, Michael Newcity takes an approach that is unique. It could be invaluable to Western businesspeople. After discussing the general profile of political risk, he hones in on the rule of law in today's Russia and the political cultural perceptions of law in Soviet and traditional Russia. We see that concrete privatization involving foreign investment can be reversed by arbitrary manipulations of the law and conflicting laws in the face of both parochial and public pressures. If law is not properly respected, the Western businessperson in Russia has at least one more frightening reason to consider him- or herself at the frontier.

John P. Entelis's case study of SONATRACH, the state oil company in Algeria, looks closely at the cornerstone structure of the Algeria's political economy as a microcosm of the dynamic of power and stability (as opposed to political risk) in that oil-endowed country in North Africa. One reason the chapter was included in the book was for its laborious analysis of the politics of state monopoly industry; the reader has an example here of the sort of intelligence work that can be performed on any industrial sector in a new foreign market. SONATRACH's leadership and policy are held together by the alternation and fusion of politics, professionalism, and personality. Executive positions at the highest level in the energy sector are often interchangeable. SONATRACH, the military, and the ideology become the sources of control in a society troubled by transition to modernization, from statism and socialism to a greater emphasis on the free market, and from Islamic traditional ways that still command grassroots loyalties to a more secular state. This study is less a study in political risk than of top-down control in a military garrison state—a case of political risk stood on its head. Society and politics are volatile in Algeria but state control routinely keeps it in check.

The last case study in chapter seven appeals to the pioneer in us and addresses the opportunities and hazards that lie ahead for the U.S. businessperson who might be eyeing Cuba as a new market. For the time being, the U.S. government's embargo against Cuba, a vestige of the cold war, puts that nearby island country beyond the pale of our propensity toward global inclusiveness. But changes are taking place with each passing month.

For a piece on investment conditions in Cuba, I invited global sleuth Rensselaer W. Lee III, who had just returned from an investigative trip to Castro's island to present his newfound data and observations. Circumstances have been changing here as well as there. With the collapse of Soviet and Eastern European communism, Cuba has been denied economic supports that kept its economy afloat—barely. By 1993, out of desperation, Castro's government decided to take the more pragmatic course of opening part of the economy to foreign trade and investment. Investment laws and infrastructure were created to pave the way for a controlled entry of foreign exchange into the economy. At the same time, the more overtly business-oriented U.S. government has been moving closer to piecemeal recognition of Cuba's needs and value in a new sort of universe.

What promise does the Cuban market hold when communism still prevails and state corporations bog down a sluggish economy? Lee points out the opportunities in oil, agribusiness, tourism, and multiple forms of trade, as well as the drawbacks for undertaking any sort of business. Can Cuba's economy modernize through exposure to a greater foreign business presence, or will progress have to await the passing of Castro?

We hope that these in-depth country studies will illuminate in greater detail some of the key points that we have made, perhaps even providing the reader with some of the practical information that can be used right now in actual work in one of the important countries under discussion.

Finally, if the reader identifies critical environmental difficulties that may jeopardize assets and personnel, and will not back off from the promised profits of the investment, the corporation can always resort to political risk insurance. In the United States, such coverage is offered by the government-linked Overseas Private Investment Corporation (OPIC) or, for exports, the Federal Deposit Insurance Corporation. The mandate of these public agencies, as well as any guarantee agencies attached to the multilaterals, is to provide support for foreign investment in the developing countries. These U.S. agencies are not in the game for profit. They try to reinforce a bridge between the American private sector and the less developed countries in order to strengthen political ties. Nevertheless, the bottom line for approving either financing or insurance from an entity like OPIC is that circumstances surrounding the deal be sound. Otherwise, neither OPIC nor the public export insurers will assume the risk. Private insurers will cover most of the same countries, perhaps at higher rates than the government sector. They also might take on investments in those countries that do not yet qualify for U.S. government backing. The preference of the private companies is to offer diversified portfolios for several countries in order to leverage the higher-risk countries.

We have included a section on this practical information because it is a safer way to shield an investment once serious vulnerabilities have been identified in the project and in the political and economic environment of a given host country. Without political risk analysis as a guide, however, businesspeople hazard mistaking headlines for risk. They indeed may deny themselves the opportunity to dispel minor risks and impediments and to develop proactive strategies for monitoring and managing the business environment.

II

Country Case Studies

4

China at the Advent of a Millennium: Planning for Contingencies

Stephen I. Levine and David M. Raddock

Investment in China remains an attractive option for many foreign companies as it has been for most of the past two decades, but the smart business planner recognizes its pitfalls and weighs these against opportunities.

In China the risks are not so different from elsewhere. The political and economic uncertainties that confront foreign investment are not unlike those in other developing countries, especially ones with parastatal industries and mixed economies. The hurdles seem more dramatic because of the mystique we ascribe to China. Our perception originates in part from the way the Chinese people view themselves. Even in ignorance of the details of their own ancient history, the Chinese people see themselves as a unique civilization and indulge a cultural penchant toward grandiosity.

In practical terms, the possibility of major political and economic upheavals within the next decade of a sort that might pose a direct threat to foreign businesses cannot be excluded. But this risk must be balanced against the current reality of an entrenched Communist party-state propped up by powerful military and internal security forces with refined skills for intimidating by persuasion and a pervasive domestic surveillance and intelligence system that delimits a citizen's privacy.

In the late 1990s, Chinese political leaders reaffirmed their intention to give market forces the dominant role in the national economy. To be sure, the path they are following toward this end has many twists and turns. The intense Sino-American negotiations that led to a breakthrough trade agreement in November 1999 seem virtually certain to clinch China's long-delayed entry into the World Trade Organization (WTO), and its entry into the WTO will generate domestic and foreign economic consequences leading to its further integration into the global economy. A return to China's revolutionary-era policies (1949–1978) of economic autarky, government control of the domestic economy, and state monopoly of foreign trade is as improbable as the revival of the manual typewriter in the age of computers.

But the road ahead is paved with uncertainties. The Western businessperson must be careful to avoid being caught between China's zeal to modernize and the obstacles with which the state must inexorably battle. China's avowed goal of reaching the level of a major developed economy in the next decade is giddy if not reckless; the zeal that is required to meet that goal is daunting. Still carrying the burden of a contradictory mixed economy, China has a population of 1.3 billion and a very different culture that is more accustomed to serving as a beacon to the outside world than adapting to it. Among the challenges confronting China are how to open up the political system without jeopardizing Chinese Communist Party (CCP) control, continue the transition from a state to a market economy, control corruption, create employment opportunities for tens of millions of redundant and new workers, and manage ethnic and regional assertiveness. Tensions between private and public and urban and rural sectors are apt to increase. The question of how the leadership will promote China's foreign policy agenda without coming into conflict with other countries in the Asia-Pacific region as well as the United States and other major powers might affect the very survival of a foreign enterprise in China. Managing these, and many other problems, will severely strain the capacity of the Chinese political system and eventually could bring it to the breaking point. Although such disaster is far from an imminent possibility, the investor may choose to monitor the factors that we discuss here and adjust his or her position accordingly over time.

STABILITY AND CHANGE

The political change that swept away communism in Eastern Europe and the Soviet Union jolted, but did not topple, the Communist system in China. Ever since its brutal suppression of the spring 1989 student-led political reform movement centered at Tiananmen Square, the CCP has been on red alert for any signs of discontent. Invoking internal stability as the precondition for economic development and prosperity, the CCP has cracked down hard on real and potential challenges to its authority. In the late 1990s, it imprisoned leaders of the fledgling China Democracy Party, sought to eradicate the popular exercise/meditation group Falun Gong, and suppressed restive non-Chinese minorities in Tibet and Xinjiang. President Jiang Zemin and other top leaders have explicitly rejected Western democratic models as unsuitable to Chinese conditions and continue to insist that only the CCP can provide the leadership China needs to achieve its international and domestic goals. The Communists maintain their monopoly of power by prohibiting the formation of any other organized political groups and exercising strict control over the media. (The Internet, however, poses a serious and ever growing problem in this respect.) Yet such authoritarian controls have not always proved successful in other countries and have given way to the tide of popular yearnings. China's domestic "great wall" also can spring leaks if positive output and the strengthening of the credibility of the system do not bolster it.

The foreign businessperson who contemplates an initial investment in China or an increase in his or her company's existing exposure must be concerned with the critical question of China's capacity to remain politically stable over the next ten years. From what directions, if any, might challenges to CCP rule in China come within this period? In addressing this key question, we focus on five different groups that might conceivably challenge the CCP leadership: (1) students and intellectuals; (2) unemployed workers and farmers; (3) ethnic minorities; (4) the military; and (5) intraparty reformers.

Students and Intellectuals

At various points in modern Chinese history, students and intellectuals have played a catalytic role in politics. The premium that Chinese still place on their "intellectuals" is a legacy of Confucian emphasis on education as a criterion for rule. Mao Zedong and the Chinese Communist elite also reinforced the notion that students could play a vanguard role in social change. In 1989, Chinese student leaders, claiming to speak for the nation, sharply criticized government policies and challenged government leaders. The boldest among them disputed the government's legitimacy. This generation seems to have invested its energies elsewhere. Spurred by the promises of modernization and the atrophy of the old ideology, Chinese students entering the twenty-first century show little interest in politics and are much more concerned with personal and career goals. The most popular college majors are business administration, the sciences, and technology. As long as the economy provides attractive opportunities for China's growing number of college graduates, this focus on personal goals will continue. But if there were to be a sudden downturn in the economy, little prospect of proper employment, and a renewed spiral of inflation, students might again vent frustration over prospects and express their adolescent experimentation and autonomy by playing a broader role as an organized political vanguard. Educated youths would rechannel their energies toward expressing discontent with the failures of their elders and reclaim their historical role as emerging adults who intend to change society.

The middle school and college student cohort and intellectuals generally will remain a threat to the administration as long as they are bereft of a cohesive set of beliefs that bind them firmly to the political system. For this reason, the Chinese government is seeking a creed of some sort—a rallying cry—to provide a broader social conscience and to cushion itself against the vagaries of everyday policy and possible setbacks. CCP education officials have undertaken the Herculean task of trying to put together a new set of values for youth to direct them as outward-looking members of society and guide them in the area of interpersonal behavior. The syncretic blend of norms that have emerged from this official effort draw on China's unique Marxism, Confucianism, and elements of Western thought. Such new ideas, whether credible or just a makeshift hodgepodge, take a while to filter down. In the interim, moral direction for Chinese students is largely dictated by self-interest.

How then does the government mobilize the emotions of the young and the restless? It has had to channel natural competitiveness with authority and the urge to protest toward outside targets. Absent a revitalized and coherent ideology, the government has stirred the young and intellectuals with an appeal to anti-Western nationalism. Issuing threats over Taiwan or railing against the accidental bombing in May 1999 of the Chinese embassy in Belgrade, CCP leaders have wrapped themselves in the flag and reminded the people of the earlier depredations of imperialism in China.

Students and intellectuals will not embrace nationalism long. Like an emotional charge, it usually is short-lived and limited. It is a shallow ruse sustained by crisis. Material self-interest too is a lonely pursuit and demands continual satisfaction in the form of economic and social rewards. Yet if students were inclined to reengage in politics within the next decade because of a need for a substantive ideology, career, or something greater than themselves in which to believe, they would likely trip over inner contradictions and a well-heeled state apparatus for controlling social protest.

The central government has refined its techniques for controlling protest activities and preventing them from escalating. Unless there were already serious divisions within the government and the party that prevented the authorities from acting decisively, students' efforts would be isolated and quashed. The students might well trip themselves up on their own arrogance. Enjoying a special sense of superiority because of their position in the social hierarchy, they have ignored older generation intellectuals in the past and distanced themselves from workers and other sympathetic social groups with their "caste-like" exclusiveness. Our interview research indicates that students since 1989 generally have been prudent about taking unnecessary personal risks unless they can achieve their subjective goals. For better or worse, students are unlikely to be a critical factor in China's political equation as circumstances evolve over the next decade.

Unemployed Workers and Farmers

Economic reforms have destroyed the presumption of permanent full employment (the "iron rice bowl") that Chinese state socialism once promised. In the agricultural sector as many as one hundred million people are underemployed, with as many as fifteen to sixteen million unemployed in the cities.

Tens of millions of rural dwellers have drifted into the cities searching for a better life. They work in the construction industry and as day laborers, living on the periphery of society. Many engage in petty crime.

Urban workers whose families have been employed intergenerationally in the numerous state-owned enterprises (SOEs), once the mainstay of the economy, now find themselves underemployed or furloughed. SOEs have been struggling to compete in a marketizing economy. Outmoded equipment, poor management, and a redundant labor force contribute to chronic red ink. The heavy burden of social welfare obligations including health and childcare, subsidized housing, and pensions have exacerbated the burden on the SOEs. If the government pursues the policies of economic rationalization it has enunciated, the number of unemployed and underemployed urban workers will grow substantially over the next decade.

Does this vast army of semiemployed and unemployed rural migrants and urban workers threaten the stability of the system? Judging by the harshness of the government's anticrime campaigns and its efforts to create employment opportunities, the answer might appear to be yes. In reality, the political mobilization of these unfortunates would require an extraordinary combination of circumstances that is hardly likely to occur. Chief among them would be a breakdown of the public security system, indecision at both central and local levels of government, and the emergence, under conditions of illegality, of one or more radical political movements probably led by charismatic leaders. Something like this sequence occurred in the mid-nineteenth century when the Taiping Rebellion (1851–1864) nearly overthrew the Manchu Dynasty. Much more likely is that these people will be forced to the margins of an otherwise prospering economy. At worst, the international businessperson must be alert to the possibility of sporadic outbreaks of violence directed at rapacious local officials. This becomes a more important issue if more foreign enterprises are located away from the coastal provinces. Over the past five years, thousands of mostly small-scale protests have occurred in many urban localities. Although they are usually driven by local grievances and a lack effective organization even on the local level, they can disrupt commerce. In the future, they could well target the more highly visible foreign installations that can be blamed for the government's failings.

Expect then isolated protests against authority. These outbursts might interfere directly or indirectly with foreign-owned businesses, but they are unlikely to coalesce and challenge the regime. Only with the severe deterioration of the system and the emergence of a special type of leader, organization, and ideology to challenge the establishment could a powerful grassroots rebellion ever take place.

Ethnic Minorities

A critical factor in the collapse of the Soviet Union was the revolt of repressed minority nationalities against the dominant Russians. China too has politically restive minority nationalities, notably the Tibetans in the southwest and the Uygurs, a Turkish-speaking Muslim people, in the far western province of Xinjiang. But unlike the Soviet Union, where minority nationalities constitute nearly half the population, China is comprised predominantly of "Han" Chinese; these make up over 90 percent of China's 1.3 billion people.

Most of China's officially recognized fifty-five minority nationalities are scattered along the periphery of the country. Moreover, for economic and political reasons, Beijing has encouraged Han resettlement in border provinces including Inner Mongolia, Xinjiang, and Tibet. Barring a collapse of CCP power at the center, it is virtually inconceivable that minority nationality resentment of Chinese rule could develop to the extent of threatening the stability of the system. So much as a murmur of protest elicits Beijing's reflex to control and intimidate; in the past year or two, this has involved the kidnapping of the infant Panchen Lama in Tibet and the arrest and liquidation of numerous Uyghurs in Xinjiang.

Intraparty Reformers

The CCP is no longer a monolithic political army such as Lenin, the father of communism, envisioned a century ago. United by loyalty to the party center in Beijing and inspired by Chinese nationalism, the working-level "cadres," or leaders, of the CCP and the party's sixty-odd million members are divided along lines of generation, region, and interest.

Top CCP leaders frequently disagree over issues of policy and power. The collapse of communist ideology, no less evident inside the party than outside it, has left a vacuum that is only partially filled by nationalist visions of a great power China—a rebirth of China as the central civilization.

To simplify a bit, the struggle that we detect inside the CCP represents a conflict between a group of more conservative, control-oriented, and ultranationalist leaders on the one hand, and a more liberal (in communist terms), market-oriented, reform-minded, and internationalist group on the other. The former is leery of change, which is seen as eroding the foundations of communist power. This group tends to view the United States as the main obstacle to the fulfillment of China's aspirations for national reunification (the Taiwan issue) and great power status. The latter, in varying measure, welcomes the challenges that change presents, sees China's future in terms of increasing integration with the global system, and is more optimistic about the possibility of working out a *modus vivendi* with a United States whose dynamism is admired. An institutional expression of the former tendency is the complex of agencies making up China's security apparatus. An institutional expression of the latter is the manifestation of organizations involved in foreign trade and foreign affairs, and the apparent strengthening of the Chinese People's Political Consultative Council (CPPCC), founded in 1949 to represent noncommunist "democratic parties" and people's groups.

The relative strength of the conservative and liberal orientations varies over time, and the triumph of one over the other is unlikely, at least in the short to medium term. Nevertheless, in the longer term, we might look for a slow evolution toward greater openness and reform. Expect increasing openness in policy to be accompanied by more visible acts of political and religious repression as the communist elite tries to change and then correct its course in anxious anticipation of undesirable consequences.

Military

China's People's Liberation Army (PLA), comprised of an army, air force, and navy of about 2.5 million, constitutes a special sort of interest group. Although all officers are party members, they are also professionals whose perspective on the political system is security-oriented and increasingly technocratic. (The PLA, for example, publishes over two thousand journals.) Like other armed forces throughout the world, their zeal toward nation and their vested interest in using the arms they bear are undeniably strong.

Since the Maoist period, the PLA has become increasingly professional and removed from the political fray. The PLA's recent emphasis has been on improving China's missile forces and expanding the navy's range of operations. Senior officers have served as members of the Standing Committee of the Party Politburo, the inner sanctum of power. The PLA is a distinctive entity inside the party, which ties it to the civil Communist leadership, but it also enjoys a significant degree of organizational and financial autonomy. The senior officer corps may be considered an important advocate for harsher stands in the area of foreign policy as well as with respect to Taiwan and the minorities in China's border regions. At the same time, as technocrats, they tend to favor modernization and support the importation of high technology from the West and from Russia.

Although soldiers in premodern China were looked down upon, the PLA rank-and-file have enjoyed a high social status since the Communist victory in 1949. Their stature compares favorably to that of CCP cadres. These heirs of the revolution are proclaimed to be the people's heroes, and occasionally even spend a day assisting civilians at their menial jobs in symbolic reenactment of their early guerrilla role. As long as the present upward trend in funding for the PLA continues, and the military budget keeps pace with increases in the overall state budget, there is no reason for the military to balk. (The military budget has been increasing in recent years by about 13 percent annually. Western estimates put the PLA's actual budget at three times what the Chinese government officially states it to be.)

During the 1980s and 1990s, the PLA acquired and managed a large number of civilian properties and businesses, including hotels, factories, and other enterprises. The profits provided supplemental funding for the PLA, and extra income for officers. In 1998, Jiang Zemin ordered the PLA to divest itself of its civilian business empire and concentrate on its primary duties. A start has been made in this direction, but it will be some time before we can gauge the success of this order.

In the final analysis, the military would only pose a threat to political stability if the CCP leadership were paralyzed and civil disorder were rampant. All these factors, in addition to the interlocking relationship between the party and the PLA, argue against the military's creating trouble. The June 4, 1989, Tiananmen massacre, in which many of the predominantly teenage rank-and-file soldiers were initially quite reluctant to fire upon the people, is further proof of the basic orientation of the PLA toward its external security mission rather than the distasteful job of maintaining domestic order.

POLITICAL SUCCESSION

The lack of an effective mechanism to transfer power from one national leader or set of leaders to another can pose potentially serious problems in any country. A prolonged struggle for power at the top may send shock waves rippling downward. Amid the resulting uncertainty, working-level officials could refrain from making timely decisions that affect foreign investment and foreign business operations. In the worst case, a political succession struggle might lead to outright civil disorder.

Unlike Japan where the prime minister is weak, China concentrates a lot of power in the hands of its top leader. In 1976, the death of CCP chairman Mao Zedong precipitated an intense power struggle in China that took more than two years to resolve. Many observers predicted that the death of Mao's successor, Deng Xiaoping, would occasion a similar, if less dramatic, political tussle. But in this instance the situation had been more carefully planned. By the time Deng died in 1997 following a protracted illness, his designated successor Jiang Zemin already had been at the helm for almost eight years. Leadership control down to the grassroots level had been consolidated, and people had a chance to get used to Deng's absence from center stage. No succession crisis ensued.

The current leader Jiang Zemin does not have the personal appeal of either of his two predecessors who led the revolution during its glory days. But his bureaucratic image is suitable to a time of calm and stability. Jiang has secured his position and has planted his own people into the pyramid of power within the party. The top positions within China are allocated by, and within, the inner circle of the Communist elite that periodically co-opts new members to its ranks from the second and third circles of power. Jiang himself was brought to Beijing from Shanghai in 1989 to assume national leadership. Having turned seventy-four in 2000, he occupies the top three national positions: state president, CCP general secretary, and chairman of the Central Military Commission. When his second term expires in 2003, he must step down as president, but there is no formal barrier to his continuing as head of the party and the army.

Even if Jiang yields all three posts, as long as he remains in good health, he could still wield great influence from behind the scenes as Deng did for many years. Jiang will play a significant, though not necessarily decisive, role in choosing the successor, within the context of a collective ruling elite that does not always see eye-to-eye on personnel or policy issues. In addition to the three positions Jiang now occupies, the critical posts of prime minister and head of the National People's Congress—China's parliament—are also filled via horse-trading within the inner circle of power.

Compared to the recent past, only a narrow spectrum of differences seems to exist among the political elite in today's China. The men who succeed to the key positions—there are no women in the pool of candidates—will likely come from the fourth generation of CCP leaders. (Mao, Deng, and Jiang represent the first three generations.) Like Jiang they are civilian technocrats, not military leaders or ideologues. They are more pragmatic and disposed to compromise than their predecessors.

The game of analyzing political succession in terms of individual leaders is a bit like blindman's bluff. Both Mao and Deng repeatedly jettisoned the men they had designated to succeed them. In fact, since the founding of the People's Republic of China, only two of those tipped to take over actually have done so. The man in Jiang's entourage who is most often tipped as his successor, Politburo Standing Committee member Hu Jintao, is a generation younger than Jiang. Whoever eventually takes over the top spots will confront a political system in which the CCP and its official ideology have become increasingly devalued over the past twenty years.

Even at times of leadership turnover, the centralized, solid structure of communist political machinery suggests the continuation of stability. It may well be that over the longer-term leadership transition will become more institutionalized and less animated by "palace politics." But given what we know of China and the Chinese Communist system, and as long as standards of behavior and general social conditions remain in a state of flux, there is still a real possibility of instability or turmoil. If Chinese, who are usually tightly controlled, take to the streets in confusion, the resulting disorder, verging on chaos, could seriously disrupt business as usual and even harm enterprises and production.

The CCP seeks to maintain the single-party, communist political system at a time when the ideological verities of the Maoist period have dissipated and the state socialist economy is rapidly being deconstructed. From a political perspective, what circumstances might generate instability in China?

1. Disagreement within the Inner Circle on the Allocation of Top Positions

If third-generation patrons engaged in promoting their own favorites cannot agree on who should get what positions, split decisions might lead to prolonged squabbling. Losers could try to get back at winners by withholding cooperation or extending their rivalry to other areas.

2. Military Intervention in Policy Process

China's expanding international role, the growth of Chinese military power, and Beijing's preoccupation with issues of national sovereignty and territorial unification (Taiwan) have highlighted the importance of military leaders in decision making. Senior military leaders appear to hold hard-line views on Taiwan and the United States. They might act as a wild card in domestic and international politics, but are unlikely to assert themselves at the center in a way that would present an integral threat to the civilian leadership. Nevertheless, in the course of the competition among civilian leaders toadying to them, they might resort to maneuvers of saber-rattling and tapping into the reservoir of antiforeign sentiments among the population. The rhetoric of political leaders and government actions could make it difficult for a time for foreign businesses to operate effectively in China.

3. Groups with Ideological and Organizational Potential

In the latter part of the 1990s, several groups, some encouraged from abroad or with overseas connections, emerged in China and attempted to play a political role or fill the spiritual vacuum in Chinese society. The fledgling Chinese Democracy Party (CDP), which advocated political freedom and civil liberties in China, quickly became a victim of political repression. The Falun Gong (FLG), a Buddhist meditation and physical exercise group, articulated a transcendental need and a spiritual path beyond the everyday materialistic reality of present-day China. In October 1999, the Chinese government banned the organization as an "evil sect" and intensified a harsh campaign of repression against leaders and followers.

The major threat posed to the CCP by such groups, whether overtly political like the CDP or nonpolitical like the FLG, is their capacity to build networks of supporters across China. The FLG, while espousing no political program, had already developed a hierarchical network that stretched across cities, towns, and villages. Like the prerevolutionary secret societies of China, the FLG protected its members' identities. The difference now is that modern telecommunications and the Internet facilitate organizing to a degree that the old secret societies could scarcely have imagined.

4. Centrifugal Power versus Regionalism

China's domestic reforms and opening of the last two decades has widened the gap between wealthy coastal and poorer inland provinces and has weakened central government control over investment, trade, and tax collection. Corruption has flourished. Efforts to reassert centralized control have been sporadic and only partially effective. Nevertheless, the possibility of China's breaking up, as the Soviet Union did in 1991, is remote. Among other reasons, Beijing still exercises effective control over internal security forces. Short of breakup, however, China could evolve further in the direction of regional autonomy. Such autonomy, as long as it does not threaten the overall structure of the state system, might actually benefit foreign business operations. Rather than having to deal with distant bureaucrats in Beijing, foreign businesspersons would have easier access to local officials and would have to cope less with overlapping authority. And in the event of disturbances in one region or at the center, business in another would be sequestered.

Although problems might arise at times from a clash of will and interest between powerful regional leaders and a weakened central authority, the astute businessperson would develop a contingency strategy to avoid being caught in such a conflict. For example, one area of contention now is the question of who is responsible for ensuring compliance with central directives regarding the enforcement of international agreements such as the U.S.–China intellectual property rights (IPR) agreement of 1996. Foreign businesses, dependent upon government officials for permits, labor supply, energy, land, and so forth, should be aware that tugs-of-war between local- and national-level can trip them up. As they position themselves in the market, they should back up their local relationships with the similar cultivation of a protective shield of individuals in power in Beijing.

As ideological controls remain lax and some regions become more enterprising and richer than others, it is also conceivable that the local military will be tempted to involve itself with political leaders to share in the corruption. Under the Communists, the prerevolutionary phenomenon of warlordism only resurfaced once or twice after 1949, held in check by the periodic rotation of regional army commanders. If civil disorder or central government paralysis were to prevail, the disciplined military command might break down and senior officers might enter local politics to feed at the trough.

LEGITIMACY IN A CHANGING SYSTEM

The CCP, the heart and mind of the postrevolutionary system since the Nationalists were defeated in 1949, has long ceased to be a "revolutionary vanguard party" pushing radical social and political change.

It does still remain in supreme command, a party that claims to be exercising the "people's dictatorship," and it has no scruples about using whatever means are necessary to prevent the emergence of opposition parties or political organizations. The arrest and imprisonment on contrived charges of the leaders of the tiny CDP is a case in point. Most Communists see their party as a vehicle for advancing their own personal careers. Membership provides a kind of political credit card that they use to their own advantage. As nonstate sectors of the economy continue to grow, the party's role in economic policymaking correspondingly diminishes. Party bureaucrats at every level scheme to maintain control, but this only serves to bog things down even more. Except for people seeking careers in politics, administration, and the military, party membership is no longer a requisite. Recent campaigns to reinvigorate the party have fizzled, and party leaders including Jiang, have become the butt of private jokes.

DEATH OF IDEOLOGY

Paralleling the party's organizational decline has been a progressive dry rot that has destroyed the core of CCP ideology, defined as an action—and usually goal—oriented belief system. Mao's vision of a future communist utopia has been replaced by a "buy now," consumer society in which personal sacrifice for the collective good is either something to do later on in life or the province of schoolbook heroes. Ronald McDonald is more popular than Lei Feng, the model Communist soldier, and Colonel Sanders has replaced Chairman Mao as a source of food for thought.

Among a significant number of the population, the absence of an inspiring party leadership and the disintegration of ideology has engendered spiritual emptiness, irreverence, and political skepticism. Some people harbor nostalgia for the "good old days" as expressed in the kitsch cult of Mao. Many members of the Red Guard generation, whose lives and education were disrupted by the Cultural Revolution of the 1960s, openly express a longing for "more meaningful and freer times." Other Chinese have turned to indigenous and Western religions in a quest for faith and spiritual meaning. Both officially sanctioned as well as unregistered Christian "house churches" have flourished despite official persecution of the latter. As already noted, in 1999 China banned the FLG and instituted a witch-hunt against its several million adherents. Acting in the spirit of their imperial Chinese predecessors, fearful and intolerant CCP oligarchs have proscribed the FLG and many similar groups as "heretical sects" whose very existence supposedly threatens public order. CCP leaders, guardians of a smoldering faith, have not formally buried the corpse of Marxism-Leninism, which they still officially venerate much as they did the sarcophagus of Mao. In its place, however, the CCP promotes an assertive Chinese nationalism and "socialism with Chinese characteristics." The latter actually sanctions private enterprise, stock markets, and foreign direct investment among other nonsocialist institutions. The ambiguous collection of values that the party promotes, an uninspired hodge-podge of borrowed ideas from the past and Western science and philosophy, is meant to suggest the rebirth of China's great civilization, and aims at capturing the upbeat mood of a young, better-educated, and affluent Chinese urban generation.

COMMUNICATIONS TECHNOLOGY'S CHALLENGE

If communications like radio and television have connected a large percentage of the rural population to the values and styles of the more modernized cities, it is now increasingly difficult to jam news and practices in the outside world from the reception of the Chinese populace. In a more relaxed environment, more and more children freely listen to Voice of America and BBC broadcasts, ostensibly to improve their English but also to learn and discover.

Among the listeners, the urban young are perhaps the most crucial group. Concentrated in the heartland cities as well as the booming seaboard provinces, the younger generation believes that they, like China itself, have come of age, and that personal as well as national goals lie within reach. They are groping for new ideas and they are finding them to a large extent outside China.

One significant indicator of their connection with the outside world is the increase in the number of Chinese with access to the Internet. In 1999 alone, the number of Chinese Internet users soared from 2.1 to 8.9 million, a figure expected to reach 20 million by the end of 2000. In Beijing, Shanghai, Guangzhou, and other major metropolitan areas, numerous Internet cafes provide cheap and easy access to the information world. Although the number of Internet users is still small relative to the total urban population, it will continue to grow exponentially over the next decade.

This phenomenon is already becoming very troublesome to government and party officials in charge of monitoring and controlling information. If Chinese can receive information instantly and with ease, they can also send it. In 1989, the Tiananmen student demonstration set off a wave of similar protests in cities across China. Between May and June 1989, students relied heavily on university and institute fax machines. In the future, to use Mao's own words, in order to "spark a prairie fire" grassroots rebels should have little difficulty igniting the web. And protest activity across China's hinterland would be no tea party.

NATIONALISM

Earlier generations of patriotic Chinese were taught to view modern Chinese history as a woeful tale of national humiliation inflicted by the imperialist West and Japan. The new generation ("Generation Now") not only believes that China is a great power, but that it can and must act like one in order to compensate for past insults. Generation Now bristles at being patronized by foreigners (perhaps particularly Americans) who presume to instruct China on such topics as human rights, democracy, intellectual property rights, abortion, Tibet, and Taiwan. Underlying this anti-Western nationalism, there seems to be a sort of envy of the West combined with a sense of destiny concerning the reemergence of a great civilization in China. The popularity of an in-your-face attitude toward Westerners who would stand in China's way underlay the success of the 1996 runaway bestseller *China Can Say No*, and a shelf of similar books. Their central theme, bluntly stated, has been that China will not let anyone kick it around anymore and, in fact, should be ready to "kick a little ass" itself.

At the same time, this generation has a consumer mentality and is fond of American popular culture and the good life. To the extent that popular attitudes mirror government positions, they reinforce official nationalism. Thus, there was genuine anger in China, directed mainly at the United States, at NATO's accidental bombing of the Chinese embassy in Belgrade during the spring 1999 Kosovo War. But unlike earlier episodes of antiforeign violence in China, such as the Boxer Rebellion of the late 1890s or the antimissionary riots of the 1920s, Americans living in China were not at risk nor was their property. What emerged was a kind of "domesticated xenophobia," directed not at foreigners, but at a foreign government, namely the United States. (Popular nationalism, however, can be a double-edged sword. It can be manipulated to divert the anger from internal leaders about domestic problems. But should the Chinese government act cautiously in the name of diplomacy, popular anger can turn against what are seen as weak-kneed Chinese officials. Such was the case over provocations by Japanese ultranationalists and anti-Chinese activity in Suharto's Indonesia. The realization that nationalistic sentiment can backfire partly accounts for China's verbal bellicosity on sensitive issues affecting national sovereignty.)

The Chinese born after 1949 believe that Taiwan is an integral part of China, which American policy and unpatriotic Taiwanese politicians have conspired to keep from reuniting with the mainland. The hand-over of Hong Kong to China in 1997, marking the end of 155 years of British control, generated great enthusiasm among Chinese. Two years later, tiny Macao, a Portuguese colony since 1557, reverted to China. In a poll taken in March 2000, 95 percent of Chinese supported Beijing's official position that force should be used, if necessary, to reintegrate Taiwan. Even an avant-garde artist-friend of ours in Shanghai agrees that the government should "blow the hell out of Taiwan with nuclear devices" if that is what is required to reunify. Yet Beijing may have stirred up a hornets' nest, because despite its tough words, it cannot move against Taiwan without risking war with the United States. It must hope that a combination of tough talk and restrained behavior will keep this issue from biting it in the back.

Can the Chinese government survive with only nationalism as an ideology? Throughout most of its long history, Chinese rulers have propagated an official orthodoxy that might be thought of as an ideology. The larger question now is whether China has changed enough so that the lack of a credible and coherent official ideology, other than a generic nationalism, no longer much matters. Nationalism is emotional, lacking in depth, and difficult to control or sustain. Furthermore, if the legitimacy of the CCP rests upon the stilts of promoting China as a great power (nationalism), and ensuring the prosperity of the country and its people (economics), then other political forces—perhaps even religious or charismatic organizations at the grassroots—could conceivably claim to offer an alternative way to advance these goals.

In our view, evolving forces within the top political elite will increasingly reflect and articulate the demands of the people. CCP leaders assert that the only alternative to their own rule is chaos, but the flaws in this self-serving argument are becoming increasingly apparent to an enlightened segment of the working leadership. A reasonable supposition is that within the confines of the government elite and the CCP itself the possibility of political reform survives even if the present is not a propitious time for it to flourish.

OTHER SOCIAL PROBLEMS THREATENING THE SYSTEM

China in some respects is a typical developing country, suffering from transitional social-economic growth pains such as uneven development, expectations that do not keep abreast of modernization, and identity problems. In this case, the country only recently emerged from a revolutionary era in which—delusion or not—China was supposed to be transformed into an egalitarian society. Many pernicious aspects of the primary modernization period are evanescent, only peripheral to foreign interests and dissipate over time. Because agencies of control at the top are perhaps stronger in China than in other countries and certainly more pervasive, we will only focus on three factors—the rural-urban gap, corruption, and obvious human rights abuses—that could be destabilizing and would be useful for foreign businesses to monitor.

Rural-Urban Gap

Transitional economies must routinely endure an economic and social differential between agrarian areas and the more industrialized cities. As many farmers come to the cities in search of better jobs, the agricultural sector wanes and the urban sector experiences overcrowding, which places a tremendous burden on the system and serves as a breeding ground for unrest.

Although opportunities for travel and freedom of residence are limited in China, tens of millions of job-seeking rural migrants find their way to the coastal and interior cities. Because of their illegal status, they live at the margins of urban society, and many contribute to the rising incidence of crime. These rural sojourners not only pose a headache to the authorities, but also disturb the settled urban population. Most destabilizing is the fact that people in rural areas, and in disadvantaged inland areas generally, are becoming increasingly aware of the gap between their incomes and life styles and those of Chinese in the coastal cities and industrial metropolises who benefit more directly from rapid economic growth. The recent import of migrant corvee-type labor from the villages to the Pudong free trade zone in Shanghai and their subsequent return to the countryside might spark new initiative in their villages, but it might also stir resentment as villagers compare their condition with their urban compatriots.

The Chinese government has been exhorting foreign enterprises to relocate inland in order to spread the wealth. In the medium term, investors who comply will be assuming a risk of antagonizing the poorer workers in neighboring state enterprises as well as those working the land. Higher wages and perhaps better working conditions not only breed envy, but could also escalate existing worker dissatisfaction. The foreign businessperson who must locate inland should expect random bursts of civil disorder that might interrupt operations.

Corruption

In pre-Communist China, a certain level of official corruption was tolerated, and it tended to trickle down the ladder of social control. When it became excessive, it contributed to the toppling of both the dynastic and Nationalist (Chiang Kai-shek) governments. At this stage in the dramatic shift from a communist administration that proclaimed egalitarian values to the current emphasis on entrepreneurship, productivity, and acceptance of economic inequality, venality has penetrated every level of officialdom. One may expect to encounter it whenever and wherever favors are sought, from obtaining licenses to arranging housing. The central government initiated yet another campaign against corruption in 2000, expelling the vice chairman of the National People's Congress from the CCP and executing a former deputy governor of the Jiangxi province for bribery, in an exercise that the Chinese call, "killing the chicken to scare the monkey." The foreign businessperson, who is safe from such punishment, may still fall prey to payoffs of one sort or another despite government crackdowns. Americans must be circumspect about violations of the Foreign Corrupt Practices Act, but the Chinese take pains to disguise corrupt activities from the outsider's eye.

More important than the impact of corruption on the costliness of conducting business is the response of the Chinese people to corruption in their daily lives. When corruption is widely perceived to be out of control, it damages the government's legitimacy. Political factions or groups will use campaigns against corruption as a means to win public support and strike at their adversaries because the fight against corruption has great appeal. If within the next decade a grassroots group gained sufficient momentum to challenge the government, the fight against corruption would likely be one of its rallying cries as was the case with the student-led democracy movement in the spring of 1989.

The Human Rights Dilemma

Denying that problems exist is not necessarily the best way for foreigners seeking long-term involvement in the China market to approach thorny questions of human rights. Sanctions against China for human rights violations, which would affect business, continue to loom on the horizon.

As businesspersons are increasingly drawn inland and engaged in infrastructure construction in remote areas, they must face the possibility of being caught in conflicts between government forces (military and police) and crowds of striking workers. Of course, the foreign corporate entity or its expatriate personnel cannot dictate behavioral norms to the Chinese authorities, but they can set certain standards with respect to working conditions and workers' rights that indicate they will not be caught in the middle between opposing Chinese interests. Moreover, if a long-term project is involved, it is in the interest of the foreign entity to set up a consultative committee that will solicit community viewpoints, not simply the voice of officialdom, and reconcile government positions with those of the discontented workforce. Foreign installations engaged in long-gestation infrastructure work or looking forward to a protracted tenure in the Chinese market should consider providing other services that demonstrate their sympathy to people's needs. From a public relations standpoint, they must carefully straddle the interests of key officials at the local level (perhaps sponsoring municipal cultural projects here and there) and the working people in their community. If foreign investors only heed the security officials and allow themselves to be sucked into the vortex of the worst aspects of the Chinese system of control, they risk making themselves the object of popular anger and a target for international human rights groups. Pragmatism, then, points to the need to take human rights seriously.

THE PACE OF DEMOCRATIZATION

The broader benefits of a freer, more open, and egalitarian political arena are as important to American and Western businesspersons as the rule of law and due process. Despite fitful progress, the rule of law in China is no more certain than its respect for its constitution and civic rights. From the foreign investor's perspective, expatriate personnel will be more comfortable living and working under the rule of law and in an environment where progress is being made toward democratization. In such circumstances, the host country people are able to move about more freely, associate as they please, and have outlets to express their dissatisfaction with the system. If the local police or military become involved in matters at the work site, foreign employers and supervisors can be more assured that they will not be implicated in a breach of human rights or an international incident.

What, then, are the prospects for democratization in China? In 1986, three years before the Tiananmen incident, intraparty reformers were riding high, and China briefly seemed to be on the cusp of significant political reform. Fifteen years later, Chinese society is significantly freer, but political reforms halted with the collapse of communism in Eastern Europe and the Soviet Union. The party elite concluded that Soviet leader Mikhail Gorbachev's half-hearted attempts at political reform were at fault. (The spring 1989 student protests in China drew inspiration from Gorbachev's "glasnost" [openness] and "perestroika" [restructuring]). Party leaders, sensing mortal danger, dug in their heels and drew a sharp distinction between economic reform, which they favored, and political reform, which they opposed.

In other countries, including Taiwan, rising levels of education, increasing affluence, and greater contact with the outside world have generated domestic pressures for political reform and democratization.

Can we expect a similar trend in China? The answer to this depends upon two factors. First is the strength of the push from below. What level of risk will Chinese entrepreneurs, professionals, and other new social groups be willing to take in order to articulate demands for political reform? Are there particular issues that are likely to engage at least a determined minority from among these groups? Rather than abstract issues of democracy and representation, such concrete questions as freedom of assembly, official corruption, government favoritism, and restrictions on information seem more likely to stimulate political engagement.

Second is the responsiveness of governing elites. Will Communist leaders have the foresight and flexibility to preempt pressure for significant political change by advancing their own reform agenda? Or will potential reformers be stymied not only by the memory of Gorbachev's failure, but by Communist diehards who view any move in the direction of pluralism as a threat to their own power and privilege?

Although it is comforting to think that education, information, and prosperity will push China toward pluralism and democracy, authoritarian regimes are not on the endangered species list. The Communist government in China might still be around for another decade or two, and the prudent businessperson need not worry too much about scenarios of collapse, civil strife, and uncontained threats to foreign property. A slow and fitful political evolution is more likely than any radical transformation. As intraelite interests become more differentiated, a natural trend toward some sort of pluralism will be harder to curb. Professional groups will become more coherent and assertive. One element in the political structure that might amplify the diversity of political ideas is the CPPCC, which articulated a more moderate public approach toward Taiwan amid the flurry of Chinese threats voiced in the run-up to Taiwan's 2000 presidential election. In recent years, the CPPCC has hosted political delegations from the United States and other countries. It has been made a channel for nonmainstream points of view. Other central government institutions, including the National People's Congress, might also evolve in the direction of pluralism and democracy. China-watching businesspersons should bear in mind that if American or other foreign groups push issues like democratization and human rights too hard, whether from genuine concern or post–Cold War frustration, official Chinese reactions are likely to be nationalistic, xenophobic, and increasingly repressive. China is especially jealous of its prerogatives with respect to internal issues, and rarely hesitates to defy international opinion. It prefers stability and order to the uncertain outcome of attempts at radical change.

FOREIGN AFFAIRS

The environment in which foreign businesspersons operate in China is greatly influenced by the state of China's relations with the world and its position in the region. A basic question is whether China will be cut off from much of the world as it was in the 1950s through the 1970s or engaged in the mainstream of world affairs as it has been ever since. Before the economic reforms and the opening of China in the 1980s ended the country's partly self-imposed isolation, most of China's very limited foreign trade was conducted at the semiannual Canton trade fair where state foreign trade corporations enjoyed a monopoly of foreign trade and foreign importers and exporters usually lacked direct access to Chinese suppliers or end-users. During the Cold War, China's foreign relations were dominated by security concerns that dictated a policy at first of alliance with the Soviet Union in the 1950s and then alignment with the United States in the 1970s. In the 1980s, Beijing proclaimed an independent foreign policy, a policy to which it still adheres.

In the thirty years after the CCP took power, China went to war on several occasions: against UN forces in Korea in 1950, India in 1962, the Soviet Union in 1969 (border skirmishes), and Vietnam in 1979. Mao left China's foreign relations in disarray. Deng normalized relations with the Soviet Union, India, Vietnam, and South Korea, while seeking to maintain good relations with the United States, Western Europe, and Japan. In the revolutionary period (1949–1978), China sought to overthrow the international status quo. Mao railed against imperialism, claiming that "great disorder under heaven" favored China's aim of world revolution.

China's regional role at the start of the twenty-first century will entail assuming the mantle of stabilizing force on the continent. Mao's China once sought to be an example for regional and third-world revolution, but generally this giant country has been relatively peaceful and self-contained. War in Korea and Vietnam and skirmishes in the Taiwan Strait and in the northeast with the Soviet Union seem to have been rather tame behavior considering the historical circumstances. Now, as one of the five permanent members of the Security Council, China plays an increasingly active role in world affairs, generally in support of regional and global stability This nation seems prepared to become a world power and its regional role is intended to project the rebirth of an eminent civilization that might hold cultural sway over the region and—with globalization—perhaps the world.

China has been party to the burgeoning interest in regional security issues. The Asia-Pacific region has lagged well behind Europe in developing multilateral mechanisms for dispute and conflict resolution. From a more self-interested perspective involving sales to North Korea, Pakistan, and Iran that enhance its nuclear capacity, China seems to be more willing to play by the rules of the game.

As the Asia-Pacific multilateral mechanisms for conflict resolution begin to diversify with the establishment and enhancement of organizations like the Asian Pacific Economic Cooperation (APEC) forum, the Association of Southeast Asian Nations (ASEAN), and the ASEAN Regional Forum (ARF), China will be drawn into a proper security network. These mechanisms now provide periodic venues for discussion among regional as well as other countries on economic, security, and other issues.

At counterpoint with its commitment to stability is the new China's compulsion to recover territorial integrity. China has been dedicated to recovering shoals, reefs, and islands in the interest of its will to become a modern maritime power. Its struggle to contest sovereignty over the Paracel and Spratly Islands in the South China Sea and rights in the East China Sea have been based as much on concerns for reclaiming Chinese turf as for offshore oil and other mineral rights. The country's power in the region will continue to grow both in economic and military terms, and its neighbors will have to recalibrate their relations periodically to take account of this reality. But China is not likely to threaten regional security by trying to acquire a formal or informal empire as Japan did in the 1930s.

China has achieved good relations with the European Union (EU) on a foundation of economics and trade. It has developed a security partnership with post-Communist Russia grounded in common suspicion of American unilateralism and lubricated by China's purchase of billions of dollars worth of Russian arms and high technology weapons systems. With Japan and India, its major Asian neighbors to the east and west, China has correct, if not particularly cordial relations. The memory of Japan's twentieth-century attempt to subjugate China still rankles, while democratic India, the dominant power in South Asia, is a potential great power rival in Asia.

In recent years, Jiang has taken his show on the road, visiting Great Britain, Canada, France, Germany, India, Israel, Japan, Russia, and the United States, among other countries. In contrast, Mao traveled abroad just twice, to the Soviet Union in 1949, and again in 1957. Seeing their president feted by world leaders on the evening news feeds Chinese national pride and self-confidence.

The sticking point in China's foreign relations involves its most important relationship of all—namely, its relationship with the United States. Many, if not most, in the Chinese elite view the United States as hostile to China's great power aspirations, and they look toward a multipolar world in which American power will be balanced by other countries, singly or in combination. They are suspicious of globalization and interdependence, which they see as new ways by which the West, particularly the United States, seeks to curb Chinese sovereignty, submerge its national integrity, and frustrate China's aspirations. Communist leaders view the United States as an ideological adversary committed to the long-term objective of undermining their power. The conservative older generation abhors American popular culture, but even Generation Now is ambivalent.

The leadership in Beijing insists that status of Taiwan is the main issue in Sino-American relations, and the resolution of the question of reunification is at bottom one of the gravest problems of the region. In 1949, Chiang Kai-shek's Nationalist forces took refuge in Taiwan, a Japanese colony between 1895 and 1945, after their defeat at the hands of the Communists in the civil war. Ever since then, the United States has provided security protection for Taiwan, under a formal security treaty until 1980, and under congressional mandate thereafter. In 1980, the United States switched diplomatic recognition from Taiwan to China, and acknowledged Taiwan to be part of China under a deliberately ambiguous formula that fully satisfied no one, but facilitated maintenance of the new status quo.

By the end of the 1990s, the reunification issue was brought to the brink of crisis. Taiwan's increasing development of a democratic process over the past fifteen years combined with the mainland's increasing need to press heavy-handedly for a renewed political commitment from Taiwan to reunite and make active steps in that direction. The election opposition Democratic People's Party (DPP) candidate and erstwhile Taiwanese independence proponent Chen Shui-bian to the presidency of Taiwan in March 2000 threatened a confrontation involving China, Taiwan, and the United States. Four years after the grouping of its troops across the Taiwan Strait in a menacing show of force, Beijing issued verbal threats about military action to thwart the election and any subsequent gestures that would suggest Taiwanese independence. Caught in the middle, the United States tried to temper emotions on both sides and contain the situation. Whether a disastrous conflict can be avoided over the longer term is an open question. It is too easy to dismiss Chinese threats as mere bluff. Although it may take five or more years for China to acquire the military capability to launch an invasion across the Taiwan Strait, there are lesser steps it can take in the immediate future. These include renewed saber rattling, a limited maritime blockade, practice missile launchings, and demonstration strikes against selected Taiwan military targets. Chinese military action against Taiwan would very likely trigger U.S. involvement and could destabilize the entire Asia-Pacific region.

China also has a number of territorial disputes with its Southeast Asian neighbors over various islands and reefs in the South China Sea. Possession of these assets would support China's bid to become a major maritime power. Beijing is concerned as well with offshore oil rights in the South China Sea and periodically has challenged the Vietnamese over the Paracel and Spratly Islands. Although there is little likelihood of conflict over these islands in the next five years, there is also no resolution of the issues in sight.

On the whole, China's foreign relations do not pose an imminent threat to the foreign investor or to companies with interests elsewhere in the region. Even with respect to the issue of Taiwan, the chances for a political *modus vivendi*, if not a solution, are still much better than those for conflict. Economically, the prospects for Taiwan and China to develop interlocking interests can only run afoul of sharp conflict in other areas. Some unresolved issues in a globalizing world lead to interim tensions that could interfere with the foreign enterprise's operations. Thorny differences between China and particularly the United States over weapons sales, persecution of Chinese individuals and breaches of human rights, and U.S. interference in the "internal" affairs of other countries could stir small retaliatory actions from slowness in issuing visas and approving licenses to delaying imported parts at Customs. Such nuisance ploys have been undertaken reciprocally over the years.

ECONOMIC OUTLOOK: BRIGHT CONDITIONS BUT STRUCTURAL TRANSFORMATION IS DIFFICULT

Since 1978, China's economy has undergone a remarkable transformation. By shelving Marxist shibboleths, unleashing the productive capacity of Chinese farmers, workers, and entrepreneurs, and promoting China's integration with the world economy through trade, investment, and technology transfer, Deng and his successors have brought China into the front ranks of the developing world. For nearly two decades China's economy has grown at the fastest rate of any in the world. According to a leading American economist, from 1978 through 1996 the gross domestic product (GDP) increased at a rate of 7.9 percent.

Foreign trade and investment, once insignificant, has become the engine behind China's growth. Exports now account for 20 percent of GDP, although China still accounts for only 3.4 percent of world trade. China's foreign reserves stood at $159 billion in early 2000, providing a downy cushion against debt service in the worst of crises requiring massive imports.

In urban and coastal China, a new middle class of relatively affluent consumers, numbering perhaps one hundred million people, has emerged with a taste for foreign consumer goods including toiletries, cosmetics, medicine, soft drinks, electronics, and so forth. Shanghai, Guangzhou, Tianjin, Beijing, Shenzhen, and other Chinese cities bustle with new skyscrapers, luxury hotels, department stores, and new housing tracts.

Nevertheless, despite significant gains in reducing poverty, a substantially larger urban and rural underclass, numbering in the hundreds of millions, persists, and the economic gap between urban and rural has grown. These contradictions underlie the comment by Yukon Huang, head of the World Bank mission to China that "China's economy is still a transitional economy." Economic reform has generated tens of millions of new jobs, but in recent years, growth has slowed and millions of workers have become redundant. The World Bank estimates that one-third of the 140 million jobs in SOEs are easily expendable. Unemployment and underemployment threaten social stability. They stir resentment of privatization and ultimately the foreign presence in the process.

China's leaders, bitterly divided among themselves, struggle with the immense task of managing the transition to a full market economy and face the reality of a diverse and fractious country and of commanding a corrupt and often unresponsive bureaucracy much of which is still wedded to old ways of doing business. Not so long ago, socialism meant state ownership and management of the economy. Today, "socialism with Chinese characteristics" means a mixed economy in which private, including foreign, enterprise and collectively owned township and village enterprises (TVEs) have been the major engines of growth, particularly in the dynamic southeast coastal provinces of Guangdong and Fujian. Yet even as the state share of the economy slowly shrinks, SOEs remain the dominant feature of the economy. (Between 1996 and 1998, the state share of industrial production fell from 75 to 67 percent.) The government's share of GDP dropped from 30 percent in 1989 to only 12 percent in 1998. The reform and economic rationalization of large numbers of technologically obsolescent, inefficient, and money-losing SOEs remains on the agenda of Premier Zhu Rongji. But the timetable for doing so has been attenuated, and the means envisioned are primarily reorganization and internal enterprise reform rather than privatization or allowing market forces to claim the weakest among them. In cases where privatization has occurred, local CCP and government officials have engaged in massive asset-stripping such as occurred in post-Communist Russia. The state, whose control of the economy was probably its major function over the past fifty years, remains unwilling to let it go, fearing that CCP control will be undermined.

Growth

During the first decade of economic reform, pent-up consumer demand long-deferred infrastructure investment, and foreign trade all fueled high-growth rates that peaked at a claimed 14.2 percent in 1992. (High growth was accompanied by inflation that reached 24 percent in 1994. Drastic government measures brought this under control by 1996.) In recent years, growth has slowed significantly, to a predicted 7.2 percent in 2000. The most significant impact has been upon employment. Between 1996 and 1998, employment by SOEs and urban collective enterprises fell by 32 million to 110 million. Private sector growth has not compensated for this loss in an economy where ten million job-seekers enter the job market every year. According to official Chinese statistics, some twenty million workers were laid off in 1997 and 1998 alone. Many more are retained on a part-time basis or forced to wait for back wages and take moonlighting jobs. In several cases where the closing of a factory affected most of a town's work force, the authorities had to call on the army to restore order after angry workers rioted in the streets.

Debt and Infrastructure

China is necessarily limited in its growth and ability to absorb foreign enterprise without infrastructure improvements. The government has resorted to massive infrastructure investments over the past several years, including $24.2 billion in 1999, to sustain high rates of growth. Taiwan reports that much of its investment in China has gone into infrastructure with no return. Much of the construction has been financed by large-scale special bonds. In 1998 and 1999, the government claimed to achieve its targeted growth rates of 8 and 7 percent, respectively, although independent economists doubted these figures. These expenditures have led to chronic large-scale budget deficits. Meanwhile, foreign indebtedness has increased rapidly to $120 billion in 1999, three-quarters of that contracted in the last three years alone. In contrast to the early 1980s when China demurred at drawing down on the credit lines available to it, debt-servicing on domestic and foreign borrowing was already absorbing 35 percent of government revenues in 1999.

Balance of Payments

Largely owing to strong American demand, China's exports remained strong even through the low point of the Asian economic crisis. In 1999, for example, China's exports increased 6 percent to $195 billion, and China enjoyed a trade surplus of $30 billion, although this was down from the year before.

Deflation

The real problem for the economy has been sagging domestic demand. This is due to a variety of factors including anxieties about unemployment, the gradual switchover in the cities from heavily subsidized housing to market-driven housing, and savings for retirement in the absence of an adequate pension system. (The graying of China's population has led to a projection that in thirty years as much as 40 percent of the state budget will need to be allocated to pensions for the estimated 22 percent of the population over the age of sixty.) China's economy is characterized by slack demand, surplus inventory, and excess capacity. This is manifest in a mild deflation (with depressed retail prices) that has stretched for more than two years.

Banking System

Another weak point in the economy, acknowledged as such by the central government, is the banking system. At every level, but the local and provincial levels in particular, banks have been under political pressure to make loans to local businesses, especially SOEs on political, rather than economic, grounds. Because of a high ratio of nonperforming and bad loans, many local and provincial banks teeter on the verge of insolvency, kept afloat only by infusions from the four major central banks. The central banks, too, have been in trouble. The central government has taken steps to control provincial banks by beginning to place overarching banking organizations above the provincial level. Ironically, a very high household savings rate of close to 40 percent contributed to some of the 60 percent of bank deposits in 1998. This high savings rate is the flip side of low consumer demand. Conflicting signals from the government continue to complicate the problem of reforming the banking system.

The Question of a Devaluation

The Asian economic crisis of the late 1990s heightened international expectations that China would devalue its currency (the yuan or renminbi) in order to boost exports, but few indicators suggest such a devaluation in the immediate future. Exports have flourished and the balance of payments is good. In fact, Chinese leaders earned a lot of political credit by keeping their pledge to maintain the yuan within a very narrow band, trading at about 8.3 yuan to the dollar. (An earlier devaluation in the mid-1990s brought the official exchange rate into line with the market rate and eliminated what had been an active black market in the currency, but the yuan is still not a freely convertible hard currency.)

The uncertain economy of China might temper the enthusiasm of the foreign businessperson contemplating entry into the Chinese market. Once China joins the WTO, it will be more open to imports but its openness will test the soundness of the economic structure. Moreover, China will continue to resist the competition. Although conservative Chinese leaders fought a losing battle with regard to the WTO, they have not lost the war. In fact, Premier Zhu Rongji, who led the campaign for WTO, paid for his victory with a significant loss of domestic authority. It is widely expected that China will resort to the extensive arsenal of non-tariff weapons available to slow or divert the impact of the market opening and economic transparency concessions it made as the price of its WTO entry ticket. If so, such measures will involve attempts to protect vulnerable domestic sectors, including agriculture, whose inefficiencies and irrationalities make them vulnerable to enhanced foreign competition.

The prognosis for China's economy, like that for its political future, is decidedly mixed. The prudent foreign businessperson must avoid excesses of enthusiasm or of despair.

CONCLUSION

Red tape, bureaucracy, corruption, an imperfect legal system, and the continuing hold of state enterprises complicate doing business in China, while the potential for worker unrest clouds the future. On the other hand, the country has come a long way from the days of Maoist autocracy and state economic monopoly, and the impulse for reform is still present even though reformers face difficult challenges. True, China's repression of dissidents and free-speaking intellectuals continues in an alarming way, but perhaps this is a manifestation of an understandably frightened reaction to the fear of change and uncontrollable avenues of communications as China faces the political and value-laden aspects of globalization.

As a mixed economy (whose statism is reinforced by political needs) and transitional society, China also faces such grave problems as unemployment and underemployment, rural-urban gaps, differential standards of living among regions, and a tendency for regional pull away from the center.

If the Chinese market is mined with risks and inconveniences for the American investor, it is also a wellspring of opportunity. As always, familiarization with the complexities of the national and local-level environments and a commitment to realism rather than romanticism are the best ways to proceed. Westerners should not be euphoric about entering the Chinese trade, but China has more to offer than many neighboring countries. The investor should be prepared to waste what he might think is a lot of time and manpower hours in getting a toehold in China, but the outcome can be very profitable. There may no longer be a market for U.S. "oil for the lamps of China," but China's oil will help us. And this burgeoning new economy will serve as a market for our heavy engineering services, advanced machinery, technology, consumer items, and service industries. In a more general sense, China's entrepreneurial spirit, productivity, and growth and the benign strategic priority that the U.S. government attaches to its stability—all are factors that ensure a favored position for the foreign investor. The premise of the Bill Clinton administration and Republicans like Henry Kissinger is that the more China is brought into the global mainstream of economic cooperation, the more it will be forced to compromise and be caught up in a web of cross-cutting obligations. If this thinking is correct, the future will be as secure for the foreign businessperson in China as for regional and global stability. Much will depend on the creativity, skill, and flexibility of leaders in Beijing, Taipei, and Washington.

5

Post-Soviet Russia for the Investor: Reliable Rule of Law and Associated Risks

Michael Newcity

The investment climate in Russia today is fraught with risks (as well as opportunities) that must be evaluated carefully and thoughtfully. The entire typology of political risks identified by David M. Raddock[1] in his first edition is present in Russia and ready examples abound.

LEGITIMACY

Communism in Russia is the ultimate faith that failed. While belief in communist ideology was certainly on shaky ground well before the final collapse of the Soviet Union, since then the Russian nation has struggled to find a common set of values and beliefs. A belief in the legitimacy of the state and its institutions has never been strong among Russians, who have always been treated as subjects rather than citizens. In the absence of a strong state that commands respect and obedience, Russian society is in flux as Russians seek new institutions that will command their loyalties. Until these new loyalties have formed and strengthened, Russian society will endure a continuing crisis of legitimacy.

REGIONALISM

Russia's crisis of legitimacy is made all the worse by intractable ethnic conflicts. Among the approximately one-fifth of the population who are not ethnic Russians, even a belief in the meaning and continued viability of Russian nationhood is not a universally shared assumption. For many of these ethnic

minorities, Russia is a post-imperial state, an agglomeration of disparate ethnic communities that were originally united through military force and now
share a limited sense of common nationhood. Now that the empire has col-
lapsed, many of the leaders in the non-Russian communities seek to exploit the
weakness at the center to expand local and regional autonomy. The effects of
these struggles between regional governments and the central government in
Moscow range from the bitter and violent conflict in the North Caucasus to the
war of laws that has characterized relations between the central government
and regions such as Tatarstan, Bashkortostan, and Sakha.

NATIONALISM

Apart from the intra-Russian nationalism of Russia's ethnic minorities, there is
also a strong Russian nationalist sentiment that bitterly resents the hard times that
have befallen Russia and that blames the West for these difficulties. To many in
this group, Russia's post–cold war humiliations and economic difficulties are the
direct result of the policies advocated and undertaken by Western governmental
and international institutions. The expansion of NATO to include Poland, Hungary, and the Czech Republic, followed by NATO's war against Yugoslavia, have
accentuated the concerns of many Russians that in the future Russia will be surrounded and dominated by a hostile military alliance. The failure of the Russian
economy to thrive, eight years after the commencement of privatization and market economic reforms, has caused some Russians to question the role of Western
governments and international organizations that have been actively involved in
Russia's reform efforts. Several years ago, a large survey of Russian attitudes towards political and economic reforms included the question: "Do you think that
the West is pursuing the goal of weakening Russia with its economic advice?"
More than 60 percent of the respondents answered "yes" and only 20 percent answered "no."[2] Since this survey was conducted, Russia has experienced a financial collapse in August 1998 and continued economic hardship, which has done
little to change these attitudes. Russia has often been suspicious of the West, and
in recent years these suspicions have often turned against foreign investors who
are seen by some to be exploiting Russia's weakened economic circumstances.
These suspicions and hostilities towards foreign investors are best illustrated by
the difficulties at the Lomonosov Porcelain Factory and the Vyborg Pulp and
Paper Mill, both of which will be discussed in more detail later in this chapter.

LEADERSHIP SUCCESSION, AUTOCRACY, AND OLIGARCHY

Prior to late December 1999, many observers both in Russia and out were eagerly
looking forward to the presidential elections scheduled for June 2000. Boris

Yeltsin was barred by the Russian constitution from seeking another term, so the June presidential elections, if held in accordance with Russian law, would mark the first time in one thousand years of Russian history that there was a peaceful, orderly, and electoral transfer of power from one political leader to another. Of course, Yeltsin's stunning New Year's Eve announcement that he was resigning and Vladimir Putin would become acting president until presidential elections could be held in late March 2000, upset these plans. Though Putin was elected (much more narrowly than anticipated) in the March elections, his accession to the presidency in this manner did not represent the anticipated victory for constitutionalism. Putin became acting president through a highly questionable arrangement with his predecessor and was then able to use the powers of incumbency to win election in his own right. The transfer of power from Yeltsin to Putin, then, represented yet another victory for the Russian tradition of oligarchic rule in which questions of leadership succession are resolved by backroom deals among political oligarchs. The tendency towards oligarchy in Russia extends from the political realm into the economic. The privatization of state enterprises created the opportunity for many of the old Soviet enterprise managers to become the owners of their newly privatized enterprises. They merely swapped the de facto control they had enjoyed under the Soviet regime for de jure ownership of the same enterprises once they were privatized. In addition to this existing economic oligarchy, which has emerged from the first phase of Russian economic reforms apparently as powerful as before, privatization has given rise to a group of super oligarchs—individuals who have exploited their political connections and sweetheart privatization deals to establish Russian versions of the Japanese "keiretsu." The interlocking corporate groups these oligarchs have created, including leading financial institutions, oil and other natural resource companies, and dominant media outlets, pose substantial challenges to market entry, and their political connections make them difficult adversaries for foreign investors (as the experience of BP Amoco with its investment in Sidanko, which is described near the end of this chapter, indicates).

POLITICAL CULTURE

Many of the factors that will determine the success or failure of economic reform in Russia are policy-oriented, structural, and technical (e.g., how to create and regulate financial institutions that will stimulate the emergence of healthy financial markets and stimulate investment; whether Russia will lower its tariffs or raise them to protect domestic industry; the question of Russia's reliance on an income tax or a value-added tax as its primary source of state revenue). Underlying all of these factors, however, are issues of culture (legal, political, and economic) that will determine the success or failure of these reform policies. Russia's legal culture and its implications for legal reform are discussed later on. As to political and economic reforms, it should be noted here that Russian history has always been characterized by reform initiatives foisted on the nation by autocratic political leadership, including Peter the Great, Alexander II, Vladimir Lenin, and Mikhail Gorbachev. In this respect, the economic and political reforms undertaken by Boris Yeltsin are no different and are likely to be no more successful. These previous reform initiatives (interestingly enough, all of which attempted to introduce various forms of Western institutions to Russia) enjoyed, at best, mixed results, due in no small measure to the fact that the population was neither ready nor receptive to them. The success of reform initiatives in Russia will depend not only on the soundness of the policies, but also on the popular acceptance of them.

THE RISKS OF RUSSIAN LAW AND LEGAL INSTITUTIONS

In addition to evaluating the various risk factors previously mentioned, any investor contemplating an investment in a foreign country must seriously evaluate the law and legal system of the country in which the investment will be made. Are the local laws adequate—do they define precisely the rights and obligations of the investor? Are those laws sufficiently stable, predictable, and transparent, or is the investor likely to experience sudden and unexpected changes in foreign exchange rules, taxation, and so forth that will materially and adversely affect the investment? There are a host of specific legal issues that must be assessed in this regard—the local laws on foreign investment, company law, securities regulation, asset securitization, taxation, foreign exchange, and intellectual property will all play a central role in determining the success or failure of the investment. But even if the laws on these and other relevant subjects are sound, the investor must also determine whether the institutions responsible for enforcing those laws are competent, impartial, and respected. So an additional question must be asked: Will the institutions of the local legal system enforce and protect the rights and obligations of the investor?

A variety of different mechanisms have been developed over the years to assist investors in reducing the investment risks associated with local laws and legal institutions. The General Agreement on Tariffs and Trade (GATT) and the World Trade Organization (WTO) process have made great progress in establishing standardized minimum expectations for the content of local investment and trade-related laws. In order to join the GATT, and now the WTO, countries have been required to adopt or amend laws so that they meet the standards specified in the relevant trade agreements. Other international treaties—in the field of copyright protection, for example, the Berne Convention for the Protection of Literary and Artistic Works and the Universal Copyright Convention—have aided in establishing international standards for laws in important investment-related fields. Other international agreements—principally bilateral investment treaties—have protected investors against adverse and unforeseeable changes in local laws. International organizations such as the Organization for Economic Cooperation and Development (OECD), the World Bank, the International Monetary Fund (IMF), and others have been heavily involved in advising developing and transitional governments on legal reform in order to assist them in establishing legal regimes that will be receptive to foreign investment.

The task of establishing an investment-friendly legal regime has been especially difficult and contentious in the transitional states of eastern Europe and the former Soviet Union. The laundry list of laws that have had to be drafted, debated, adopted, and implemented in these countries is astonishing. A partial list of this legislative agenda and a brief overview of the attendant issues and controversies illustrates the Herculean task that has faced legislators in this region:

- *Constitutional reform:* In addition to the multitude of political and democratic reforms that have had to be adopted, new constitutions throughout this region must be adopted that permit, among many other activities, the private ownership of property, including land.
- *Civil law:* New civil codes, with provisions on contract and property law that are suited to market economies, must be adopted to replace the communist-era civil codes that reflected Soviet-style command economics. The Soviet-era contract law that did exist in the former Soviet Union was designed to facilitate the Soviet-style planned economy in which enterprises entered into contracts on the basis of government orders, not freedom of contract. Consequently, the new post-Soviet contract law introduced principles of freedom of contract as well as consumer protection provisions to protect individuals in weak bargaining positions from being exploited by parties in strong bargaining positions.
- *Privatization:* One of the first legislative tasks that all the nations of eastern Europe and the former Soviet Union have to face is the privatization of state enterprises. The centerpiece of any effort to convert a Soviet-style communist economy into a market economy has to be the transfer of ownership of state enterprises into private hands. This huge undertaking has necessitated the preparation of many different laws and regulations to define the process and procedures to be followed in privatizing large and small enterprises throughout this region.
- *Property law:* New, sophisticated laws on property are a prerequisite to the creation of a market-oriented legal regime in the former communist countries. These laws must define the nature, rights, and conditions of property ownership. They must also precisely specify how property may be acquired, used, and disposed. Establishing the legal basis for a system title to property is no small feat in countries where, under the Soviet system, the right to use assets was more important than holding actual title to those assets. The post-Soviet legal systems must provide the legal and administrative mechanisms for converting de facto control over property to de jure ownership of that

property. All of these changes must be undertaken against the backdrop of an acrimonious dispute throughout the former Soviet Union over the extent of private property rights. One of the most contentious areas of legal reform in Russia and elsewhere throughout the former Soviet Union is land law. The Russian president and the legislature have been deadlocked for years over the adoption of a new land code. President Yeltsin insisted on legislation that would permit the free buying and selling of land; the conservative politicians who dominate the legislature have refused to adopt such legislation. Instead, they adopted legislation that would sharply limit market activities in land and that would prohibit foreign ownership of land. Yeltsin vetoed this legislation and they have remained deadlocked ever since.

- *Commercial law:* Transition from a Soviet-style command economy to a market economy has necessitated the adoption of new laws to regulate market-oriented commercial transactions. Commercial laws and codes intended to establish standard terms and introduce uniformity in commercial transactions have been adopted in a few eastern European countries.

- *Competition law:* Obviously, the Soviet economic system had no need for antimonopoly laws. The post-Soviet economies, however, require the adoption and enforcement of such laws in order to prevent disruption of the market by enterprises that enjoy dominant positions in the market. Typically, the laws that have been adopted also include provisions outlawing various unfair and deceptive trade practices, including misleading advertising and misappropriation of trade secrets.

- *Investment law:* Investment laws are intended to establish the rules under which foreign investments can be made. Most of the nations of eastern Europe and the former Soviet Union have already adopted laws on foreign investment, but they differ significantly in their scope, content, and how favorable they are to investment. Important issues typically covered by such laws include the convertibility and repatriation of profits earned by foreign investors, protection against expropriation and nationalization, tax and other investment incentives, and the stabilization of tax rules.

- *Company law:* One of the first laws required in the transition from a Soviet-command economy to a market economy was a law defining the creation, powers, and governance of companies. Before state enterprises could be sold to private investors, they first had to be transformed from ill-defined state-owned entities of uncertain legal character and powers into companies with independent legal personality and well-defined powers and characteristics. Of special importance to foreign investors are the provisions in these company laws on corporate governance, especially the provisions protecting the interests of minority shareholders.

- *Securities law:* In addition to transforming state enterprises into companies, it was also necessary to create the legal basis on which those companies could capitalize themselves, especially through the public sale of their shares. Thus, new laws (and administrative agencies) are required to regulate the issuance and sale of shares by those companies, as well as the securities markets and securities firms that have arisen to assist in these activities.

- *Bankruptcy law:* Just as laws on the creation and capitalization of companies are required, so too are laws that govern the process by which the assets of insolvent companies are divided among their creditors and the companies are terminated. Drafting workable bankruptcy laws has been especially urgent in eastern Europe and the former Soviet Union because they are littered with insolvent and unprofitable enterprises that must be reorganized or wound-up if the new market economies are to achieve modest improvements in efficiency and productivity.
- *Taxation:* In the Soviet-style economy, taxation was a sideshow of economic policy. In a market economy, taxes are used to raise revenue, allocate resources, and redistribute income. However, in the Soviet-command economy, indirect methods for achieving these ends were unnecessary. The Soviet planners allocated resources and distributed income directly via the state economic plan. Transferring revenues from the private sector to the public sector via taxation was unnecessary because everything in the Soviet system was part of the public sector. However, with the collapse of the Soviet system and the transition to a market-oriented economy throughout eastern Europe and the former Soviet Union, taxation went from being a sideshow to being the main event in state economic policy.

Foreign investors have a substantial vested interest in all of these subjects. An investor could easily lose control of an investment, for example, if the local law does not provide adequate protection for shareholders' (especially minority shareholders') rights, if changes in foreign exchange rules prevent the investor from repatriating profits, or if amendments to tax laws sharply reduce the profitability of an investment. In addition to these general-interest subjects, there are specific legal issues that have substantial significance for investors in specific sectors. For instance, international petroleum companies have great interest in the adoption of legislation on production sharing agreements, which govern the conditions under which petroleum companies explore for oil and natural gas, extract it, and then divide the oil or natural gas with the government. Adoption of such legislation has consistently been viewed as a prerequisite to extensive investment in the petroleum sector in countries like Russia and other former Soviet republics.

Drafting and adopting legislation on all of these subjects is obviously an extraordinarily time-consuming and complex undertaking. It is even more complex in countries like Russia that are organized on federal principles. In Russia, the operative laws governing many aspects of investments, especially those relating to the ownership or use of land and natural resources, include local and regional laws and decrees, as well as the legislation adopted at the federal level. In considering and negotiating such an investment, a foreign investor must work with both the federal, regional, and local authorities to define the terms and conditions of the investment. Since relations between the Russian federal government in Moscow and the local and regional governments are frequently less than harmonious, reconciling the legal requirements of these various government bodies may pose a substantial challenge to the prospective investor.

The task of drafting and adopting legislation in the many areas relevant to foreign investment is truly daunting. But once legislation has been adopted, other substantial hurdles must be faced. First, the meaning of the legislation must be made clear before it can be implemented. Legislation and regulations adopted in eastern Europe and the former Soviet Union are often poorly drafted, vague, internally inconsistent, and inconsistent with other legislation. This latter problem is especially acute in Russia, which since the early 1990s has been the battleground for the so-called "war of laws." Initially, the term referred to the struggle prior to the collapse of the Soviet Union between the federal government in Moscow and the governments of several of the union republics, in particular the Russian Republic. In order to assert greater autonomy from the federal government, the union republic governments would issue laws and decrees that were in conflict with laws on the same subject that had been promulgated by the federal government. During this period, the thorny question for anyone attempting to determine their legal rights and obligations under Soviet law was which of these conflicting laws and/or decrees was authoritative. One of the great ironies of the collapse of the Soviet Union is that after the collapse these same tactics were used to limit the power of the Russian president, Boris Yeltsin, who had earlier pioneered their use against the Soviet president, Mikhail Gorbachev. In Russia, the war of laws has been fought on several fronts. These tactics have been used in the power struggles between the Russian president and legislature and between the Russian federal government and the regional governments. Thus, it is not uncommon that when one of the combatants in the war of laws adopts a law or issues a decree on a particular subject, another combatant will adopt a law or issue a decree on the same topic that is not consistent with the first law or decree. As before, the great challenge for anyone, especially a foreign investor, is to determine which of these seemingly contradictory laws or decrees trumps the other. As a result of poor legislative drafting and these intentional and unintentional conflicts between laws, the meaning of Russian legislation on many subjects is often murky.

A second major hurdle facing anyone attempting to interpret and implement legislation is that Russian legislation has frequently proved to be unstable once it has been adopted. Legislation in several key areas has often been amended or otherwise modified. This phenomenon has been most frustrating in the field of taxation, where tax legislation has been amended, seemingly, on a monthly basis. The resulting uncertainty has been occasionally compounded when the legislative modifications have been given retroactive effect. Taxpayers in Russia, for example, have on occasion actually been required to recalculate tax returns that were already submitted in order to give effect to subsequent changes in the legislation.

A third hurdle is simply finding the law. Though the texts of laws adopted by the national legislature and decrees adopted by the president are published in official and unofficial publications, they are not codified, indexed, or otherwise organized in any meaningful way. Relying on the official publications to find the up-to-date text of the law on the value-added tax, for example, which was originally adopted in December 1991, would necessitate browsing through all of the issues of those official publications from 1991 to the present. Unofficial publications, especially several commercial computer databases of Russian legislation, are very helpful in this regard. Their limitation, however, is that while they are extensive, by their very nature they are not all-inclusive, and it is never quite clear what may have been left out. Finding the texts of statutes and presidential decrees, however, is a walk in the park compared to finding the texts of regulations issues by government ministries and agencies. They are published occasionally in official newspapers and journals, but the coverage is spotty at best. One of the biggest worries for anyone concerned with Russian law has to be whether he or she has found all of the relevant legal texts—and ultimately there is just no foolproof way of knowing for sure. There will always be the fear that somewhere out there an obscure, but important, unpublished amendment or regulation will be waiting to cause mischief.

A fourth (and perhaps the highest) hurdle for someone evaluating his position under Russian law is determining how Russian laws and regulations are implemented on the street. Even if one is convinced that the president and legislature, acting in concert, have adopted comprehensive, well-drafted legislation on a particular subject; that there are no contradictory decrees at the regional and local level; that the government ministries or agencies charged with the responsibility of applying and implementing the legislation have issued clear, precise, and con sistent regulations and interpretive rulings; and that these laws, decrees, and regulations are conspicuously published, an even more daunting task must then be undertaken—with all this accomplished, the legislation must still be put into effect and applied in society. While legal texts (constitutions, laws, decrees, and regulations) are important, experience with the Russian legal system certainly teaches us that what those texts say and what people (judges, administrators, and other government officials) actually do are frequently quite different. The impediments to the effective implementation of new legislation include ignorance, lack of training, poor communications, bureaucratic intransigence, willful disregard of the law's requirements, and pervasive corruption.

In order to assess the investment posed by the Russian legal system, it is necessary to examine the state of Russia's laws as they relate to foreign investment and then review how the legal system deals with investment-related disputes. In the following sections, we will look at several of the more important investment-oriented areas of the law to assess their comprehensiveness and stability. We will then consider several recent cases in which foreign investors have been forced to turn to the Russian legal system to protect their rights in their investments. In the final section, we will draw some conclusions about the risk and uncertainty.

THE STATE OF RUSSIA'S LAWS RELATING TO FOREIGN INVESTMENT

A full analysis of all Russian legislation that is relevant to foreign investment is much too ambitious an undertaking for the present. Rather, we will review the state of Russian legislation in several areas of the law that are of greatest impor- tance to investors. Our purpose is to assess whether those laws provide a clear, comprehensive, and unambiguous framework that will permit existing and prospective foreign investors to understand and perform their legal rights and ob- ligations and that will encourage foreign investment.

The New Russian Law on Foreign Investment

The cornerstone of any legal regime relating to foreign investment is a law on for- eign investment that clearly specifies the protections and incentives accorded to foreign investors. The Russian Republic adopted the Law on Foreign Investments on July 4, 1991, months before the final collapse of the USSR. This law remained in effect until it was superceded by a new Law on Foreign Investment in the Russ- ian Federation, signed into law by President Boris Yeltsin on July 9, 1999.

The new law contains many of the same provisions and protections that were contained in the 1991 law. However, the 1999 law is considerably more sophisti- cated than the earlier law and contains several new and valuable protections for foreign investors.

The most notable innovation in the new law is a tax stabilization provision found in Article 9. Under this provision, any new federal laws or regulations that change the rates of certain specified federal taxes and customs duties, or any amendments to existing laws and regulations that increase the aggregate tax bur- den on foreign investors, will not apply to a foreign investment project for a pe- riod of seven years or until the foreign investor has recovered its investment, whichever comes first. This protection against adverse changes in Russian legis- lation is only applicable to certain foreign investment projects in which the for- eign investment accounts for more than 25 percent of the project's capital or to priority investment. A priority investment project is defined in the legislation as projects in which the aggregate amount of foreign investment is at least one bil- lion rubles (or its equivalent in foreign currency—approximately $40 million) or the amount of foreign investment in the equity capital of the project is at least 100 million rubles (approximately $4 million).

Other provisions of the legislation suggest that this tax stabilization provision may, in fact, be intended to apply to all direct foreign investment projects in which the foreign investment accounts for 25 percent of the equity capital. This ambiguity illustrates one of the more significant problems with Russian legislation in general—it is frequently ambiguously drafted, which of course creates opportunities for arbitrary and sometimes corrupt implementation of legislation as government officials interpret ambiguous legislative provisions to suit themselves.

This provision illustrates a second weakness of Russian legislation in that the tax stabilization provision in Article 9 will require corresponding amendments in Russian tax legislation and the promulgation of appropriate regulations before it can be fully effective. Frequently, Russian legislation anticipates the adoption of other legislation or the amendment of existing legislation. If and when these necessary legislative changes are not promptly forthcoming, the effect of the original legislation is substantially diminished.

In addition to the tax stabilization provision in Article 9, the 1999 law contains other provisions (similar to those contained in the original 1991 law) protecting foreign investors:

- *National treatment:* Article 4 stipulates that foreign investors will be treated no less favorably than Russian investors, "except with the exceptions provided by federal law." The law does state that more restrictive limitations on foreign investors may be imposed only in cases where the national constitutional system, morals, health, defense, security, and the rights and interests of others must be protected. Special incentives for foreign investors are permitted. The scope of the guarantee of national treatment contained in the new law appears narrower than the comparable guarantee contained in the 1991 law. The earlier law provided that the legal status of foreign investors and their investments could not be less favorable than the corresponding status of Russian individuals and legal entities as it related to "property and property rights." The nondiscrimination clause contained in Article 4 of the new law only guarantees nondiscrimination with respect to investment activities and the use of profits. This certainly suggests that Russian law will continue to countenance discrimination against foreign investors in regards to their use and ownership of property.
- *Protection against expropriation:* Article 8 of the law provides a guarantee against expropriation or nationalization of a foreign investment similar to that contained in the 1991 law (and bilateral investment treaties to which Russia is a party). Under this section, the assets of a foreign investor shall not be seized, requisitioned, or otherwise nationalized except "in cases and on the grounds provided in a federal law or international treaty of the Russian Federation." If a foreign investment is confiscated or nationalized, the investor will be compensated for the value of the seized property. This investment guarantee is relatively weak; it does not ensure "prompt, adequate, and effective compensation," which is the international standard for

such investment guarantees. Indeed, Article 7 of the 1991 law contained precisely this "prompt, adequate, and effective compensation" formula. The new law, however, has abandoned this standard. It is silent on the question of the timing for compensation or how the value of the seized asset will be determined. It also does not define what is meant by "seizure, including nationalization" for purposes of this provision. Would it include a case in which a Russian court holds that the original privatization of a Russian enterprise was improperly done and that the ownership of the enterprise must revert from the foreign investors, who subsequently purchased the enterprise, to the Russian state. This has recently become a very loaded question in light of the controversy over the ownership of the Lomonosov Porcelain Factory.

* *Repatriation of profits:* The law provides that foreign investors have the right to freely transfer abroad or otherwise make use of their after-tax profits earned in Russia.

These are among the more significant protections for foreign investment that are contained in the new Russian Law on Foreign Investment. Most of these protections were contained in the 1991 law, but the 1999 law adds the tax stabilization provision and defines the relevant terms more precisely than the earlier legislation. The 1999 law, however, has narrowed several of the protections for foreign investors that were contained in the 1991 law. The long-term benefit or effect of this new law is unclear and will remain unclear until the various amendments to other legislation and regulations that are necessary to give effect to its provisions are adopted and implemented.

Company and Securities Laws

Prior to the late 1980s, all enterprises in the Soviet Union were state controlled. The notion of an autonomous, self-governing legal entity was anathema to the Soviet economic and political system. In 1990, the Soviet Union adopted legislation that permitted the creation of the first real corporations in Russia in many decades—joint stock companies. Since this original decree was adopted, Russian company law has evolved through the adoption of several discrete laws that have created a relatively sophisticated legal regime governing the creation, governance, and termination of a variety of different kinds of legal entities. At present, the most important laws dealing with company law issues are the Russian Civil Code, the Joint Stock Company Law of 1995, and the Law on Limited Liability Companies of 1998.

The company law currently in place in Russia closely resembles its counterparts in western European countries, especially Germany and the Netherlands. The law permits the establishment of an array of different corporate legal entities:

- *Full partnership:* Partners are fully and jointly liable for all partnership obligations, and all partners act with equal authority on behalf of the partnership.
- *Limited partnership:* The partners are divided into two classes—general and limited partners. In this corporate form, the limited partners are liable for the partnership obligations only to the extent of the capital they have actually contributed. The general partner is liable for all of the partnership's obligations, but the general partner can be either a natural person or a company. Thus, ordinarily the general partner would be a company especially established for the purpose of acting as general partner and would have limited assets.
- *Limited liability company:* In such companies, there is a limit on the number of investors—no more than fifty. Moreover, the membership interests in a limited liability company are not freely transferable; there are strict limitations on the right of an investor to sell his membership interest to another.
- *Additional liability company:* In this relatively unusual corporate form, the investors in a company will be liable for the obligations of the company to the extent of their individual investments as well as any additional amount that is specified in the corporate charter. The purpose of such an arrangement in which the investors expand rather than limit their liability is to increase the creditworthiness of the company while actually limiting the liability of the investors to fixed, specified amounts.
- *Joint stock company:* By far the most common and popular corporate form, the joint stock company can be established in one of two forms: A joint stock company of the open type permits an unlimited number of shareholders and free alienability of shares. Obviously, this is the requisite form for publicly-traded companies. The joint stock company of the closed type has a limit of no more than fifty shareholders and also restricts the alienability of shares—the other shareholders arc given a right of first refusal to purchase the shares of any selling shareholder.

Under Russian legislation, a company will be managed based on the annual shareholders meeting. At this meeting, the shareholders will elect corporate management (including a board of directors if the company has more than fifty shareholders). The Joint Stock Company Law also includes a requirement that interested parties (directors, management, or 20 percent of the shareholders) who engage in transactions with the company must report those transactions to the board of directors and auditors.

There have been many scandals and controversies arising out of dubious corporate transactions. One of the most notorious of such cases involved action by the entrenched management of a major aluminum company that deleted the name of a British investor from its share registry, thereby depriving the investor of 20 percent interest in thc company. High-level political interventions were ultimately required to reverse this action. This and other similar overmanipulation of the share registries led to the adoption in October 1993 of a presidential decree regulating the manner in which companies maintain their share registries. Under this decree, all joint stock companies are required to maintain share registries following the specified format. Companies with more than one thousand shareholders are required to use the services of an independent share registry.

To anyone familiar with western European company law, the basic contours of Russian company law will seem familiar. The form and characteristics of the various legal entities are similar to their western European counterparts, and the basic principles of corporate governance and management are also basically similar. But as the following case studies amply illustrate, some of the most pressing issues arising under Russian company law relate to shareholder management and the protection of minority shareholder rights—and the niceties of Russian company law are sometimes overridden by political and economic pressure. But more of this in connection with the case studies will be examined.

Intellectual Property Protection

A recent survey of American businesses in Russia indicated that intellectual property protection is one of the four most important issues for U.S. companies doing business in Russia. The others mentioned were taxation, licensing, and official corruption. The issue of intellectual property protection in Russia is not a problem arising from inadequate legislation. In 1992 and 1993, the Soviet legislature adopted an array of new legislation on the protection of patents, trademarks, copyrights, computer software and databases, and integrated circuits. These laws, in general, were prepared by leading Russian experts acting in consultation with international organizations such as the World Intellectual Property Organization. They are fully up to the world standard in terms of the sophistication and protections provided by these laws. Since these statutes were originally adopted, the Russian criminal code has also been amended to include intellectual property piracy as a serious criminal offense.

The major weakness in these laws is that they are somewhat vague on the enforcement powers granted to Russian courts. Nevertheless, they do provide the legislative foundation for the effective protection of intellectual property rights. Russia also has taken action to further the protection of the rights of foreigners to their intellectual property. Most notable was Russia's accession to the Berne Convention for the Protection of Literary and Artistic Works in 1995.

The Russian Law on Copyright and Neighboring Rights, adopted in July 1993, represents a substantial advance over previous Soviet-era legislation. Among its more noteworthy features are:

- extension of the term of copyright to the life of the author plus fifty years.
- inclusion of computer programs as a protected work.
- provision of considerably more extensive protection to sound recordings than was previously available.

Under this copyright law, courts have the power to issue orders affirming the rights of copyright proprietors, awarding damages, and enjoining violations. Unfortunately, the courts have limited powers to enforce such injunctions.

A new patent law was adopted in September 1992, and it also considerably expands the scope of protection and represents a shift from old Soviet-style to western-style protection. Among the major features of this law are:

- Industrial designs and utility models are protected.
- Patents are valid for twenty-year terms from the date on which the application is filed.
- The criteria for patentability are generally similar to comparable criteria in western legislation.
- Protected inventions include microorganisms, chemical and other substances, and plant and animal cell cultures, which had not previously been protected.
- Priority is given on a "first-to-file" basis.
- A patent license must be registered with the State Patent Agency in order for it to be valid.
- If a patentee fails to exploit adequately a patented invention within four years of issuance, the Supreme Patent Chamber may grant a nonexclusive license to another party who will exploit it.

The statutory provisions concerning remedies for infringement are extremely sketchy. For example, they are not nearly as detailed as the comparable provisions in the copyright law, though they do recognize the right of the patentee to receive compensation for damages. One other limitation on the effectiveness of the patent legislation is that when the Law on Patents was adopted in 1992, it was anticipated that a Supreme Patent Chamber would be established. The Supreme Patent Chamber would be the highest appellate body for patent disputes and would be responsible for supervising the operations of the patent system. However, to date, the Russian government has not established the Supreme Patent Chamber and its functions go unfulfilled.

A new law on trademarks was also adopted in September 1992. Under this law, trademarks are entitled to ten years' protection from the date on which an application is filed, with the right to extend protection for additional ten-year terms. Trademarks, like patents, must be registered with the State Patent Agency and foreigners must register them through registered patent agents.

The trademark law introduced two new concepts:

- collective mark—used by a group of enterprises or a union to designate goods that they produce that have common characteristics; and
- designation of the place of origin of goods—a place name used to identify products.

Again, the provisions in this law concerning remedies for infringement are extremely general.

Trade secrets are also protected. Provisions in the Russian Civil Code that
came into effect in 1995, as well as provisions in Russian antimonopoly law and
elsewhere, provide protection for such sensitive information. Under Article 139
of the Russian Civil Code, the criteria for protection of trade secrets is comparable to similar laws in the United States and elsewhere. The information must have
actual or potential commercial value due to the circumstances that it is unknown
to third parties, that there is no free access to it, and that the possessor of the information has taken steps to maintain its confidentiality.

As previously stated, the problem with Russian intellectual property protection
is not the laws. Though there are deficiencies and gaps in the legislation, they are
certainly workable. Unfortunately, they are also very difficult to enforce. The
problem of intellectual property piracy, counterfeiting, and trademark infringement is virtually pandemic throughout Russia. It involves both goods produced in
Russia, as well as pirated or counterfeit goods imported from China, Bulgaria,
Korea, and elsewhere. Intellectual property protection illustrates one of the most
significant legal risks associated with investing in Russia. The gap between what
the law says and what people do is frequently enormous.

The violation of intellectual property rights is open, brazen, and very widespread, as illustrated by the following anecdotes:

- Recently in Moscow, the author was shopping in a large bookstore for computer software. He wanted to buy Cyrillic TrueType fonts to use in his Windows operating system. At one stall, where Windows was running on a
  demonstration computer, the proprietor said that he had no fonts for sale, but
  that once presented with blank diskettes purchased next door, he would
  download all of the fonts that were included with the Russian version of
  Windows.
- The world premiere of a movie version of Vladimir Voinovich's novel, *The
  Life and Extraordinary Adventures of Private Ivan Chonkin*, was scheduled
  for showing at a film festival. As the lights went down to begin showing the
  film, its producers noticed that video equipment had been set up throughout
  the theater and that some members of the audience were pulling small video
  cameras out of their bags in order to pirate the film. The producers then
  withdrew the film from the festival.
- The book and movie of *Gone with the Wind* have been extremely popular in
  Russia, so much so that book stalls there have been flooded with unauthorized sequels to the book, written by Russian authors under pseudonyms.
  These sequels have involved every conceivable permutation of events and
  characters from the original: In some, Scarlett lives, in others she dies, and
  still others explore the circumstances of her birth. As the manager of the trading company that distributes these books stated, "Copyright laws are like all

laws in Russia. We have them, but nobody ever abides by them. It's getting to be an epidemic." The people behind these books were certainly aware of copyright law requirements. According to Russian press accounts, the distribution of these books was organized in such a way that the books are published in Belarus, which at that time had not yet adopted new copyright legislation. As one of those involved said, "The books are written by citizens of Belarus, and Belarus has no copyright laws. So we have rights without limits."

- A young Russian film director completed a movie in Russia, only to see pirated copies of it circulating in Russia's video stores and being broadcast on television within weeks of its commercial release. When asked whether he would consider going to court to protect his rights, the director said that "Everything is corrupt and there is nowhere to turn. . . . To go to court is expensive and besides, it just means more bribes."
- Russian street vendors have attempted to capitalize on the great success that McDonald's has enjoyed in Russia. Some of them have begun selling fake Big Macs, infringing the McDonalds trademark in the process. These vendors buy supplies of precooked hamburgers from local distributors and then warm them up in microwaves at their kiosks, selling the "copies" at almost half the price at which authentic Big Macs are sold in Moscow.

The piracy of intellectual property in Russia is obviously extremely widespread and the consequences for foreign investors whose projects rely on intellectual property are substantial. The International Intellectual Property Alliance (IIPA), which represents eight trade associations representing copyright-based U.S. industries, estimated that Russia is "in the same class as China in terms of losses suffered by U.S. industry" from copyright piracy. Video piracy "approaches 100 percent," with unauthorized copies of films such as the Sylvester Stallone-Sharon Stone movie *The Specialist* on sale on the streets of Moscow a week before the U.S. premiere. The IIPA estimates that trade losses from copyright piracy in Russia in 1994 were $805 million, compared with $866 million in China. With respect to computer software, the Software Publishers Association estimates that the rate of piracy in Russia was 95 percent in 1994, with monetary losses of $144.5 million.

These statistics date from 1994, when the Russian copyright law was relatively new. More recent statistics, however, do not give much hope that longer experience with the copyright law has improved Russia's record in intellectual property piracy. Some estimates suggest that piracy has declined somewhat. For example, one estimate said that software piracy was down from 91 percent of the software sold in 1996 to 89 percent in 1997, and 64 percent in 1998. However, the Software and Information Industry Association estimated that 92 percent of the computer software used on personal computers in Russia during 1998 was pirated, and the Interactive Digital Software Association estimated that in 1998,

97 percent of the computer and video games sold in Russia were pirated, representing a loss to the entertainment software industry of $2.4 billion.

The Russian pirates are nothing if not energetic. Pirated copies of Microsoft's latest operating system, Windows 2000, were on sale in Moscow for approximately $3 for several months prior to its official roll-out in early 2000. Pirated works from Russia and the former Soviet Union have also begun to make their way into markets in western European countries. For example, bootleg tapes and records of performances by Benjamin Britten that were produced in Russia have appeared on the shelves of stores in the United Kingdom.

The Russian government has taken some steps to fight intellectual property piracy. It has sponsored antipiracy announcements on television, and the police have raided kiosks and street stalls that sell counterfeit goods. The Interior Ministry has established a unit to fight piracy, the Intellectual Property Police. In Moscow in 1999, the police conducted approximately three hundred such raids and seized tens of thousands of counterfeit video tapes and pirated CD-ROMs. However, only seventy-five individuals were fined as a result of these actions, only ten criminal investigations were begun, and only one conviction for intellectual property piracy has been obtained.

The high level of intellectual property piracy in Russia produces repercussions for many foreign investors. The most drastically affected are those like Microsoft, that heavily rely on intellectual property protection for their business. Other foreign investors may be adversely affected because of the fallout from Russia's failure to solve this problem. The ineffective enforcement of intellectual property rights may delay Russia's admission as a full member of the WTO. It is also possible that the U.S. government may decide to impose trade sanctions against Russia; already, industry groups have asked the U.S. Special Trade Representative to place Russia on the Priority Watch List under U.S. trade legislation.

The foregoing summaries of Russian law give a snapshot of the state of Russian legislation in a few of the fields of law that are of greatest interest to existing and prospective foreign investors. The next task is to examine how Russian law works in practice by reviewing several recent cases of investment disputes.

INVESTORS' ADVENTURES IN RUSSIA: RECENT CASE STUDIES

The challenge of how to make law and legal institutions work in Russia today is illustrated in the following case studies of foreign investors and their experiences in the Russian legal system. A series of recent court cases involving foreign investors in Russia has raised concerns over the prospects and conditions for direct foreign investment in Russia. In one case, a Russian court ruled that the privatization of a leading Russian porcelain manufacturer was invalid, threatening a substantial investment made in the company by U.S. investors. This judgment is currently on appeal. In a second case, Russian workers have seized control of an enterprise despite court orders requiring that the workers permit the enterprise's new foreign owners to take control. Troops were called in to restore order, but the case remains unresolved. In yet a third recent case, a major international oil company announced that it was reviewing its operations in Russia following a Russian bankruptcy proceeding that resulted in the sale of a valuable asset—a Russian oil company—in which the international oil company had invested. The sale, according to the oil company, was made against its wishes and at below-market prices. In the fourth case study, American investors who established a fast-food restaurant in St. Petersburg were locked out of their restaurant by their Russian general manager. Although they were given a favorable verdict by international arbitrators who adjudicated the dispute, they have so far been unsuccessful in enforcing that judgment through the Russian courts.

Lomonosov Porcelain Factory, or KKR Meets Their Match

The Lomonosov Porcelain Factory is the oldest and most famous porcelain manufacturer in Russia. The factory was founded in 1744 as the Imperial Porcelain Factory and was the first such factory in Russia and only the third in Europe. Its distinctive products are popular with collectors around the world. The 225-year old factory was originally privatized in 1993, with the majority of its shares retained in the hands of factory employees. In 1998, a group of foreign investors that included the U.S.–Russia Investment Fund (USRIF) and the well-known U.S. investment company, Kohlberg Kravis Roberts & Co. (KKR) acquired a majority interest in Lomonosov Porcelain. USRIF was founded in 1994 by the U.S. government and capitalized with funds from the U.S. Agency for International Development for the purpose of promoting direct investment in Russia. The USRIF invested $4.25 million and KKR invested $4 million in Lomonosov, and together they acquired a controlling interest in the company.

The transfer of ownership in Lomonosov from the management and employees to the new foreign investors was contentious from the outset. During the summer of 1998, shares in Lomonosov that were then held by employees were bought up by Rendezvous, a St. Petersburg investment company. Economic conditions at the plant were poor, payment of wages had been delayed for up to three months, the Russian economy and financial institutions appeared to be in free-fall, and many workers were ready to sell their shares. Rendezvous was able to buy approximately 60 percent of the shares in the company within three months. Although Rendezvous acknowledged that it was buying the shares on behalf of foreign investors, it did not disclose the names of those investors. Apparently, the shares purchased by Rendezvous were transferred to several offshore companies, and it is from these offshore companies that USRIF and KKR acquired their shares.

Soon after foreign investors, acting through Rendezvous, purchased a majority of the outstanding shares, they scheduled a shareholders' meeting to elect a new supervisory board. However, Rendezvous's purchase of shares was fiercely resisted by the incumbent factory management and employees, who accused Rendezvous of taking advantage of the factory's adverse financial conditions to persuade workers to sell their shares. Once the identity of the foreign investors was publicly disclosed, the Russian press reported that factory employees barred USRIF and KKR representatives from entering the premises or attending shareholders' meetings. The foreign investors were accused of failing to produce an investment plan and of seeking to seize the factory museum's valuable porcelain collection. The foreign investors, the incumbent management and its supporters argued, were intent on taking advantage of an important Russian cultural institution that had fallen on hard times.

The incumbent management of Lomonosov Porcelain announced plans to bring an action before the Russian State Anti-Monopoly Commission seeking to block the USRIF and KKR takeover. In addition, the Russian Ministry of State Property initiated a suit before the St. Petersburg and Leningrad Oblast Arbitrazh Court,[3] also seeking to overturn the purchase. On October 11, 1999, the St. Petersburg Arbitrazh Court ruled that the original 1993 privatization of Lomonosov was invalid. The court held that the decision to incorporate Lomonosov Porcelain Factory in the form of a joint stock company of the closed type as part of the privatization process had violated applicable laws and that the company should have been incorporated as a joint stock company of the open type.[4] Under Russian company law, in a joint stock company of the closed type, shareholders are barred from selling their shares to an outside third party without the approval of the other shareholders. According to Russian press reports, Rendezvous had circumvented this limitation by purchasing a single share of Lomonosov stock from a former employee. Then, as an existing shareholder, Rendezvous purchased a majority interest in the company from the other existing shareholders. The court ruled that this strategy was inconsistent with Russian law and that because the 1993 privatization process was flawed, Lomonosov Porcelain Factory must be renationalized (i.e., returned to state ownership) or privatized yet again.

The St. Petersburg court decision sparked an immediate and intense response in the Russian and foreign media, and Russian and U.S. government agencies quickly became involved. USRIF and KKR announced plans to appeal the court ruling in spite of their technically not being parties to the suit between the Ministry of State Property and Lomonosov Porcelain Factory. The chairman of the Russian Federal Securities Commission, Dmitrii Vasilev, wrote a letter soon after the court ruling to the Ministry of State Property, which had brought the lawsuit, taking exception to the ruling and the ministry's position in the case. According to Russian press reports, Vasilev wrote that "from our point of view, this precedent taken by the State Property Ministry deprives existing shareholders and investors of the confidence that the state protects them and calls into question their ownership rights to bonds and shares in any Russian enterprise formed as a result of privatization." USRIF, which is, after all, a U.S. taxpayer-funded organization complained about its treatment to the U.S. Congress and to Acting President Vladimir Putin of Russia.

The efforts by the U.S. investors to persuade the Russian government to intervene to prevent the loss of their investment was unsuccessful. Two weeks after the Arbitrazh Court's decision was handed down, First Deputy Prime Minister Nikolai Aksenenko approved a proposal prepared by the Ministry of State Property for renationalizing the Lomonosov Porcelain Factory. Under this plan, the existing factory would be divided into two enterprises, one of which would be retained by the state and the other of which would be privately owned. Under this plan, the property of the existing Lomonosov Porcelain Factory would be divided between the two enterprises in a manner and following a procedure to be determined. This renationalization plan would be submitted to the St. Petersburg Arbitrazh Court for approval.

In the meantime, USRIF and KKR appealed the decision of the St. Petersburg Arbitrazh Court to the appellate division of the St. Petersburg and Leningrad Oblast Arbitrazh Court, which upheld the lower court's ruling on December 21, 1999. Despite these adverse judicial decisions, the foreign investors were able to take control of the management of Lomonosov Porcelain Factory at a shareholders' meeting held on January 20, 2000. At that meeting, the foreign investors elected five of the nine directors, including the chair.

At the time, this victory may have seemed like a Pyrrhic one since the Russian Ministry of State Property was proceeding with plans to renationalize Lomonosov. However, USRIF and KKR appealed the adverse decisions of the local courts to the regional arbitrazh court, and on March 2, 2000, the Northwestern Circuit Arbitrazh Court overturned the initial decision. This decision, at least temporarily, has aborted the Russian government's plans to renationalize the Lomonosov Porcelain Factory. Douglas Boyce, the general director of Lomonosov Porcelain and vice president of USRIF, was quoted in the Russian media after the appeals court decision was handed down as stating that "justice has been done, and Russia has narrowly once again avoided destroying its reputation among international investors."

It is possible that the Ministry of State Property will appeal the regional court's decision to the Higher Arbitrazh Court in Moscow, which is the final court of appeals for the arbitrazh courts. However, it is not a foregone conclusion that the Higher Arbitrazh Court will hear such an appeal. The appellate function of the Higher Arbitrazh Court of the Russian Federation is limited and whether it will review the decision of a lower court is solely within the discretion of the chairman and deputy chairman of the Higher Arbitrazh Court and the procurator general and deputy procurator general of the Russian Federation.[5] However, the struggle for Lomonosov Porcelain has become highly politicized, involving a struggle for power and economic policy between the Ministry of State Property, the entity that initiated the lawsuit to renationalize, and other government officials who worry that the initial decision will ruin Russia's reputation with foreign investors. In such an environment, however, it is possible that the Higher Arbitrazh Court will end up making the final decision.

If the initial court decision is reinstated and the Lomonosov Porcelain Factory is renationalized, it will mark the first time that the privatization of a Russian enterprise in which foreigners have invested has been ruled invalid and the enterprise has been renationalized. In any event, it may not be the last such case. In any atmosphere charged with antiwestern resentment, the Russian press has already reported that the privatizations of the ports in Vyborg and Vysotsk have also been challenged and that the procurator in St. Petersburg has expressed plans to investigate the procedures following in privatizing the port of St. Petersburg.

Vyborg Pulp and Paper Mill

At the same time that the dispute over the nationalization/renationalization of the Lomonosov Porcelain Factory was being decided by the courts in St. Petersburg, another dispute over foreign investment in a Russian factory was attracting extensive press coverage in Russia. On October 14, 1998, thirty troops from the Russian Ministry of Justice were called in to raid the Vyborg Pulp and Paper Mill in Leningrad Oblast.[6] The troops were asked to remove mill workers who were attempting to prevent the mill's new foreign owners from taking control. The Justice Ministry troops actually opened fire on the workers who had barricaded themselves in the mill. Two workers were wounded and several claimed they were beaten. Hundreds of workers then surrounded the building that the troops had entered. Fifteen hours after they entered the mill, the Justice Ministry troops left, arresting eight members of the mill workers' strike committee. These eight individuals were charged with resisting the authorities, and the Leningrad Oblast procurator's office announced plans for a criminal investigation of the strike committee. Russian newspapers reported that the new managing director of the mill, who represented the British owner Alcem U.K. Ltd., was beaten up by mill workers in the melee.

The mill workers were protesting an order issued by a court in St. Petersburg in May 1998, which ordered that Alcem be allowed to take control of the mill. Vyborg Pulp and Paper Mill had been under the effective control of the workers' collective for twenty-one months. A British company, Nimonor Investments had originally acquired the mill, but the workers seized control of the plant soon after Nimonor purchased it, and in essence forced them to withdraw. Nimonor sold the mill to Alcem U.K. Ltd. in June 1999.

The mill workers said they were concerned that the new British owners of the mill would turn it into a plywood factory, a metamorphosis that would lead to substantial layoffs. Vyborg Pulp and Paper Mill is located in the town of Sovetskii in Leningrad Oblast and employs two thousand of the town's seven thousand people. The mill also supplies heat and electricity to the town.

In July 1999, officials of Alcem were able to enter the mill's administration building with the help of police officers and private security guards. The managing director appointed by Alcem announced that the new owner would not lay off any workers and would pay $1 million in wage arrears as well as a large outstanding tax obligation of the mill. Alcem also told the workers at that time that it would spend up to $20 million to purchase new equipment. The workers, however, did not trust these promises and were further angered by Alcem's use of force to enter the mill. The workers threatened to block the highway that connects Leningrad Oblast with Finland in protest.

Soon after the Justice Ministry troops entered the mill, the Russian State Duma passed a resolution protesting the use of force against the mill workers. Union organizations also protested the Justice Ministry's actions.

On October 19, five days after the Ministry of Justice troops raided the mill, the governor of Leningrad Oblast announced plans to request that the St. Petersburg and Leningrad Oblast Arbitrazh Court—the same court that ruled on the Lomonosov Porcelain nationalization and that had earlier ordered the Vyborg Pulp and Paper Mill workers to permit Alcem to take control of the mill—review the legality of the mill's privatization.

The dispute between Alcem and the mill workers appears to have been resolved by an agreement finalized on January 15, 2000, between Alcem and the mill's trade union. Under the agreement, according to a trade union official who was quoted in the Russian media, Alcem has agreed to continue to employ twenty-five hundred workers, each of whom will be given an advance payment of one thousand rubles and average monthly wages of twenty-five hundred rubles. It is uncertain whether this dispute might have been averted at the very outset through worker-management committee and sensitivity on the part of Vyborg and then Alcem to the anxieties associated with macroeconomic privatization. This case serves as much as a lesson about the critical importance of the will of human beings collectively. It teaches us a lesson about the critical importance of appreciating cross-cultural sensitivities at a human level and the devastating risk that interference can pose.

BP Amoco and Sidanko

BP Amoco made an investment of more than half a billion dollars in Sidanko, a Russian oil company and owned 10 percent of the shares in the company. In May 1999, Sidanko was declared bankrupt. As part of the liquidation process, Sidanko began to sell off its assets under court supervision, and on October 21, 1999, Tyumen Oil Company, another large Russian oil company, purchased a Sidanko subsidiary, Kondpetroleum, for $52 million. This sale price was considerably less than BP Amoco thought the company was worth—the original asking price for Kondpetroleum had been $145 million.

Sidanko next announced plans to sell another of its subsidiaries, Chernogorneft, for $200 million, also to Tyumen Oil Company. BP Amoco criticized these actions on the grounds that Kondpetroleum and Chernogorneft were valuable assets of

Sidanko and that their sale at lower-than-market values unfairly reduced the value of BP Amoco's investment in Sidanko. BP Amoco complained that these sales violated its rights both as a shareholder in, and in fact a creditor of, Sidanko.

BP Amoco accused Tyumen Oil of manipulating and influencing the bankruptcy proceedings, thereby stripping Sidanko's most valuable assets for unreasonably low prices. BP Amoco officials pointed out that the head of Tyumen Oil's board of directors was also the governor of Tyumen Oblast, the center of the Russian oil industry and the location of the court considering the Sidanko bankruptcy case.

BP Amoco has been one of the major foreign investors in Russia, with total investments of approximately $1 billion in Russia. In addition to its $571 million investment in Sidanko, it also owns 22 percent of the output in Russia Petroleum, and has opened gas stations in the Moscow area. However, BP Amoco complained that it has been stymied in its attempts to realize value from its investment in Sidanko and that the bankruptcy proceedings, in which the court consistently decided against the foreign investor, were manipulated and abused. As one BP Amoco spokesman stated concerning the sale of Chernogorneft, "[it] in no sense can be described as bankrupt. It is a viable company. The bankruptcy law is being used to enforce transfer of ownership even though the business is not bankrupt. Chernogorneft is making more than enough money to satisfy the creditors."

On November 26, 1999, BP Amoco announced that it was reviewing its operations in Russia. Whether the threat of pulling out of Russia was a bluff or not, it apparently motivated the various interested parties to negotiate a settlement of this major investment dispute. On December 22, 1999, it was announced that BP Amoco and the other principal shareholders of Sidanko had reached agreement with the principal shareholders of Tyumen Oil Company. Under this agreement, ownership of Chernogorneft reverts to the control of Sidanko. Sidanko will then be released from bankruptcy, with BP Amoco retaining its 10 percent interest; the other current principal shareholders of Sidanko will own 65 percent of its shares, and the principal shareholders in Tyumen Oil Company will acquire 25 percent of the shares plus one share in Sidanko. Thus, in essence, Chernogorneft, the principal remaining asset of Sidanko, will be divided between the current shareholders of Sidanko and the shareholders of Tyumen Oil Company. Sidanko and Tyumen Oil Company have also agreed to cooperate through a joint venture in the development of the Samotlor oil field, which had previously been divided between Chernogorneft and a subsidiary of Tyumen Oil Company. According to officials of BP Amoco, this settlement agreement satisfies the interests of Sidanko's shareholders and creditors.

Subway in St. Petersburg

In 1994, a U.S. company, East-West International Ltd., entered into a joint venture with a Russian company, Minutka Ltd. Their joint venture—Subway Petersburg—was created to open a Subway sandwich restaurant in St. Petersburg. The restaurant was located on Nevsky Prospekt in St. Petersburg. By

1995, the Russian partner had locked out the Americans from the restaurant. The Russian company transferred joint venture funds into its own accounts and announced the dissolution of the joint venture. Although the layout and decor of the restaurant was recognizably Subway's, the restaurant was re-opened under the name Minutka.

Under the joint venture agreement, disputes between the partners were to be re-solved by arbitration in Sweden, a very common form of dispute resolution for foreign investors in Russia. The American partner took its case before an arbitral panel of the Arbitration Institute of the Stockholm Chamber of Commerce and ul-timately received a favorable verdict in 1997 in the amount of $1.2 million.

The successful American plaintiff then attempted to enforce its award against the defendant in Russian courts. Although Russia is a party to the international treaties on the mutual recognition and enforcement of arbitration awards, the Russian defendant attempted to delay and defeat the plaintiff in its actions before the Russian courts. Eventually, the Russian courts upheld the arbitration award, first at the local level and then by the Russian Supreme Court in Moscow in 1998.

Will this matter? The obvious challenge, of course, is to take this Russian court judgment and enforce it against the defendant. Although this might seem like a relatively easy task, it certainly is not. The Russian courts have limited resources to enforce their judgments. They can issue rulings, but seizing and liquidating as-sets to satisfy those judgments is very difficult for them because of limits on their powers, personnel, and resources. The courts have recently been given bailiffs to assist in this task, but a wily and determined judgment debtor can make it very difficult on the court and plaintiff seeking to enforce a judgment. In the Subway case, for example, when bailiffs arrived at the restaurant to serve a writ of exe-cution on Minutka Ltd., the defendant, they were told that a new company had taken over management. Since that new company's name was not on the writ, they were unable to serve it. The Minutka restaurant—complete with its Subway wallpaper, fittings, and decor—remains open for business on Nevsky Prospekt, St. Petersburg's busiest thoroughfare.

Despite these legal travails, the Subway restaurant chain has not been deterred from opening other restaurants in Russia. In 1999, a new Subway restaurant, lo-cated in a Moscow defense institute, was opened. According to Subway chair-man David Worrell, "We don't want to give the impression that there are nega-tive feelings. . . . We have a very enthusiastic and strong view of Russia and we are extremely interested in participating in developing the local economy."

WHAT SHOULD FOREIGN INVESTORS UNDERSTAND ABOUT RUSSIAN LAW AND THE RISKS IT POSES FOR THEIR INVESTMENTS?

Ordinarily, law and legal institutions are supposed to reduce risks for investors by promoting predictability and stability. The irony of the Russian system is that while it is intended to serve this purpose, the legal system also creates its own risks for investors. The obvious risks for investors that emanate from law and legal institutions are:

- Legislation on a particular issue may not exist.
- Legislation and, especially, regulations may be difficult to find.
- Legislation and regulations may be incomplete, vague, contradictory, or otherwise deficient.
- Legislation may change frequently.
- Legislation may be interpreted and implemented in inconsistent ways by government officials.

What all of this means, of course, is that legislation and regulations may not always provide reliable guidelines for the conduct of business in Russia. All that being said, a foreign investor should take some solace from the outcomes in each of the case studies that have been recounted: In each of the case studies, Russian legal institutions either sided with the foreign investor or a negotiated settlement was concluded.

In the Lomonosov Porcelain case, the regional appeals court ruled in favor of the foreign investors in the face of substantial political pressure brought on by those who opposed foreign ownership of the factory. In the Vyborg Pulp and Paper Mill case, the Ministry of Justice forcibly raided the mill and arrested striking workers on behalf of its foreign owners. In the BP Amoco-Sidanko case, though the legal system did not side with the foreign investors, a negotiated settlement was reached. In the Subway restaurant case, the Russian Supreme Court set a valuable precedent in holding that a foreign arbitration award was enforceable by Russian courts. Actually enforcing that judgment, however, remains difficult.

Thus, as in so many other aspects of Russia today, the real question is whether the glass is half full or half empty. Russia has undertaken a legal (not to mention political, economic, and social transformation) that is unparalleled in modern history—peaceably transforming its fundamental constitutional, economic, and political structures. In less than ten years, Russia has made substantial progress in establishing the legal foundation for a market-oriented economy that permits and values foreign investment. Statutes have been adopted covering most (but certainly not all) of the important legal issues that affect foreign investment. Drafting these laws has been the easy part of the job. What remains is assimilating the values and principles embodied in these laws into Russian legal and popular culture so that they are obeyed rather than resisted.

The Problem of Culture

Foreign investors must be aware of the effect that Russian history and culture have on shaping popular attitudes toward them, their investments, and the legal system. The Lomonosov Porcelain case and the Vyborg Pulp and Paper Mill case are good examples of popular suspicion directed toward foreign investors. In the Lomonosov Porcelain case, many Russians were deeply concerned that foreigners would take control over a factory that was widely regarded as a landmark of Russian culture. Perhaps the resistance to the foreign investment would have been somewhat ameliorated if the new foreign owners had demonstrated a proper respect and understanding for the place that the factory plays in Russian culture. In the Vyborg Pulp case, the workers at the mill were worried that new foreign owners would convert the mill into a plywood mill, resulting in significant layoffs and economic and social distress. One legacy from the Soviet era is that large mills and factories frequently were the only major employers in town and, consequently, bore the responsibility for providing valuable social and other services. Substantial layoffs and downsizing would leave laid off workers with few job opportunities and might also be accompanied by elimination of the clinics, day cares, and other services provided by the factory. Again, a greater sensitivity to these concerns by foreign investors might have minimized the acrimony that ensued. The sort of consultative committees and crisis management that Raddock suggests in the first part of the book as part of his discussion of human rights and the rule of law is certainly commendable.

There is another very important issue of culture that foreign investors must understand if they are to have a proper feeling for how Russian law and its legal system operate. It is simply this: Russian experience of the law and legal institutions has been quite different from the comparable experience in western European and North American societies. As a result, it is naive to assume that Russians will regard law and legal institutions in the same manner as their western European and North American counterparts.

The traditional Russian attitude toward law, drawn from the country's long historical experience of arbitrary and autocratic governments, is that "The law is like an axle. It will turn whichever way you want, depending on how much grease you apply." Many factors have combined to produce a culture in which most people are deeply suspicious of the state; doubt that they have little ability to influence the decisions made by government; feel that the laws and regulations issued by the government are burdensome and illegitimate; and attach little opprobrium to evasion of many aspects of the law (tax and intellectual property laws are obvious and immediate examples). The factors that have shaped this culture that disrespects and distrusts the law and legal institutions include centuries of arbitrary and autocratic rule by the tsars, followed by seventy-four years of Soviet rule, a central characteristic of which was that law was a subset of politics, a tool to be used to maintain the dominant class in society. The widespread corruption and cynicism that characterized the Soviet Union during the 1970s and 1980s then burnished these traditions and beliefs. Russia's historical experience of law and legal institutions has been to witness their use to oppress and punish. Engendering respect for law and legal institutions in this environment will have to overcome this experience.

Russia is also a nation that has had little experience of capitalism. Prior to the Bolshevik Revolution in 1917, capitalist enterprises were a relatively thin layer between the feudal nobility and the peasants, who constituted the vast majority of the population. Moreover, many of those peasants lived in communes where the land was owned in common and distributed and periodically redistributed on the basis of the needs of each family in the commune. The basic notions of capitalism and private property have not held sway in Russian culture to nearly the same degree or for as long a time as they have in western Europe and North America. The semifeudal tsarist state was succeeded in 1917 by a Soviet regime that spent nearly seven decades demonizing entrepreneurs and capitalists as being exploiters. Why would anyone who understands Russian culture and tradition be surprised in this post-Soviet era, when economic hardships have been so extreme, that many Russians look on foreign capitalists with anything other than distrust and suspicion?

The Russian legal environment into which foreign investors must venture is one of a government working hard to reconstruct its legal system but with many pitfalls. It has made great progress in laying the legal foundation for a market economy that is receptive to foreign investment, but some of the laws, however, are unreliable and legal institutions are often ill-prepared and corrupt.

NOTES

1. David M. Raddock, *Navigating New Markets Abroad* (Lanham, Md.: Rowman & Littlefield, 1993).

2. Jerry Hough, "Why Ivan Mistrusts Us: A New Poll Shows Russians Suspect Economic Reform is a Western Trick," *Washington Post*, February 11, 1996, p. C2.

3. The Russian arbitrazh courts are sometimes referred to as the arbitration courts. However, the term "arbitration courts" in this context is something of a misnomer. The Russian arbitrazh courts do not involve arbitration in the same way as it is handled in U.S. courts. Rather, these courts are genuine courts of law. The Russian Federation has two separate judicial systems for resolving civil law disputes. There is a system of regular civil courts that have jurisdiction over disputes in which at least one of the parties is an individual or a nonbusiness corporate entity. There is a separate and parallel system of arbitrazh courts that has jurisdiction over disputes between legal entities that are engaged in business or other economic activity, and over complaints against those state agencies that affect the conduct of business or economic activities. The arbitrazh courts consist of a Higher Court of Arbitration and inferior circuit and local arbitrazh courts.

4. The difference between joint stock companies of the open and closed type under Russian company law is that there are limits on the number of shareholders permitted in joint stock companies of the closed type and there are restrictions on the alienability of their shares. Companies with more than fifty shareholders that anticipate public trading in their shares must be organized as joint stock companies of the open type.

5. The Procurator General is, in essence, the chief prosecutor for the country.

6. In the Russian federal system, the "oblast" is one of several different forms of regional government. The city of St. Petersburg, for example, is located within Leningrad Oblast.

6

SONATRACH—The Political Economy of Algerian Energy Resources: Risk Assessment in a Transitional Environment

John P. Entelis

It should be considered that the recovery of national wealth and the development of hydrocarbons form part of the struggle of the people of the Third World for their economic liberation and the establishment of a new international economic order.

Resolution of 31 December 1980 passed by the Central Committee of the National Liberation Front (FLN), at the time Algeria's single governing party, regarding the country's long-term energy policy.

More so than in most countries, the Algerian economy is dependent on politics. This dependency is only partially due to geography and history, which have combined to give the economy its political character; more influential has been the deliberate decision of Algeria's technocratic elites to bring the economy under the direction of the state. Only in the last decade of the twentieth century and the beginning of the twenty-first have government leaders begun to alter this orientation. Market considerations have forced a rethinking about state-society relations and the role of the private sector in economic development. Yet the key to Algeria's economic future in the near and intermediate term remains concentrated in the hydrocarbon sector, which continues to be monopolized by the most powerful economic enterprise—SONATRACH, Algeria's state-owned gas and oil industrial giant. Despite the political upheaval resulting from the military coup d'état of January 11, 1992, which witnessed the return of army rule following a brief period of democratic experimentation, and the subsequent bloodbath that ensued, which has claimed over one hundred thousand lives, Algeria's

Note: Portions of this chapter first appeared in "SONATRACH: The Political Economy of an Algerian State Institution," *The Middle East Journal*, vol. 53, no. 1 (Winter 1999), pp. 9–27.

military-industrial complex remains strongly in place and is more than ever committed to protecting the country's vital economic interests, encouraging foreign investment, participation, and collaboration, and insulating society from the most direct and extreme forms of physical violence carried out by radical Islamist groups.

This chapter seeks to highlight the way in which Algeria's military-dominated regime manages the country's key hydrocarbon resources through its principle institutional agent—SONATRACH—in the face of an ambiguous political legitimacy, economic uncertainty, and chronic social unrest. Upon such military statism rests the stability that ensures security and the predictable for foreign investment.

THE PAST AS PRELUDE TO THE PRESENT

In the decade following independence in 1962, Algeria nationalized all major foreign business interests as well as many private Algerian companies. Nationalization ranged from the assumption of a controlling interest in some cases to complete takeover in others. By the late 1970s, the Algerian economy was almost totally government controlled. State enterprises and government agencies ran much of the foreign trade, almost all of the major industries, large parts of the distribution and retail systems, all public utilities, and the entire banking and credit system. Despite government measures to disperse and decentralize the massive state bureaucracy and to create new incentives for private sector initiative in the late 1980s and early 1990s, there has not been a single major strategic enterprise denationalized and returned to private ownership in the whole of the postindependence period.

The Algerian commitment to a state-centered technocratic thrust evolved out of the radical nationalism of Houari Boumedienne and his group, who took power in mid-1965. They were convinced that true national independence could only be realized through control of natural resources, especially hydrocarbons, and through rapid industrial development—objectives that, in the context of global economic relations and the dominance of advanced industrial societies, could be achieved only through nationalization and state control of the economy.

The 1965–1971 period witnessed an intensive state-directed public sector expansion. Initially, the state created new industrial ventures with public investment. Simultaneously, foreign firms were taken over. Later a portion of the self-management or *autogestion* sector was absorbed into state enterprises. The banks, insurance companies, and some mines were socialized in 1966. Two years later, the state nationalized sixty-six of three hundred French enterprises that were operating in diverse fields such as construction materials, fertilizers, electrical supplies, textiles, and foods. State control of marketing of gas and oil products, the first step toward state control of the oil and gas industry, was effected in 1968, and takeover was completed in this crucial sector in 1971.

In 1965, an Algerian national oil and gas corporation (SONATRACH) was created, followed by a network of state industrial combines. By 1967, thirteen other state corporations had been set up, including the National Iron and Steel Company (SNS), the National Company for Textile Industries (SONITEX), and the Algerian Insurance Company (SAA). These and the related state corporations later constituted the underpinning for the Algerian development strategy: to secure full control over the natural resource base and convert the oil and gas revenues into a broad-based industrial sector.

Since the late 1960s, industrial development has been given priority over agricultural development, and within the industrial sector most investment has gone into basic industries. In the past this industrialization-first strategy was defended by two arguments.

First, continued emphasis on the export of raw materials and agricultural products would prevent Algeria from achieving the type of economic independence deemed necessary to make political independence truly meaningful. Second, not only could Algeria's petroleum and gas resources finance industrialization, but they could also be used to develop a petrochemical industry that would be the foundation of the entire strategy of industrialization.

THEORY

The industrialization-first strategy has its theoretical roots in the notion of *industries industrialisantes* ("industrializing industries") as articulated by G. Destanne de Bernis, a French adviser for the Algerian industry. He argued that given Algeria's limited agricultural resources, the rural population could not maintain a reasonable standard of living and therefore had to find employment in the industrial sector. In any case history, an agricultural revolution was shown to follow, and never precede, an industrial revolution. Once industry was in place, it would supply the fertilizers and machinery for agriculture, as well as form a market for the resulting agricultural output. With Algeria's impressive hydrocarbon base, this industrialization-first approach seemed compelling. In addition, Algerian planners had always recognized that although better endowed than many other third world states, Algeria possessed diminishing resources. The planners' dilemma, therefore, was how best to convert these resources, before they were exhausted, into a self-sustaining and self-propelling economic infrastructure capable of supporting the country's expanding population at increasing levels of per capita income.

The manner in which this industrialization-first program would achieve effective self-sufficiency would be as follows: Some industries, particularly the power-producing ones, have stimulating capacities that give rise to a series of associated industries, both upstream and downstream. The entire national economy is thereby stimulated. The industrializing industries include energy-related industries, such as petroleum and gas, which provide fuel, feedstock, and finance for the industrialization process with petrochemicals representing the basis for a whole range of new industries: iron and steel, metallurgical and mechanical industries, and chemicals (e.g., phosphates). These huge capital-intensive projects are based on Algeria's own natural resources and utilize the most modern production processes. They act as the "motor" of the development process producing raw materials and machinery for other sectors of industry engaged in the production of finished goods such as vehicles, farm machinery, pumps and irrigation equipment, electrical goods, and plastics, thus strengthening the interindustry matrix. In turn, the products of the new industries would contribute to the modernization of the more backward sectors of the economy, notably agriculture, forging new linkages that would eventually create an integrated economy reducing Algeria's dependence on the world capitalist market.

The implementation of this economic strategy was begun with the three-year program of 1967–1969. It was expanded in two back-to-back, four-year plans (1970–1973, 1974–1977), according to which industry was supposed to place at the disposal of the socialized economy the basic requirements of energy and heavy industry to meet important needs of the population and to achieve the greatest possible capitalization of the country's natural resources. The 1967–1969 program was actually a "preplan" with modest objectives. Nevertheless, it was during this period that the structure of state-directed industry was built up and the major national companies—purchasing and marketing agencies, cooperatives, and other institutions—were created. Special development programs also began during this three-year period.

The thrust toward industrialization was implemented in earnest with the four-year plan of 1970–1973, which marked the first real effort at comprehensive economic policy in the postindependence era. The conceptual framework within which this four-year plan was devised rested on a number of fixed objectives: the top priority of heavy industry; the increasing substitution of domestically produced consumer goods for imported ones (import substitution); and the training of the various specialized personnel required by a rapidly developing economy. The plan allocated 45 percent of total capital investment to the establishment of a capital-intensive industrial sector that was to be the basis of economic growth. Fifteen percent went to agriculture, and the remaining 40 percent of investment was allocated to social and economic infrastructure. The investment strategy was called "planting Algeria's oil" (semer le pétrole pour récolter l'industrie), thereby using petroleum revenues to create a strong industrial base. At the same time, an agrarian revolution policy, as it was called, aimed at improving efficiency through land reform and a system of cooperatives. The latter program was not only undercapitalized but, owing to resistance from the rural population, it failed to increase agriculture's percentage of the gross national product (GNP), which in fact declined from 13 percent in 1969 to 9 percent in 1973.

The second four-year plan (1974–1977) attempted to remedy the apparent imbalance and malfunctions of the previous plan without jeopardizing the heavy emphasis on rapid industrialization. The new plan, nevertheless, placed more emphasis on developing consumer industries that would create jobs, fight regional economic disparities, encourage small- and medium-sized industries, and promote land reform. The 1974–1977 plan also placed a major emphasis on housing, an area that had been conspicuously neglected in the first four-year plan.

HYDROCARBON POLICY

Algeria's development strategy of rapid industrialization has been made possible by petroleum and gas revenues. The country owns the world's fourth largest proven natural gas resources and significant reserves of crude oil. It is the seventh largest Middle Eastern–North African oil producer but accounts for only 4 percent of the total output of the Organization of Petroleum Exporting Countries (OPEC), which it joined in 1969, and no more than 2 percent of total world output. The development of these reserves has been central to economic planning since independence in 1962. Despite (or because of) policy shifts since 1980 toward decentralized decision making in the hydrocarbon and other large industrial sectors, the strategy of using these natural resources to finance other industrialization continues to govern energy policy and helps explain Algeria's constant determination to obtain as high a price as possible on world markets for its natural resources. As recently as the first quarter of 2000, for example, Algeria, joined by Iran, resisted attempts by OPEC, under pressure from the United States, to moderate global oil prices whose rapid rise seemed on the verge of threatening global economic growth. While it finally succumbed to these pressures, Algerian oil pricing policy remains consistently "hard-line" and inflexible with its broader developmental objectives in which finite energy reserves remain central.

Under the regime of Houari Boumedienne (1965–1978), the emphasis was placed on as rapid and as extensive exploitation of energy resources as technology and world market conditions would allow. The underlying concept of the hydrocarbons development plan of the period was that essentially all of the presently known reserves of oil, condensate, and liquefied petroleum gas (LPG) and most of the known gas reserves would be used up over the next four decades or by the middle of the twenty-first century. According to the reasoning of the time, because the sale of a large portion of the country's hydrocarbon reserves was necessary for the creation of a large and integrated industrial base for the national economy, it was important to maximize the production rates of gas, crude oil, LPG, and condensate, consistent with obtaining the highest total recovery of hydrocarbons as economically as possible.

A significant shift in policy took place with the ascent of Chadli Benjedid to the presidency of the republic in February 1979. In December of that year, a special parliamentary commission was established to investigate the

Algerian oil ministry's sales of liquefied natural gas (LNG) to the El Paso Company of Houston, Texas. A year later, on December 25, 1980, the commission submitted its report and held El Paso "morally responsible" for causing SONATRACH to lose earnings estimated at $290 million in the ten-year period following the signing of a contract in 1969. These charges led to the dismissal of the two officials responsible for the rapid recovery policy and the discrediting of their policies.

Several days later, at crucial meetings of the Central Committee of the FLN on December 29–31, 1980, a new energy policy that gave greater emphasis to resource preservation and energy conservation, and improved the means by which Algeria could control and utilize its natural resources and hydrocarbon industry was formulated. In addition, the Central Committee emphasized the need for creating new industries that would be self-generating and less vulnerable to external energy and market considerations.

The energy policy that emerged had carefully identified aims including:

- much more emphasis on the use of natural gas for domestic purposes in industry and residential homes;
- a broader national effort at energy conservation by preventing unnecessary energy waste;
- a broader and more intensive effort at discovering and exploiting national energy resources and a concomitant development of indigenous technical and scientific expertise;
- a concerted effort at discovering and developing alternate energy sources such as wind, geothermal energy, and solar power, along with increasing mining of coal and nuclear raw materials;
- the creation of more efficient and extensive capacity for hydrocarbon storage, distribution, and transportation;
- more careful monitoring of domestic hydrocarbon output in relation to the world market supply-and-demand balance;
- continued firmness and determination in pursuing price increases for hydrocarbons;
- diversification of export markets for hydrocarbons;
- greater coordination and cooperation with other hydrocarbons producers and exporters in achieving a "just" price for natural gas exports;
- a restructuring and more efficient management of the hydrocarbon industry, beginning with the state oil and gas company;
- accelerated development of domestic technological expertise in the oil and gas industries so as to reduce the dependence on foreign technical assistance;
- improving the coordination between the scientific, technical, diplomatic, security, and defense institutions in matters relating to hydrocarbons; and
- the establishment of a Higher Energy Institute empowered to coordinate national energy policy and monitor its impact on the economy as a whole.

Despite its modest reserves of petroleum deposits and its rather late entry into OPEC, Algeria has consistently argued for a maximum return on its oil exports. This attitude is in part due to rational economic calculations but also has strong emotional and ideological roots. Even during the war of national liberation, the Algerian revolutionary movement made reference to French oil exploration in the Sahara, and awareness of the possibilities of an oil industry increased the insistence of the FLN on the unity of Algerian territory. After independence, oil came to occupy a crucial place in Algerian political emotions. There was a strong sense that the natural resources of Algeria belonged to the Algerian state. To this was added the aspiration to economic independence without which political independence was not truly meaningful and the resistance to "back door" imperialism or neocolonialism.

By 1972, a mere decade after independence, all petroleum exploration and production facilities, natural gas concessions, and gas and oil pipelines and other transport facilities had come under the control of the Algerian state. The historic turning point had occurred on February 24, 1971, when Boumedienne, in announcing that Algeria had decided to "'carry the revolution to the petroleum sector," nationalized 51 percent of all French oil companies operating in the country and 100 percent of all natural gas concessions. This "victory" in the oil battle against French and other multinational petroleum companies enhanced Boumedienne's prestige at home and abroad and became a constantly recurring theme, associated with the cultural and agrarian revolution, in his speeches. The nationalization decrees opened the door to a new era in the international oil industry, allowing other OPEC members, for example, to progressively take control of their own hydrocarbon resources.

The quadrupling of oil prices following the 1973 Arab-Israeli war enabled foreign exchange derived from petroleum expenditures to reach $5 billion, dramatically increasing Algeria's investment opportunities for national economic growth. Since that time, Algeria has consistently argued within OPEC for higher prices. Except for the 1977–1978 period preceding the overthrow of Mohammad Reza Pahlavi, the shah of Iran, and two major "slack" periods of 1981–1984 and 1994–1998, Algeria has successfully raised the price of its oil. During 1979, for example, the price of its highest-grade crude was increased from $14.10 per barrel at the beginning of the year to $30 in December. Two further increases in 1980 and one in 1981 brought the price by May 1981 to $40, to which was added a $3 surcharge for oil exploration. The surcharge was intended as a way by which foreign oil companies would be encouraged to participate with SONATRACH in oil exploration.

By early 1982, however, the world oversupply of oil forced Algeria to drop the surcharge and, in line with other OPEC producers, charge $37.50 per barrel. This trend of decline continued through 1983 reflecting a broader pattern of petroleum political economy: OPEC ministers agreed in March to set their oil reference price at $29 per barrel, and the price for high-grade Algerian oil was set at $30.50.

Algeria joined Venezuela in supporting Iran's request in mid-November 1983 to raise OPEC prices by as much as $5 a barrel, arguing that the group's $5 price reduction eight months earlier had failed to revive oil demand. This pattern of politically determined price-fixing was replicated in late 1999 and early 2000.

While the 1990–1991 Persian Gulf crisis and war temporarily raised oil prices, the overall trend has been one of steady decline. Short of a major global oil reduction caused by war or political turmoil in the Middle East or elsewhere, it seems unlikely that Algeria can succeed in forcing a sustained price increase in the near and intermediate future. As a consequence, crude oil sales as a percent of total hydrocarbon export earnings have been declining steadily over the years. Revenues from sales of crude oil accounted for 61 percent of Algeria's total hydrocarbon export earnings in 1980 and had fallen to less than 20 percent by the middle 1990s. The dramatic change in the composition of Algeria's hydrocarbon exports caused by the continuing oil glut worldwide and the recognized paucity of Algerian reserves vis-à-vis other OPEC and non–OPEC producers have led Algeria increasingly to shift attention to its expansive natural gas reserves as the instrument for implementing its developmental policies.

THE POLITICAL ECONOMY OF NATURAL GAS

With the decline in oil production and the remaining doubt about substantial future expansion of recoverable petroleum reserves, natural gas is quickly becoming Algeria's most valuable export. The 5.1 billion tons (2000) of proven recoverable gas reserves (4 percent of the world total) are for the most part unassociated with the oil fields. This unassociated gas is free of sulfur and, consequently, both easy to handle and inexpensive. It is not only suitable for commercial and domestic uses but also readily adaptable to petrochemical transformation by the extraction of a condensate and for liquefaction for shipment abroad.

The exploitation of natural gas in Algeria on a massive scale is a relatively recent phenomenon of the postindependence era. Taking advantage of new gas technology, particularly in the transport across the sea by liquefaction (which confines the transport to a limited number of liquefying and deliquefying points of entry and exit), Algeria has taken the lead in a new world industry. SONATRACH has been responsible for the planning, management, and financing of pipelines and liquefaction plants. The result has been the creation of a state-of-the-art industry that has been economically worthwhile, thus justifying the large-scale capital expenditure. Yet it is these huge capital outlays and the increasing dependency on gas for export earnings that have led Algeria to seek substantial price increases for its LNG to bring it to par, based on energy value, with the price of crude oil.

Algeria has bargained stubbornly with potential customers for its expanding natural gas exports. Shifting exports from the fluctuating oil markets to the more stable demands for gas has been a central part of Algeria's international economic strategy in the last two decades and a principal means of financing development. SONATRACH has been in the forefront of Algeria's efforts to achieve parity with oil prices, thereby increasing OPEC's potential control over the structure of world energy costs.

The attempt to organize a worldwide gas cartel similar to OPEC and the use of tactics involving threats of boycotts, embargoes, and cessations of oil deliveries, as well as promises of greatly increased (or threats of decreased) trade and bilateral commercial agreements, have all been part of a concerted effort to increase the price Algeria charges for its natural gas. Failure to extract the necessary economic and political benefits from this policy have had direct consequences on regime stability as the bloody riots of October 1988, the rise of political Islam, and the descent into civil war have so clearly demonstrated. As the transition from a state-centered to a market-oriented economy takes place, serious social dislocations are expected that only ample hydrocarbon revenues can serve to cushion. In the early and mid 1980s, this strategy led to three major "successes" with the Belgians, French, and Italians and four "failures" with German, British, Spanish, and U.S. companies, save for a few minor contracts. As global energy needs have receded and new discoveries of natural gas been made elsewhere, close economic partners of Algeria such as France and Italy have challenged even signed contracts.

The manner in which Algerians have negotiated or renegotiated gas contracts with western customers reveals much about the political economy of development that has been pursued by past and present Algerian leaders. Pricing disputes with U.S. contractors began less than a year after the first LNG deliveries to the United States had been made. SONATRACH requested in early 1979 that the price paid to Algeria be renegotiated, complaining that in the decade since the contract was originally signed SONATRACH's costs had substantially increased. After several months of intense negotiations, the U.S. companies capitulated, approving a not-so-insignificant increase over the original price of Algerian natural gas entering the United States.

For his part, the newly appointed energy minister, Belkacem Nabi, indicated that the price of energy was still too low. Accounting for shipping and regasification, the cost of Algerian gas at the pipeline entry was $3.43 per million BTUs (British Thermal Units; one million BTUs equals about thirty cubic meters of natural gas). The minister wanted gas priced according to a new principle: namely, a price equivalent to the energy content of Algerian crude oil at the point of export. Because shipping gas in liquid form is more expensive than shipping oil, and because the liquid must be regasified, the delivered gas would be higher in price per BTU than oil.

Nabi initiated talks with Gaz de France in early 1980 to renegotiate the price of LNG from $3 per million BTUs to $6 per million BTUs. He subsequently made the same demand of El Paso Natural Gas, giving it until April 1, 1980, to accept a doubling of the price of the 1.05 million cubic meters of gas the company had planned to buy in 1980. Algeria also told customers in West Germany, Belgium, and Italy that they too would have to accept a doubling of prices for future gas deliveries.

Unwilling to renegotiate contracts, the major U.S. and European customers were cut off from all supplies of Algerian gas in the first week of April 1980. A month later, the Algerians stepped up their campaign to make gas prices rise in line with oil prices by threatening to close their gas-exporting business altogether unless they received substantially higher prices. They also threatened to cancel plans for a third liquefaction plant (at Arzew), which was to be built by the Foster Wheeler Corporation of the United States. (Ultimately it was canceled for economic reasons.) As part of Algeria's strategy, Nabi argued that oil sales alone were sufficient to meet all of the country's foreign currency needs.

By September 1980, it was evident that Algeria's campaign to raise the world price of natural gas and to create a cartel of natural gas exporters like OPEC was failing. Algeria unilaterally canceled a twenty-year contract to supply LNG to the Netherlands and West Germany, hoping to apply pressure on its customers to accept a doubling of the world price of natural gas. Algeria took the offensive again in November 1980 when SONATRACH informed France that the ten-year contract to sell 230,000 barrels of oil a day to the French-controlled Compagnie Française de Pétroles would be abrogated unless France accepted higher prices for the 4 billion cubic meters of Algerian natural gas that it had planned to import in 1980. In linking oil supplies with higher gas prices in this way, the Algerians hoped to exploit the increased importance of their oil contract with France. By the end of 1980, it had become clear that none of these measures had produced the desired results, and Algeria was losing millions of dollars in foreign revenue.

The major breakthrough occurred in February 1982 when the new socialist government of François Mitterrand agreed to a "political" price for Algerian natural gas. For two years, negotiations between Algeria and the previous French government of Valéry Giscard d'Estaing had failed to achieve agreement on price and quantity of gas sales. Following political talks between Benjedid and Mitterrand in late 1981, a new agreement was struck. According to contract terms, Gaz de France, the French state gas utility, agreed to pay $5.20 per million BTUs, with the price indexed to a basket of six crudes, for 9.63 billion cubic meters per year. That price was well above the $4.28 that France paid for Algerian gas in 1981 and much higher than the $3.70 to which the price would otherwise have fallen in 1982 under a formula that had linked the price of natural gas to the cost of certain grades of crude oil. Essentially, nearly 14 percent of the contract was to be subsidized by the French government as a sign of political goodwill.

The agreement constituted a major victory for Algeria in its long campaign to increase gas prices so that they would be equivalent in energy terms to world oil prices. France's decision also greatly reinforced Algeria's hand in negotiations with Italy for the supply of 13.02 billion cubic meters of Algerian natural gas annually through a pipeline crossing Tunisia under the Mediterranean (Transmed).

MARKET PRESSURES FORCING POLITICAL FLEXIBILITY

Several developments made themselves evident in the decade of the 1980s making uncertain whether Algeria's strategy of price parity between oil and gas could pay off in the long run. By the mid-1980s, there was a worldwide glut of natural gas and a relatively weak demand. In addition, exploration and discovery of new sources, along with continuing efforts in the former Soviet Union, Saudi Arabia, and elsewhere to bring to market large quantities of natural gas, made it increasingly difficult for the Algerians to maintain their hard-line bargaining position. The contracts that had been signed with the nearly dozen foreign customers tended to be relatively small in volume. The U.S. market, which still constitutes the greatest potential customer, was effectively removed as a major importer after El Paso pulled out in 1981. The Panhandle (Houston) and Distrigas (Boston) agreements were exceptions, but they constituted minuscule percentages of total U.S. gas imports at the time. Even successfully concluded contracts with French, Spanish, and Belgian customers were soon being renegotiated with all seeking substantial reductions in contracted supplies because of weak demand. Finally, Algeria's indexation formula became detrimental to the country as a result of the movement of the market.

These setbacks came at a particularly critical time for Algeria. The country's development goals had been predicated on Algeria's hydrocarbons policy as originally put forth by the Boumedienne regime and later modified by Benjedid. In both cases, first oil, then natural gas, were to be the financial catalyst for an industrially based development. Given Algeria's limited crude oil reserves and the depressed demand for OPEC oil in the world market, the role of natural gas had assumed increased importance in Algerian economic calculations. However, Algerian officials continued to articulate and implement a broad-based political strategy of maximizing natural gas revenues through a system of indexation and long-term contracts with western customers. In such agreements, the customers were tied to specific pricing formulas but were only "promised" increased commercial and trade agreements with Algeria.

The complexity of the natural gas industry and the massive investments and large capital outlays involved, including over $3 billion in equipment, terminals, and specialized giant tankers, made it difficult for the Algerians to shift quickly or radically their energy policy. It was therefore no real surprise in subsequent contract dealings to see Algerians exhibiting greater flexibility. This was the case, for example, in the negotiations for contract modifications with the U.S., Belgian, French, and Spanish customers although a protracted pricing dispute with Spain's national gas company, ENAGAS, forced the Algerians to go to the International Chamber of Commerce for arbitration. The Spanish company's attempts to extricate itself from earlier contracts—now considered "exorbitant"—led to Algerian trade reprisals and a worsening of Spanish-Algerian economic relations. Despite an amicable resolution of this dispute in mid-1985 to the official satisfaction of both Madrid and Algiers, it was a pattern that had the potential of being repeated with other European customers.

By the late 1980s, it had become clear to the Algerian leadership that it could no longer afford to significantly reduce the outlays for the socioeconomic programs that had been identified in various development plans. These programs constituted the centerpiece of Benjedid's economic strategy of liberalization, private sector initiative, and other forms of decentralization, deconcentration, and democratization that were being promoted in the middle and late 1980s as the solution to the country's numerous social, economic, and bureaucratic problems. Ultimately, Chadli's reformist strategy proved too little too late to overcome the wide gap that had evolved between a decreasing energy-driven revenue base and the pressing demands of an increasingly restive civil society. This combustive combination led to the nationwide riots of October 1988 that resulted in the deaths of hundreds of innocent civilians by the once-idolized Algerian military.

The immediate political consequence of the "October events," as they came to be known, was the rapid liberalization and democratization of the country, including the rise of political Islam in the form of successive electoral victories by the Islamic Salvation Front (FIS) in June 1990 and December 1991. Fearful of the rise of an Islamic "threat" and the possible loss of its privileged position in state and society, the army staged a coup on January 11, 1992—an event that catalyzed a wide-ranging civil war that by 2000 has resulted in the deaths of over one hundred thousand people. The current government of Abdelaziz Bouteflika, elected to the presidency in an uncontested vote in April 1999, has been unable to affirm its political legitimacy although it has forced a reduction in the frequency and scope of the killing. Like its predecessors during the state-centered socialist era, the new market-oriented regime, apparently responsive to multilateral pressures for financial reform and economic restructuring, including accelerating privatization policies, remains tied to the hydrocarbon sector for its developmental and political salvation. As such, attention has returned to the future status of SONATRACH—the institution around which revolves all future hopes for development, investment, and democratization.

Since its founding in 1963, SONATRACH has been an integral part of the Algerian state. Because of Algeria's overwhelming financial dependence on hydrocarbon resources—which provide 97 percent of the country's foreign exchange revenues—no government has been willing to disengage the state national oil and gas company from its bureaucratic moorings. Despite the systematic pressures that various multilateral financial lending institutions (such as the International Monetary Fund [IMF], the Paris Club, the London Club, and the World Bank), foreign governments, and economic advisors have applied on Algerian authorities to radically restructure their mismanaged socialist system of rule, SONATRACH has always been considered "off-limits." Thus, while widespread reforms have been implemented since the late 1980s—which were intended to streamline an otherwise stagnant economy through the introduction of such market-oriented policies as privatization measures, liberal foreign investment codes, and the elimination of government subsidies—none of them have been allowed to undermine the government's control and operation of SONATRACH.

Along with the important economic factors explaining this condition are deep political considerations as well. The most important of these revolve around the ongoing conflict between competing elites in state and society who have different agendas, constituencies, and purposes. Intraelite conflicts have long dominated Algerian politics, within both the civilian and military sectors of society. This applies as well to the economy's "golden goose"—SONATRACH, the world's ninth largest oil company.[1] The current condition of civil unrest created by the campaign of Islamic violence directed against the military-dominated government has worked to sustain rather than diminish elite conflict over SONATRACH—Algeria's largest and most lucrative source of patronage, privilege, and power. The current competition is between the efficiency-minded middle-level managerial technocrats of the oil and gas industry—who are pushing for greater market-sensitive reforms including full-scale privatization—and the bureaucratic elites in the government and the military—who are fearful of losing control over national authority. By 2000, the latter was winning over the former.

Since its founding in December 1963, only a year and a half after Algeria achieved its independence in July 1962, SONATRACH[2] has been a fully integrated part of the national governmental structure of the Democratic and Popular Republic of Algeria. For the last thirty-five years, it has served as a crucial instrument in the formulation and implementation of the government's domestic and international political economy. The integrative nature of Algerian hydrocarbons resources with Algerian government policy can only be understood in the context of five distinctive yet interrelated factors: history, ideology, economics, administration, and law.

History and Elite Competition

Algeria achieved its political independence on July 5, 1962, after a bitter war of national liberation against the French who had colonized the country beginning in 1830.[3] While the country became free, its polity was fractured, its society divided, its culture ruptured, and its economy devastated. Only one sector showed any promise of growth—hydrocarbons. The new leadership in Algiers envisioned exploiting this crucial sector as a way by which to overcome the vast legacy of political and economic backwardness left by the colonizing power. Thus, almost from the very beginning, oil and gas production were envisioned as central to the country's efforts to socialize the economy, expand state control over civil society, develop civilian and military infrastructures, and position Algeria as a future "great" power in the southern Mediterranean region. To achieve these grandiose goals, the state undertook simultaneous political, social, economic, and international transformations.

In the political realm, a single-party authoritarian regime was established using "revolutionary socialism" as an ideology of popular mobilization. While the first postindependence president, Ahmed Ben Bella (1962–1965), was ambiguous in this regard, his successor, Houari Boumedienne (1965–1978), fully institutionalized this political project. In the social realm, Boumedienne deepened and expanded the regime's socialist character by providing broadly based nationalized social services (medicine, schooling, pensions, and so on). Economically, the regime completely nationalized all "strategic" interests—this included the important gas and oil sector, which came fully under government control in February 1971 with the nationalization of all French hydrocarbon interests.[4] Lastly, in the area of foreign policy, Algeria assumed a visible if not militant posture in numerous international forums as part of its effort to establish a "new international economic order" (NIEO) in which gas and oil were to be used to coerce fundamental changes in the international economy and thereby shift global political power away from the industrialized north and towards the underdeveloped south.

While the liberalization policies of Boumedienne's successor, Chadli Benjedid (1979–1992), significantly ameliorated both the militancy of third-world revolutionism and the suffocating effects of state bureaucratic control of the economy, the critical hydrocarbon sector remained firmly in the hands of the state. SONATRACH served the important function of expanding oil and gas production—now in close collaboration with multinational oil companies—while also providing the government with the revenue necessary to try to satisfy the increasing social needs of a young, restless, and expanding population, as well as to maintain state power in general.

The government of Liamine Zeroual (1994–1999) simultaneously accelerated the liberalization process in several areas in an effort to contain and defeat the Islamist insurgency that emerged in early 1992 when the army staged a coup d'état on the eve of the second round national legislative elections in which the now-banned FIS was about to achieve a decisive victory. The army-imposed regime has undergone an institutional transformation with the successful completion of several electoral mandates—a presidential election in 1995, a constitutional referendum in 1996, and legislative and municipal elections in 1997. Yet, the country continues to face daily violence which has cost the lives of nearly one hundred thousand people since early 1992.[5]

None of the violence, however, has slowed the regime's economic transformation in which a socialist economy is gradually being replaced by a market-oriented one. Many sectors of the once nationalized economy are now being privatized except for one—hydrocarbons. And despite the expansive role now being played by scores of foreign oil and gas companies in exploiting Algerian resources, SONATRACH remains state owned. Indeed, while in the past historical, ideological, economic, and global considerations were once fused to justify maintaining national control of oil and gas production, today's *raison d'être* is pure political economy. In order to remain power, the narrowly based, army-supported regime depends almost exclusively on the national rents that oil and gas production provide in order to remain in power—that along with corruption, coercion, and co-optation. As long as the regime is viewed by the majority of its citizens as illegitimate if not dangerous, it seems unlikely that SONATRACH will at any time in the near or intermediate future be privatized or spun off as an independent enterprise unit.

Almost from the beginning of its modern political history, Algeria has been racked by deep cleavages among its dominant elites. Rather than creating unity and a sense of common national purpose among these elite, the bloody war of independence (November 1954–July 1962) exacerbated and extended existing tensions, rivalries, and differences. As one noted scholar of the subject has written: "[T]he [Algerian] revolution not only perpetuated old antagonisms but also created new sources of strain and tension among political leaders. . . . Rather than developing into a 'political class' that jealously guards its prerogatives and power, the Algerian political elite has been composed of numerous clans, factions, and cliques, none of which has been powerful enough to dominate the entire political system."[6]

In the last three decades, these intraelite conflicts have not completely disappeared; rather, they have been submerged within ruling state institutions of which the army has been the most dominant. In practice, this has meant that competition over power, privilege, and patronage operates at the highest level of authority in a continuous albeit opaque way. This applies in particular to the revenue-rich hydrocarbons sector from which flows valuable state patronage. Understanding the contested nature of elite political power in Algeria helps explain the ambiguous and sometimes contradictory nature of public policy towards economic enterprises. During nearly all of Algeria's postindependence period, both ideology and public policy converged to keep SONATRACH squarely under the control of state. When faced with serious economic crises, however, reform measures were introduced to overcome the vast legacy of bureaucratic mismanagement. Yet even these reforms did not go forward unchallenged, including the efforts to improve SONATRACH's financial performance. While alternating elite interests continue to influence decision making in Algeria's political economy, including determining the fate of SONATRACH, no single elite constituency either in the military or the bureaucracy has gone so far as to call for SONATRACH's total privatization. Indeed, as long as Algeria continues to be governed by the army in an authoritarian manner, it seems unlikely that the state will formally relinquish control over the most valuable resource of its political economic power.

Ideology

Algeria owns the world's fourth largest proven natural gas resources and substantial reserves of crude oil.[7] The development of these reserves has been central to economic planning since independence—its functions have included financing the creation of other industries as well as providing essential services intended to improve living standards.

More than any others, these sociopolitical considerations govern hydrocarbons strategy in Algeria and explain why Algeria is determined to obtain as high a price as possible on world markets for its natural resources preferably through the instrumentality of OPEC production quotas and other cartelization mechanisms. The ideological underpinning of this strategy was reconfirmed and reinforced at the December 29–31, 1980, meeting of the Central Committee of the FLN. Despite major political and institutional turmoil since then, the ideological configuration of Algeria's energy policy put into place nearly two decades ago is still in effect today.

As discussed earlier, the 1980 meeting laid down specific recommendations that have had major implications for the country's energy policy. The first of these is that hydrocarbons are a nonrenewable resource, and the second that the "most effective guarantee for the development of the country lies in a permanent mobilization of the workers in order to develop other sectors and thus achieve a more diversified and more integrated economy, which is therefore less vulnerable in its relations with the outside world."[8]

This recognition of the limited nature of resources and the importance of creating other industries that will be self-generating led the FLN to carefully formulate identified aims that were discussed earlier in this chapter.[9] What is remarkable about this hydrocarbons blueprint, articulated twenty years ago, is how very much it remains in effect today. Only the addition of extensive foreign investment and participation in the oil and gas industry constitutes a new but complementary aspect of the original plan.

Economics

The first major discovery of oil was made in the Sidi Aissa region in 1948, and by 1958 the country's main oil field—Hassi Messaoud—was coming onstream. In 1961, gas production began at Hassi R'Mel. Not surprisingly, these developments led France, the colonial power, to reassess its view of Algeria's future. Shortly before it finally conceded on the issue of full independence, Paris was prepared to give up the three northern departments—previously thought the only part of the vast territory worth economic exploitation ("useful Algeria")—but hoped to hold onto the territoires du sud (southern territories), where oil and gas rather than welfare of the native Touaregs caught the French imagination. However, the French Sahara was not to be, and Algeria after gaining its independence (1962) secured the region's hydrocarbons wealth for itself—a situation it consolidated with full nationalization in 1971.[10]

In the 1960s and 1970s, Algeria became increasingly dependent on oil and gas to finance its investment in industry and the social welfare of a fast-growing population. The centralized socialist state that Boumedienne created was constructed on a sea of hydrocarbons revenues, allowing Algeria to push ahead with its social experiments and industrialization—a strategy labeled "industrializing industries,"[11] discussed in detail earlier.

Algeria is one of the major oil and gas producing countries of Africa. In 1994, 1995, and 1996, it set the record for the most oil discovered of all oil producing countries. Yet, the country's full hydrocarbon potential has still to be fully and reliably established. In addition to its upstream strength, Algeria has a strong downstream sector that includes refining, distribution, marketing, and chemicals.

More than ever, the hydrocarbons industry is key to the Algerian economy, earning nearly $11 billion in 1996 or 97 percent of its foreign exchange revenue. Its current proven hydrocarbon reserves are estimated to be 4.2 thousand million tons of oil equivalent of which 1.2 thousand million tons are of crude oil (9.2 thousand million barrels) and 3.6 trillion cubic meters (tcm) or 128 trillion cubic feet (tcf) of natural gas. This represents nearly 1 percent (0.9 percent) of the world's crude oil reserves and nearly 3 percent (2.6 percent) of the world's natural gas reserves. At current production levels—1997 average: 846,000 barrels of oil per day (bpd); 1996 natural gas production: 65.9 billion cubic meters (bcm)—its reserve-to-production ratio is twenty-two years for crude oil and eighty for natural gas.[12]

There are currently about thirty-five major producing oil fields in the country. The main fields are located in the east-central region of the country at Hassi Messaoud and around In Amenas near the Libyan border. Recently, a cluster of new fields with commercial potential have been discovered at Hassi Berkine, east of Hassi Messaoud towards the Tunisian border.

Algerian oil fields generally produce light crude oils with a low sulfur content. The principal crudes are Sahara Blend and Zarzaitine. Exports of crude oil and refined products from Algeria have varied in recent years reflecting the highly competitive oil market, erratic global weather patterns, and a weakened Asian economy. In 1994, for example, over 1.2 million bpd were exported while in 1997 only about 850,000 bpd were exported, 18 percent of which were in the form of crude oil, 24 percent condensates, 25 percent gas, and 19 percent refined products. The bulk of Algeria's exports of crude oil goes to western Europe (85 percent), with about 5 percent going to the United States.

Algeria is particularly rich in condensates and natural gas and the government has instituted a strategy of investing in facilities that exploit these resources. The country has now become one of the world's leading exporters of condensates, with a volume of some 400,000 bpd. While Algeria's crude oil constitutes 30 percent of the country's recoverable hydrocarbon reserves, its natural gas constitutes 70 percent. It also ranks fourth in the world—after Qatar, Russia, and Iran—in terms of gas reserves. Output of natural gas in Algeria has grown steadily over the years, from 36.5 bcm in 1986 to 49.2 bcm in 1990 and 65.9 bcm in 1996. By 2000, conservative analysts say this figure could approach 70 bcm annually; some more optimistic SONATRACH officials forecast the volume to reach as high as 170 bcm.[13] Apart from encouraging foreign oil companies to develop Algeria's gas fields, the government is also promoting the use of natural gas in the domestic market—especially in the industrial sector where plants can easily be converted from fuel oil to gas.

Commercial production of natural gas began in 1961. Proven reserves, which are mainly wet, stand at 5.1 billion tons, although actual reserves are probably much higher. According to SONATRACH, natural gas represented 57 percent of Algeria's total proven hydrocarbon reserves in 1996. Algeria accounts for 25 percent of European Union gas imports. Two-thirds of known reserves are contained at Hassi R'Mel, in central Algeria, five hundred kilometers south of Algiers. Other important fields include Rhourde Nouss, Alrar, Rhourde El Chouff, Rhourde El Adra, Gassi Touil, and Bassin d'Illizi. Four plants at Arzew and Skikda, all owned by SONATRACH, liquefy gas for export. LNG production from these complexes was 18 bcm in 1994 but is expected by 1999 to rise to about 49 bcm when a radical but protracted overhaul is completed.

The estimated $1.5 billion revamping and upgrading of the Arzew liquefaction plants is nearly complete and further progress is expected at Skikda, where contractors ran into problems, which will provide more LNG capacity. Revamping and expansion at Arzew and Skikda will bring their production to around 29 bcm a year by the end of 1998. Of this, 21.2 bcm is to be produced by the GL1-Z and GL2-Z plants at Arzew. The Skikda gas liquefaction plant is now expected back on stream in late 1998 or early 1999.

A network of export pipelines link the oil and gas fields to terminals and refineries at the Mediterranean coast. There are seven terminals for the export of Algerian hydrocarbons at Algiers, Annaba, Oran, Arzew, Skikda, and Bejaia, and at La Skhirra in neighboring Tunisia. The most important terminal is at Arzew, which handles over 40 percent of all hydrocarbon exports and 100 percent of condensate exports.

Despite gas liquefaction facilities producing below capacity during an extended period of renovation and expansion work, SONATRACH became the world's fourth biggest gas exporter—after Russia's Gazprom, Shell, and Exxon—when the taps were opened to a new pipeline in late 1996. Algeria has built two major gas pipelines to facilitate exports to Europe. The $1.3 billion Maghreb-Europe gasline (GME) was completed in November 1996, allowing the transportation of 10 bcm per year to Spain, Portugal, and Morocco. The existing twenty-one-hundred-kilometer Trans-Mediterranean gasline (TME) to Italy via Sicily has been expanded, providing throughput capacity of 25 bcm per year to Italy and neighboring markets. Both pipelines run from Hassi R'Mel through neighboring countries—the TME through Tunisia and the GME through Morocco—before crossing the Mediterranean seabed.

Increases in export pipeline capacity are necessary for a projected gas export capacity of 75 bcm a year in the early twenty-first century. There are plans to boost GME's throughput capacity to some 11 bcm a year, and to add a further

5 bcm capacity to the TME line through the construction of new compression stations. Other projects include: development of the Alrar-Hassi R'Mel pipeline, consisting of a gasline 42 to 48 inches in diameter with four compression stations; completion of the 42-inch Hassi R'Mel-Skikda gasline to come onstream in 1998; and construction of the 521-km In Salah-Hassi R'Mel gasline, with a capacity of 7 million cubic meters per year.

Given the centrality of the hydrocarbons industry to Algeria's political economy of development now and into the future, SONATRACH, which is both the state-owned operator and the parent company of the industry, continues to serve as the country's institutional bulwark against autonomous political and economic interests. SONATRACH retains overall responsibility for hydrocarbon policy, exploration, production, transport, and export. Over the period 1996–2000, SONATRACH plans to invest nearly $30 billion to increase exploration and further develop reserves. It remains the country's main export earner.

The chief planks in SONATRACH's current development program are its multibillion dollar strategic alliances formed with overseas operators. Since 1991, international companies have been allowed to work in or even buy into existing oilfields. By the end of 1996, for example, twenty-three exploration and production-sharing contracts were in place with eighteen international companies, involving investments worth $1.5 billion. The foreign firms involved in Algeria's hydrocarbons sector take a long-term view of the political risks, and major investments are underway or planned in all areas of the production. To protect foreign installations against attack by Islamic militants, private security arrangements and a strong army presence have been put in place.

Administration

SONATRACH's relationship to the state is direct, intimate, and long-standing. High government officials and their counterparts in the national company exchange positions regularly with the current minister of energy and mines. Such a pattern has been in existence virtually since SONATRACH was formed but has been reinforced in the last decade or so as the country has struggled to transform its socialist economy into one based on market principles. Although names of ministries have changed, reshuffled, or eliminated altogether, those in charge of the hydrocarbons sector have remained key actors in the management and direction of SONATRACH.

In the government of Abdelhamid Brahimi formed on February 15, 1988, for example, Belkacem Nabi was appointed minister of energy, chemicals, and petrochemicals, while Youcef Yousfi continued as director general of SONATRACH. The new government of Prime Minister Mouloud Hamrouche, a reformist, was formed on September 16, 1989, following the disastrous nationwide riots of the year before. There was a marked shift in the composition of the new government away from ministers with military and party backgrounds towards professional technocrats. The energy sector was folded into a reconstituted ministry of mines and industry with Sadek Boussena as its new head. Boussena had replaced Yousfi in the general directorship of SONATRACH in 1987 and later made chairman of the state energy company before his appointment as minister of energy and mines. As minister, he was responsible for the first of several major restructurings of SONATRACH undertaken since the company divested some of its specialized divisions to form separate companies in the early and mid-1980s. Although a new general manager was appointed to run SONATRACH (Abdelhaq Bouhafs), as minister overseeing the energy sector Boussena was personally responsible for the initiative that led to the creation of five SONATRACH subsidiaries— Sonatrach Exploration, Production, and Marketing; Sonatrach Transportation; Sonatrach Liquefaction; Sonatrach Refineries; and Sonatrach International. In effect, he retained control over the entirety of the country's energy sector until he was removed from the government in the cabinet reshuffle of June 18, 1991 to be replaced by another high-level SONATRACH official, Nordine Aït-Laoussine.

The new government of Sid Ahmed Ghozali separated the ministry of energy from the ministry of mines and industry and appointed a long-time collaborator of the prime minister in the oil and gas industry under President Houari Boumedienne, Nordine Aït-Laoussine, to replace Boussena as energy head. Aït-Laoussine was once a senior SONATRACH official when Ghozali ran the energy company in the 1970s and later became a consultant to a Swiss-based energy company. Several important elements in Algeria's political economy practices in the energy field are reflected in these moves—the role of intraelite alliances and associations established and maintained over time, the importance of technical skills and bureaucratic experience, and the direct ties to SONATRACH.

Another government reshuffle on October 16, 1991, saw the removal of the contentious Economy Minister Hocine Benissad leaving Ghozali and Aït-Laoussine as the two front men in the country's effort to reform its economy as well as its important energy sector. This personal, professional, and political alliance between the two was maintained even following the military coup d'état of January 11, 1992, which saw the removal of President Chadli Benjedid from power and the shutting down of Algeria's infant democratic experiment. Both men also maintained their positions in the cabinet reshuffle of February 23, 1992.

The ruling military junta struggled to keep control of the political situation following the assassination of its hand-picked president, Mohammed Boudiaf, on June 29, 1992. Fearful that both political and economic reforms initiated by the Chadli presidency and sustained by the Ghozali government were fostering "antistate" behavior and encouraging "populist aspirations," the regime shifted course when it reshuffled the government on July 19, 1992, appointing as premier and minister of the economy Belaïd Abdesselam, an old-line Boumediennist socialist. The new government was populated with men who had worked for the huge state conglomerates favored during the Boumedienne era when Abdesselam structured Algeria's "industrial revolution," but which were broken up into autonomous companies during the Chadli years (1979–1992).

Revealingly, and despite the apparent shift in the new government's economic policy orientation, the energy portfolio was given—once again—to Hacen Mefti, a former SONATRACH official.

Born on July 3, 1937, in Algiers, Mefti earned a master's degree in electrical engineering from Dresden University (former East Germany). From 1966 to 1984, he was a project manager, pipeline division head, production director, and finally executive vice president (heading the hydrocarbons division) with SONATRACH. After leaving SONATRACH in 1984, he became the senior advisor in the now defunct planning ministry before becoming chairman of Fonds de Participation Mines, Hydrocarbures, and Hydraulique in 1988. He also served as a consultant for several international institutions and hydrocarbons sector companies. Mefti survived numerous cabinet reshuffles on October 24, 1992, November 24, 1992, February 3, 1993, and July 10, 1993. When a new government was formed on September 4, 1993, by the new prime minister Redha Malek—an old-line Boumediennist militant known for his antidemocratic tendencies—Mefti was replaced by Ahmed Benbitour, the first and last energy minister with no direct links to SONATRACH.

Benbitour was then a forty-seven-year-old economist with a doctorate from the University of Montreal who had previously worked as a director in both state-owned companies and government ministries. Benbitour had represented Algeria at general meetings of the IMF and other financial institutions. At the time of his appointment as energy minister, observers were surprised that he had been selected since it was expected that another technocrat trained by SONATRACH would take the job. Some believed the move "inspiring" since SONATRACH was to serve as the linchpin of the economy, with a long-established group led by president-director-general Abdelhak Bouhafs staying in place to oversee its transition into a major international company. If Bouhafs had joined the government, as some believe, he would have become vulnerable, which explains why he refused the job when it was offered. Benbitour meanwhile was expected to use his economics background well while holding hydrocarbons policy on a steady course.

Although he managed to survive one cabinet reshuffle on January 31, 1994, Benbitour was shifted out of the energy ministry to head the ministry of finance in the government changeover that took place on April 15, 1994. His replacement was Amar Makhloufi—a former SONATRACH official. Thus Benbitour's experience represented but a brief interruption in a pattern that had been established early on and that continues until today—the inseparability of SONATRACH from its governmental roots and vice versa.

Amar Makhloufi was born on November 17, 1943, at El Madher in Batna province. He studied mathematics and petroleum engineering before joining SONATRACH as an engineer in the late 1960s. He later headed one of the company's chemical subsidiaries, but left the oil industry for a period when he was appointed governor of Annaba province (wilaya). Makhloufi returned to the Energy and Industry Ministry in the early 1990s and was named director of planning and then deputy minister.

Makhloufi remained energy minister until the government reshuffle of June 25, 1997, when former SONATRACH chief executive officer and director of the office of President Liamine Zeroual since 1996, Youcef Yousfi, assumed the portfolio. Yousfi had served as a SONATRACH director general in the 1980s. He is a member of the RND, the majority party in parliament created by former president Zeroual. With Yousfi's appointment, the fusion of political, personal, and professional attributes was once again reaffirmed as a key consideration in the deliberation and implementation of national energy policy. In the December 23, 1999, cabinet reshuffle following Abdelaziz Bouteflika's election to the presidency the previous April, Yousfi became foreign minister ceding the energy and mines portfolio to Chakib Khelil. Khelil's appointment, a one-time energy advisor at the World Bank, intended to signal a new willingness to cooperate with foreign investors in the energy sector. However, a series of political gaffes got him into trouble when he was quoted as saying, in a March 2000 press conference, that SONATRACH "was no longer off limits for privatization." He was forced to quickly retract this statement indicating, on more than one occasion, that "there were no intentions of privatizing the national oil company SONATRACH."[14]

Another recent related example of the already mentioned process of political-administrative fusion in the energy sector was the July 14, 1997, appointment of Abdelmajid Attar as the head of SONATRACH. A trained geologist, the fifty-one-year-old Attar was a SONATRACH insider who had worked as director of the state company's exploration and international affairs divisions. While no details were provided about the fate of outgoing Director-General Nazim Zouioueche—whose marshaling of Algeria's opening to international oil companies won appreciation abroad—it had prompted speculation that increased political influence and government control was to be extended to SONATRACH, following the creation of a National Energy Council chaired by the Algerian president. The reappointment of Abdelhak Bouhafs as SONATRACH's chairman in the new December 1999 government of Prime Minister Ahmed Benbitour, himself a former energy minister, represents an attempt to reestablish institutional continuity in that important office. Head of SONATRACH from 1989 to 1995, Bouhafs is a close associate of Bouteflika, who has acted as the president's advisor on economic affairs.

Finally, as Algeria has begun moving slowly towards opening elements of its energy sector to foreign investment, Algerian expatriates with ties to SONATRACH have emerged as key players. This is the case with the 1997 creation of a joint venture in which the Algerian state pipeline company ENAC would become a commercial entity into which Anderson, a British oil services company, would buy. A framework agreement to establish the venture was signed by ENAC and the British-based Anderson, led by an Algerian expatriate Amara Korba Aziz, a former official with SONATRACH. This underlines the important role being taken by Algerian expatriates in the country's new generation of private sector–led investments.[15]

These diverse examples reflect the interactive nature of elite involvement in the Algerian oil and gas industry in its dual and at times conflicting roles—individuals selected to maintain close political scrutiny of the industry alternating with those intended to foster greater autonomy and private-sector involvement.

SONATRACH has undergone a number of major restructurings almost from its inception, beginning with the nationalization of the industry in 1971 that entailed the full transfer of the country's oil and gas resources to SONATRACH. SONATRACH's organizational restructures, pricing policies, investment strategies, international alliances, and overall development planning originate within high government circles in collaboration with the company's technocratic elite. Responding to political and market pressures over the years, SONATRACH has modified its production and pricing policies to ensure adequate national income not only to sustain the country's developmental goals but, as important, to fortify the power and privileges of the ruling elite in the army and government bureaucracy. Simply put, SONATRACH is organized and administered by and for the state's political economy interests.

During the Boumedienne years (1965–1978), SONATRACH was an extremely large company, responsible not only for oil and gas production, distribution, refining, and processing (petrochemicals production), but also for oil and gas industry engineering and exploration. This made SONATRACH both a powerful and highly centralized institution, two attributes that hampered its efficiency and ability to coordinate with the other economic sectors that it was ultimately meant to serve.

As a consequence, in the early years of Chadli Benjedid's presidency (1979–1992), it was decided that the mighty SONATRACH would be decentralized—but not denationalized—with the subdivision of many of its responsibilities into separate enterprises. Several major companies were created from divisions of SONATRACH in April 1980, and others have since been set up in a further process of decentralization.[16] SONATRACH oversees the industry and organizes the exploration, production, and marketing of hydrocarbons, but these companies work autonomously for much of the day-to-day business. SONATRACH also has a marketing company, SONATRADING (located in Amsterdam), through which its U.S. gas deals have been transacted.

Further restructuring, undertaken in the middle 1980s, was intended to make SONATRACH into a holding company responsible for planning, marketing, and financial policy. This left such aspects as management, labor relations, investment, and commercial transactions to the newly created autonomous subsidiaries.

Following a sometimes radical reassessment of its economic policy after the oil shock of 1985–1986, Algeria modified its energy pricing policy in an attempt to increase sales and export revenues. This was especially apparent in the case of gas sales. In the 1970s, Algeria developed a policy of charging the highest price possible—to a level at which, in the case of contracts with major partners such as France, customers were paying what came to be known as the "political price"—and enforcing rigid long-term contracts (which were to undermine a promising transatlantic gas trade). The revised policy of the middle 1980s aimed to provide more competitive and market-sensitive terms, to win new customers, and to maintain market share with traditional clients. The 1982 hydrocarbons law was amended in 1986[17] in order to stimulate oil and gas exploration by attracting foreign partners.

Almost from the beginning of the reform and restructuring efforts undertaken by the Chadli government to make the Algerian economy more responsive to market forces, the status of SONATRACH has been considered "special." Initially, when asked whether Algeria's enterprise reforms would extend to SONATRACH, most public officials answered that it was a company like all the others and would become autonomous. In reality, of course, SONATRACH has always been *unlike* any other Algerian enterprise since it accounts for nearly all of Algeria's hard-currency earnings. Thus, as much as government officials might wish that SONATRACH become independent and operated "like all other companies," no one is about to let go of the goose that lays the golden eggs.

This does not mean that pressures for change have not existed. Indeed, like the current combat at the highest level of the Algerian political system between army "hard-liners" and "soft-liners" over how much and when to open up the system to genuine political change, so too SONATRACH has its counterpart of bureaucratic-managerial infighters struggling over how much and how fast the deregulation, decentralization, and denationalization process should proceed.

Practically speaking, profit-oriented management of SONATRACH is badly needed. The company has been an inefficient organization for decades. It has been overstaffed, and its equipment and installations are antiquated and badly in need of maintenance if not outright replacement. Under the gloss of the company's highly profitable sales of Algeria's oil and gas is an operation that would show major losses if evaluated by normal business standards.

While middle-level management and company technocrats push for dramatic changes to overcome these handicaps—beginning with transforming SONATRACH into a truly independent private corporation—top bureaucrats and their political allies in the government are unable or unwilling to let go of the company given its importance to the national economy. Authorities are anxious to maintain control over the company in order to keep control over its earnings, particularly since hard-currency earnings often linger elsewhere and only slowly make their way into government coffers. This has become particularly critical in recent years given the fluctuation of global oil and gas prices and the need to satisfy pressing social demands in the face of an ongoing political challenge from militant Islam.

Beyond the political will, there has been the need to effect new legislation. Since SONATRACH was originally created by law, it could not simply be reorganized as the other state-owned companies could; instead, it had to be changed by modifying the existing legislation.[18]

Law

Since the middle 1980s, the Algerian government has put a high priority on attracting the international oil companies because it needs their help in order to expand oil and gas exports to get through the economic crisis facing the country. SONATRACH has fallen far behind in technology and equipment and has been unable to carry out the necessary exploration and production on its own. An important new development in this regard has been the shifting away from contracts negotiated based on "political" criteria to those employing standard international legal and arbitration procedures. Thus, participation has become more attractive to foreign companies as economic reforms continue and Algeria increasingly adopts international business practices.

Under Algeria's 1986 Petroleum Law, SONATRACH continued to enjoy full control over all activities in the hydrocarbons sector. At that time, any foreign company interested in doing business in this sector had to have SONATRACH as a partner. There were two ways for foreign companies to go into the oil business in Algeria: through a production-sharing contract or a participation contract.

Under the terms of a production-sharing contract, the foreign company sets up a local office in its own name and funnels the financing for its operating expenses through that office. The company's share of exportable oil is delivered to it free on board and free of all taxes. Taxes levied on its operation are paid by SONATRACH through the sale of part of the oil produced by the foreign company. The participation contract is much more complicated and costly. It involves the setting up of a joint venture company in which SONATRACH, by law, maintains a majority interest; this company is then bound to follow all Algerian accounting and tax procedures, including having the tax status of an Algerian company with a turnover and taxable profit. Because of such complications, these types of contracts have not been used by foreign companies.

In the late 1980s, Anadarko was involved in protracted negotiations with SONATRACH that almost failed because of the lack of an international arbitration clause in the production-sharing contract. The impasse was resolved by the inclusion of a clause providing in effect that if Algerian law were to change so as to permit international arbitration, the new law would be retroactively applicable to the contract.

While international arbitration has been introduced in other sector's of Algeria's economy, applying it to the oil and gas sector required changes in the 1986 law—a decision that could only be taken at the highest political levels.

New Hydrocarbons Investment Law

On the eve of the military coup d'état of January 11, 1992, the Algerian parliament passed a new hydrocarbon investment law intended to make investment in Algeria's oil and gas sector more attractive to foreign oil companies.[19] The major features of the 1991 law were that:

- foreign firms were authorized to explore for and develop gas deposits in partnership with SONATRACH, "the state-owned hydrocarbons firm";
- foreign firms were authorized to exploit existing oil fields in partnership with SONATRACH;
- international arbitration was permitted for disputes between foreign firms and SONATRACH; and
- royalties and petroleum taxes were reduced for oil and gas found in certain remote or otherwise difficult areas of exploration or production.[20]

Other important aspects of the new law included provisions regarding:

- *Oil Pipelines:* Article 4 of the new law amended the 1986 law to allow foreign firms to finance, build, and operate oil pipelines under contract with SONATRACH, which continued to have exclusive right to transport oil.
- *Separate Agreement with Government:* Formerly, foreign firms had to negotiate an agreement with the government defining their proposed activities and their obligations to Algeria, in addition to the contract they negotiated with SONATRACH. Article 6 removed that requirement.
- *Profits to Foreign Firms:* The new law did not change the forms of profit-sharing available to foreign firms, but Article 8 stated that payments to foreign firms would depend on two factors: first, the financial and technical risks incurred by SONATRACH in exploring and developing the field in question; second, the technological and financial contribution foreign firms made to the field's development.
- *Incorporation in Algeria Not Always Required:* Under Article 9, foreign firms that had formed a joint venture company with SONATRACH were no longer obliged to incorporate separately in Algeria.
- *Reduced Royalty and Tax Rates:* Article 11 stated that oil found in inaccessible or difficult production zones would be subject to a 10 percent royalty and 42 percent tax rate, well below the standard rates of 20 percent for royalties and 85 percent for taxes.
- *Dispute with Government:* While disputes between foreign firms and SONATRACH could be submitted to international arbitration, those between foreign firms and the government still had to be resolved under Algerian law.[21]

Short-Term Reversal

The reforms by liberal governments in 1991 and 1992 were reversed by the new government that was installed by the ruling army group, which came to power through a military coup. Also reversed was a program to restructure SONATRACH, prepared in the first half of 1992 under the government of Ahmed Ghozali—the man who had built up SONATRACH in the 1970s. In July 1992, the premiership was assumed by his former boss, Belaid Abdessalam, a hard-line nationalist-socialist who was the "father" of Algeria's industrializing industries strategy of the 1960s and 1970s. Abdessalam insisted on strong control by the state, imposed tough terms on foreign companies, and reversed the reforms.

By mid-1992, fifteen companies had bid for eight of the fields with their total investment offers coming to nearly $4 billion. Abdessalam rejected their offers immediately as he came to the premiership, saying they were "below the minimum acceptable" to his government—even though SONATRACH and Nordine Aït-Laoussine, till then the energy minister, had worked hard to attract these companies. It seemed at the time that the "political" pricing strategy of the Boumedienne years was being invoked again, to the serious detriment of the country's economy. More accurately, it reflected the kind of interelite political struggle over power, patronage, and privilege that has long characterized Algerian decision making whether in the political, military, or economic spheres. Fortunately for the Algerian economy, after Abdessalam was removed from office in 1993, SONATRACH revived its efforts to attract foreign companies and again took up its reform and restructuring program. The time, costs, and opportunities wasted were considerable.

Labor Union Challenge

Another challenge to current reform and restructuring efforts of SONATRACH has come from trade unions in the hydrocarbons and energy industries. Feeling the combined pressures from political Islam on one hand and acute financial requirements on the other, the military's newly appointed Algerian president in 1994, General Liamine Zeroual, was unprepared to tackle head-on the large and powerful trade union movement, whose members have gone on strike whenever government policies aimed at reducing state employment have been announced or about to be implemented. Such was the case in early 1995 when consideration was being given to reintegrating the units spun off from SONATRACH in the early 1980s such as ENAFOR (drilling), ENAGEO (geophysics), ENGTP (oil well projects), and ENTP (oil well servicing), all of which provide services to SONATRACH and to foreign oil companies active in Algeria. Other companies being considered were NAFTEC (oil refining) and NAFTAL (oil products distribution). While their equipment and technology were not always modern, these companies were said to be basically sound financially.

For their part, the unions have long campaigned to have the companies regrouped under SONATRACH. The unions fear layoffs that might result from foreign competition and want wage provisions similar to those of SONATRACH. SONATRACH, on the other hand, has strongly opposed the unions' demand and has refused to take back control over the companies. It wants to continue to concentrate on its core business to develop oil and gas exploration and production activities.

Faced with SONATRACH's opposition, the unions have proposed that the companies be regrouped under a holding company led by SONATRACH and become SONATRACH subsidiaries. Seeking to avoid labor disruption in this crucial sector of the economy, the government intervened in both 1995 and 1998 to avoid strikes by the union's 120,000 workers. The idea of creating a holding company was subsequently agreed upon by all parties.

SONATRACH's Modernization Project

Evidence that SONATRACH continues to hold center stage in the current government's effort to stave off challenges to its monopoly of state power from civil society can be seen in the Modernization Project (Promos). Unveiled by SONATRACH in January 1998, it involves a five-year, $19.3 billion expansion program. The plan provides valuable insight into the strategic thinking of both government officials and SONATRACH insiders as they conceptualize about the market, financial, and political-economic challenges facing them in the twenty-first century. It also further elaborates the ongoing symbiosis between Algerian officialdom and SONATRACH.

Mourad Preur is one of the key architects of this Modernization Project who currently serves as a strategy advisor to SONATRACH's managing director. According to Preur, along with the ongoing deregulation of Europe's gas industry, spot transactions in gas and the growth of a short-term market could set the spur to gas competition and a cut in prices, as was initially the case in the United States. As such, prices are expected to harden up after 2010, but the growth in the electricity market will lead to a decoupling of gas vis-à-vis oil prices. Thus, there is a danger that the market will become "fragmented" and prices too influenced by "stock market mechanisms" (future market). As a result, SONATRACH, like several European gas companies, believes there is a need to "seriously study the mechanism of regulation that must be established. Concerted measures between market players will be necessary."[22]

Preur predicted that "turbulence" in the gas market would probably compel the European gas industry to undertake a major overhaul and adopt "mechanisms enabling receipts to flow back towards the upstream side." For instance, vertical integration with two-way cooperation between the upstream and downstream sectors would enable part of the upstream risk to be passed along to consumers while involving producers in the most profitable part, that is, the downstream. The recently concluded multibillion dollar SONATRACH–BP gas contract creating a new joint venture company, In Salah Gas, could serve as a model of the kind of "strategic alliance" that would prompt companies in producer countries to open up their upstream operations to international companies, which would gain a significant competitive edge. In return, the companies in producer nations would be given "real openings to both the downstream in consumer countries and to the international upstream."[23]

According to Preur, SONATRACH's strategy is aimed at "hoisting the Algerian national oil and gas company into the front ranks of international companies."[24] SONATRACH firmly believes, Preur indicated, that competition surrounding oil prices tended increasingly to be based on good management and technology and that developments in the industry are increasingly being dictated by companies that obey competitive logic, and no longer by governments alone. Additionally, the concept of solidarity between producer countries will give way to solidarity between oil companies in the producer nations who will exhibit increased cooperation. SONATRACH believes cooperation between oil companies in producer countries and international oil companies will be "a stabilizing factor destined to mark the oil and gas industry in coming years."[25]

Although it couches its activities in the language of the free market, in which efficiently run independent oil companies in the producing and consuming countries will collaborate to advance their mutual interests free of government interference, the Algerian government in reality maintains actual control of all key aspects of the industry. These include selection of key personnel, determination of pricing policies, distribution of profits, and access to the domestic market, among other things. This appears to be a continuation of a long-established Algerian strategy of formally acceding to an international norm—democracy, human rights, and "free" market—while in fact continuing to promote cartelization policies that impose "political" prices in order to achieve the highest income for the state.

The Algerian "reality" became abundantly clear when a March 16, 1998, presidential decree announced that the "state energy company SONATRACH was to remain under state ownership according to a new law, which defines its legal status for the first time."[26] According to this presidential edict, SONATRACH is to be converted into a joint stock company with a capital of $4.1 billion, which is entirely subscribed by the state. It will be headed by a director-general answerable to a board of directors, which will be headed by the energy minister. The move precludes foreign investors taking stakes in SONATRACH, although the company has recently invited investors to participate in downstream projects, in addition to the upstream sector where international companies are already active. After a restructuring in early 1998, three previously independent companies became part of SONATRACH: petrochemical company (ENIP), oil products distributor (NAFTAL), and pipeline company (NAFTEC).[27]

The operational and legal control of SONATRACH is now embedded within the newly created Conseil National de l'Energie (CNE; the National Energy Council) that is headed by the president of the country and includes key government ministers and high-level members of the security establishment. The CNE has been given the authority to oversee the implementation of SONATRACH's previously mentioned multibillion dollar restructuring and development plan. In short, SONATRACH is to become a public company with all its shares owned by the government.

Underlining the company's importance to the wider economy, SONATRACH launched in January 1998 Algeria's first domestic bond issue, the first also to involve the new Algiers Stock Exchange. The five-year, $85 million bond, which was fully subscribed by February 12, was underwritten by a group of local banks. The issue comprised 115,000 shares, with 25,000 priced at AD100,000 (Algerian Dinar), 40,000 priced at AD50,000, and 50,000 priced at AD10,000. Interest was set at 13 percent tax-free, with a 2.5 percent premium. The Banque Extérieure d'Algérie headed the banking group, which also included the Banque de l'Agriculture et du Développement Rural, the Credit Populaire d'Algérie, the Banque Nationale d'Algérie, the Banque de Développement Local, and the Banque de l'Habitat—all state-owned banks.[28]

The most financially compelling phase of the modernization plan was revealed in March 2000 when BP Amoco announced that it was planning to invest $2.4 billion in the In Salah gas field between 2000 and 2002. This agreement could serve as a landmark in the history of Algerian gas constituting the biggest ever foreign investment made in North Africa's largest economy. Yet it could also serve as a challenge to the gas strategy that was put into place a decade ago when there was general pessimism about the oil sector. Now that this sector has been revived and new oil fields exploited in the boom region of Berkine, it is expected that oil production will double from the 1995 base, when production began in partnerships with foreign companies, to some 1.5 million bpd in 2005. Developing gas reserves further afield and from costly reservoirs may not be the best option from the point of view of the government—lower taxes—and the company—lower returns on investment.

These are just some of the challenges thrown up by domestic and international pressures. In a speech in late 1999, Bouhafs said that "partnerships entailing cross shareholdings could allow Algerian companies to gradually internationalize their operations." Such companies could include those that operate downstream in refining and petrochemicals, such as NAFTEC and NAFTAL, where SONATRACH is today the sole shareholder, and foreign companies operating upstream such as Anadarko, Arco, ENI, Repsol, and Cepsa Total Fina. The latter have both the capital and the managerial expertise to undertake such a task.

The manner in which the government faces up to the many challenges ahead will be crucial to Algeria's main source of income. It may also send signals as to how the regime intends to associate foreign capital with other sectors of the economy, which remain under the sole ownership and management of the state. President Bouteflika never tires of stating his wish to attract foreign capital to work in Algeria: how the SONATRACH saga unfolds will be a litmus test.

CONCLUSION

This chapter has sought to demonstrate the deeply integrated nature of Algeria's state-owned oil and gas company, SONATRACH, into the country's broader political economy through an operational analysis of this integration within five key areas—history, ideology, economics, administration, and law. This interactive analysis has also highlighted the competitive if not conflictual character of intraelite relations over time that have made it difficult (if not impossible) for the government to fully denationalize, deconcentrate, or decentralize SONATRACH in the manner that it has only just begun to do in other sectors of the Algerian economy.

NOTES

1. *New York Times*, January 20, 1998.
2. Société Nationale pour la Recherche, la Production, le Transport, la Transformation et la Commercialisation des Hydrocarbures (National Enterprise for the Exploration, Production, Transportation, Processing, and Marketing of Hydrocarbons [petroleum, natural gas, and their products]).
3. The most referenced English-language publications concerning Algeria's political history are: William B. Quandt, *Revolution and Political Leadership: Algeria, 1954–1968* (Cambridge: Massachusetts Institute of Technology Press, 1969); John P. Entelis, *Algeria: The Revolution Institutionalized* (Boulder, Colo.: Westview Press, 1986); Rachid Tlemcani, *State and Revolution in Algeria* (Boulder, Colo.: Westview Press, 1986); John Ruedy, *Modern Algeria: The Origins and Development of a Nation* (Bloomington: Indiana University Press, 1992); and Helen Chapin Metz, ed., *Algeria: A Country Study* (Washington, D.C.: Library of Congress/Federal Research Division, 1994).
4. Ordinance 71-8 of 24 February 1971.
5. The most authoritative account of the killings can be found in a publication jointly sponsored by Amnesty International, Human Rights Watch, International Federation of the Leagues of Human Rights, and Reporters without Frontiers, *Algérie: Le Livre Noir* (Algeria, the Black Book) (Paris: La Découverte, 1997). The best analytical work on the Algerian civil war is that of Luis Martinez, *The Algerian Civil War* (New York: Columbia University Press, 2000).
6. William B. Quandt, *Revolution and Political Leadership: Algeria, 1954–1968* (Cambridge: Massachusetts Institute of Technology Press, 1969), p. 11.
7. *Algeria: The Giant Market of North Africa* (London: The Economist Intelligence Unit, 1982), p. 55.
8. *Algeria: The Giant Market of North Africa.*

9. *Algeria: The Giant Market of North Africa*, pp. 55–57.

10. Algeria fully nationalized its hydrocarbons industry through a series of separate ordinances, decrees, and presidential edicts in which foreign territorial rights and resource assets were transferred to the national oil and gas company, SONATRACH, beginning in mid-1970 and ending in early 1971. The most important of these decrees were: Ordinance 70-44 of 12 June 1970, Nationalizing CREPS, CPA, SRA & TRAPSA, & Société Shell Petroleum N.V.; Ordinance No. 70-43 of 12 June 1970, Nationalizing Rights and Interests of Société Française des Petroles Elwerath (SOFRAPEL); Decree No. 71-98 of 12 April 1971, declaring the creation of 51/49 SONATRACH/Private Companies for Each Private Company Nationalized; Presidential [Houari Boumedienne] Statement of 24 February 1971, Nationalizing French Oil Companies; Decree No. 71-99 of 12 April 1971, Declaring the Transfer of the Property Nationalized Under Ordinance No. 71-23 of 12 April 1971, to SONATRACH; Ordinance No. 71-10 of 24 February 1971, Nationalizing the Companies SOPEG, SOTHRA, TRAPES, CREPS, TRAPSA, & Pipelines "PK 66 In Amenas Mediterranée à Ohanet" & "Hassi R'Mel-Haoud El Hamra"; Ordinance No. 71-9 of 24 February 1971, Nationalizing Associated Gas; Ordinance 71-8 of 24 February 1971, Nationalizing All Interests of the Société d'Exploitation des Hydrocarbures de Hassi R'Mel (SEHR), and All Mining Interests Held by All Companies in Nord In Amenas, Tin Fouyem Sud, Alrar Est, Alrer Ouest, Nezla Est, Bridas, Toual, Rhourde Chouff, and Rhourde Adra, and Mining Interests Held in Gas Derived from Deposits in Gassi Touil, Rhourde Nouss, Nezla Est, Zarzaitine, and Tiguentourine (Including El Paso, Francarep, & Petropar); Decree No. 71-66 of 24 February 1971, Transferring All Concessions Nationalized by Ordinances No. 71-11 to SONATRACH; Decree No. 71-65 of 24 February 1971, Transferring All Concessions Nationalized by Ordinance No. 71-10 to SONATRACH; Decree No. 71-64 of 24 February 1971, Transferring All Concessions Nationalized by Ordinances Nos. 71-8 & 71-9 to SONATRACH; and Ordinance No. 71-11 of 24 February 1971, Nationalizing the Companies CFP (A), CREPS, PETROPAR, SNPA, SOFREPAL, COPAREX, OMNIREX, EURAFREP, & FRANCAREP.

11. Jon Marks, *Algeria: Towards Market Socialism* (London: Middle East Economic Digest, 1989), p. 45.

12. See *Algeria: Country Profile 1997–1998* (London: The Economist Intelligence Unit, 1998), pp. 28–33.

13. *Algeria: Country Profile*, p. 32.

14. *The Middle East Economic Digest*, 14 April 2000, p. 20.

15. Jon Marks, "The Maghreb Quarterly," *Middle East Economic Digest* (May 1997), pp. 52–53.

16. Companies spun off from SONATRACH in 1980–1981 were the following: Entreprise Nationale de Raffinage & de Distribution de Produit Pétroliers (ERDP); Entreprise Nationale de Grands Travaux Pétroliers (ENGTP); Entreprise Nationale de Plastiques & Caoutchoucs [rubber] (ENPC); Entreprise Nationale de Forage [drilling] (ENAFOR); Entreprise Nationale des Travaux aux Puits [wells] (ENTP); Entreprise Nationale de Géophysique (ENAGEO); Entreprise Nationale de Génie Civil & de Bâtiment [engineering & construction] (GCB); Entreprise Nationale de Services aux Puits (ENSP); and Entreprise Nationale de Canalisations [pipelines] (ENAC).

17. Law 86-14 of 19 August 1986.

18. See "Restructuring SONATRACH," *Middle East Executive Reports*, vol. 14, no. 1 (January 1991), p. 8.

19. Law 91-21 of 4 December 1991 amends the 1986 Hydrocarbon Investment Law 86-14 of 19 August 1986.

20. See "New Investment Law for Hydrocarbons Area," *Middle East Executive Reports*, vol. 15, no. 2 (February 1992), p. 10.

21. "New Investment Law."

22. "Sonatrach Outlines Strategy," *Africa Energy and Mining,* 11 February 1998, p. 29.

23. "Sonatrach Outlines Strategy."

24. "Sonatrach Outlines Strategy."

25. "Sonatrach Outlines Strategy."

26. *Middle East Economic Digest*, 27 March 1998, p. 18.

27. *Middle East Economic Digest.*

28. *Algeria*, 1st Quarter 1998 (London: The Economist Intelligence Unit, 1998), p. 19.

7

Market Prospects in Cuba

Rensselaer W. Lee III

$\mathbf{F}$aced with economic ruin following the collapse of the Soviet Union and the cut-off of Soviet subsidies, Cuba took steps in the 1990s to open its doors to foreign investment and tourism, and to strengthen trade links with capitalist countries. Though this effort was partly successful (as will be discussed in this chapter), long economic isolation and years of socialist mismanagement have damaged Cuba's economy, in effect limiting near-term opportunities for profitable business ties with that country. An embargo on commerce with Cuba of nearly forty years' duration effectively prohibits U.S. investment in the island and severely circumscribes (though does not eliminate) possibilities for U.S.–Cuban trade. Although the end of the embargo might help some U.S. companies (especially those in agribusiness fields), the size of the Cuban economic "pie" is relatively small and will remain so for some time. Nevertheless, increased integration of Cuba with the world economy and an expanded U.S. commercial and official presence on Cuban territory would enable increasing numbers of Cubans to appreciate the irrelevancy of the Castroite system and to press for appropriate economic and political reforms. U.S. business interests lie both in an end to the embargo and the inevitable institutional changes that would lead to a more open and democratic society in Cuba.

IMPETUS TO REFORM

Cuba's efforts to promote direct foreign investment on a large scale are of relatively recent origin. Fidel Castro's accession to power in 1959, the subsequent nationalization of all U.S.–owned businesses, and the imposition of a Soviet-style command economy severely restricted opportunities for foreign investment in Cuba from the early 1960s to the early 1990s. During much of that thirty-year period, the Castro regime's main priorities were to promote socialist transformation in Cuba, to forge close economic and military ties with the Soviet Union, and to export the Cuban revolutionary model to other countries, primarily in Latin America, the Caribbean, and sub-Saharan Africa. Such ideologically driven pretensions, however, were no longer sustainable by the late 1980s. The winding-down of the cold war, the disintegration of the Soviet bloc, and above all the collapse of the Soviet Union itself—Cuba's foremost trade partner and its main economic lifeline—in 1991 had far-reaching consequences for the Cuban system. The regime was forced to change course, to jettison (at least temporarily) its revolutionary goals, and to open its doors to trade, tourism, and investment from noncommunist countries.

The end of the "special relationship" with the Soviet Union highlighted the quintessentially dependent and dysfunctional nature of the Cuban economic system. Generous Soviet trade subsidies (preferentially high and low prices respectively for Cuban sugar and nickel exports and for Soviet petroleum sold to Cuba) as well as soft loans used to cover Cuban trade deficits with the Soviet Union had been vitally important to Cuba's economy. According to one careful study, subsidization could have amounted to $2 billion to $3 billion annually, equivalent to 25 to 45 percent of Cuba's national income during the 1980s.[1] The Soviet successor states, though, have terminated most economic assistance to Cuba and now trade with the island at world market prices. The loss of these benefits has plunged the Cuban economy into a crisis from which it has not altogether recovered.[2] Between 1989 and 1993, Cuba's gross domestic product (GDP) fell 35 percent according to Cuban official figures (and up to 70 percent according to unofficial U.S. estimates), and total Cuban imports dropped 70 percent. Shipment of petroleum—the most vital single commodity supplied by the Soviet Union—fell from 13.3 million tons to 4 million tons over the period. Endemic power shortages and increased scarcity of food and medicine prompted antigovernment violence (including street demonstrations, looting, and attacks on police) and a huge increase in the exodus of refugees. In sum, the Cuban economy has become a shambles, threatening Cuba's internal stability and possibly even the political future of the Castroite order.[3]

The Cuban leadership's response to these dire conditions has been selective decommunization. Major policy initiatives have included sweeping changes in economic administration, a significant reorientation of foreign economic policy, and a retreat (perhaps a permanent one) from the egalitarian goals of the revolution. Ideology, in other words, "had to give way to practical answers," and reform became the order of the day. As Castro said in July 1993, "Life, reality . . . forces us to do what we never could have done otherwise . . . we must make concessions."[4] Beginning in 1993, the regime implemented a number of economic initiatives designed to stimulate domestic production of goods and services, and to increase inflows of foreign hard currency. In mid-1993, for example, the regime officially "depenalized" the holding and exchange of dollars by Cuban citizens; previously, possession of foreign currency by Cubans had been a criminal offense. The regime also established state-owned retail stores where Cubans could buy goods for hard currency.[5] By the late 1990s, foreign remittances to Cuba, usually by Cubans residing in the United States, had increased to an estimated $800 million annually, which (with great irony) made the United States the most important provider of foreign exchange to the island.[6] In the agricultural sector, large state farms were converted to collectives in which farmers "set their own goals and shared in profits"; by 1998, some 70 percent of the agriculture was said to be nonstate owned. Farmers were allowed to sell up to 30 percent of their production in private markets, or "agros," and to receive dollars in payment. Limited free markets in manufactured and consumer goods and in artwork and crafts were introduced in 1994. In addition, the regime authorized a degree of privatization of the margins of the economy. Self-employment was legalized in some 150 to 170 different occupations encompassing small service trade (electricians, barbers, mechanics, and the like) as well as small, family-owned restaurants, known as "paladares." By 1996, the number of registered self-employed Cubans exceeded two hundred thousand, and many more doubtless worked without official permission or descended into the underground economy.[7]

Important changes also occurred in the conduct of foreign economic relations, particularly in the areas of trade, tourism, and investment. For example, Cuba sought with some success to cultivate wider trading links in the wake of the Soviet Union's collapse. As of the late 1980s (1987), roughly 85 percent of Cuba's foreign trade had been with countries of the Council of Economic Mutual Assistance (CEMA)—that is, with the Soviet Union and Eastern Europe.[8] The Soviet Union was the dominant factor in this relationship; as noted, Soviet trade subsidies were a virtual life support system for the Cuban economy. Since that time, Cuba has worked to expand commercial ties with developed market economies such as Canada, the Netherlands, and Spain, with Latin American states such as Mexico and Argentina, and with communist states in Asia, primarily China and Vietnam. As of 1997, the Russian Federation—the principal successor state to the former Soviet Union—accounted for less than 15 percent of Cuba's foreign trade volume, though Russia remained Cuba's single most important trading partner.[9] Also significant in economic terms was the regime's decision to strengthen the tourism industry. Cuba never had been closed to tourism, but that activity had been a low economic priority before the 1990s. For instance, some 207,000 tourists visited Cuba in 1984, producing gross direct and indirect revenues of $84 million. By 1994, the number of visitors and revenues respectively had reached 630,000 and $850 million. In 1998, 1.4 million tourists visited the island, generating $1.8 billion in total revenues in that year. The number of hotel rooms more than doubled, from 13,664 to 28,000, between 1994 and 1998. Table 7.1 documents the extraordinary pace of expansion of tourism during the 1990s. Assuming that 60 percent of these revenues flowed back out of the country to pay for goods that tourists consumed, tourism amounted to approximately 5 percent of the Cuban economy in 1998; however, its percentage of total legal inflows of foreign exchange (including export income, foreign investment, and remittances, as well as tourism) was substantially higher, at least 15 percent.[10]

A third development was the opening of Cuba's economy to broader foreign participation. Foreign investment had not been excluded in earlier years; in 1992, the regime had enacted a joint venture law designed principally to encourage upgrading of Cuba's increasingly obsolescent manufacturing enterprises. However, that law limited the number of sectors open to investment and generally held the foreigners' stake to a maximum of 49 percent of the venture; hence, few foreign businesses were willing to take the plunge. Also, the overall ideological orientation of the Castro regime at the time (it was still advocating revolution in the third world) was not particularly pro-Western investment or supportive of private property rights. Beginning in the early 1990s, however, the Cuban government began to solicit foreign investment more aggressively, offering the prospect of joint ventures in a wide array of industrial, transportation, and agriculture enterprises. In 1992, Cuba—doubtless to reassure investors that Cuba was a safe place to do business—added a clause to its constitution to the effect that the government recognizes "ownership of property" by joint Cuban-foreign entities "established in accord with domestic law." In 1993, Cuba took the unprecedented step of granting international oil companies the right to participate in hydrocarbon development on Cuban territory.[11] As of 1999, nine foreign oil companies were helping Cuba to explore for oil and gas on twenty concession blocks, sixteen onshore and four offshore. In 1995, a new law was passed allowing foreign investment "in all sectors, excluding the population's health and educational services and the armed forces institutions with the exception of their commercial systems." The law also permitted "totally foreign capital companies"—that is, 100 percent ownership by foreigners—as well as majority foreign partnerships in joint ventures. The law further provided for the establishment of duty-free zones and industrial parks with special customs privileges, labor regulations, and tax benefits "in specially delineated areas of the national territory."[12] The results of the regime's new commercial strategy were generally positive. The number of Cuban joint ventures or economic associations with foreign companies increased from eighty in 1993 to almost four hundred in 1999 (see table 7.2). As of March 1999, according to figures supplied by the U.S. Department of State, foreign entities had announced plans to invest $6.12 billion in Cuba, of which $1.7 billion represented funds committed or actually delivered to the island. According to Cuban government sources, committed funds had reached $2 billion by year-end 1999.[13]

Finally, in an effort to spur trade and investment and to diversify commercial dealings, the regime took steps to decentralize administration of the foreign trade sector. A plethora of more or less self-financing trade cooperatives and holding companies have been set up—Cubanacan S.A., Cubalse, CIMEX

Table 7.1 Growth of Tourism in Cuba

Year	Number of Visitors	Gross Revenue
1984	207,000	$84 million
1993	500,000	NA
1994	630,000	$850 million
1995	800,000	$1.0 billion
1996	1,004,000	$1.375 billion
1997	1,170,000	$1.54 billion
1998	1,400,000	$1.8 billion
1999	1,620,000	$2.0 billion

Source: U.S.–Cuba Trade and Economic Council, <http\\:www.cubatrade.org>.

Table 7.2 Joint Ventures and Economic Associations with Cuban Government-operated Companies

Year	Number
1992	80
1993	129
1994	180
1995	212
1996	260
1997	317
1998	345
1999	374

Sources: U.S.–Cuba Trade and Economic Council, <http\\:www.cubatrade.org>; media reports.

S.A., Cuba Export, and the like—that are allowed to operate independently of the central state apparatus while remitting part of their revenues to the state.[14] (Some such entities predate the demise of the Soviet Union.) One of the largest of these companies, Panama-based CIMEX S.A., comprises more than forty separate subsidiaries covering spheres of trade, manufacturing, banking, consulting services, shipping, tourism, warehousing, shopping, real estate, and cattle ranching. Some CIMEX subsidiaries may transact business on a global scale. For example, the tourism enterprise Havanatur S.A. maintains offices in at least four countries: Cuba, Panama, France, and the United States. CIMEX earned revenues in 1991 of more than $200 million, some of which was allegedly derived from clandestine or illegal activities, such as contraband trade with the United States and cocaine smuggling.[15]

REFORM'S LIMITED REACH

The previously mentioned reforms, introduced mostly in the early to mid 1990s, helped avert an economic meltdown in Cuba. The Cuban economy, which was in virtual free fall from 1989 to 1993, turned around in 1994 and registered gains every year thereafter (see table 7.3). Particularly impressive successes were recorded in sectors most influenced by foreign investment; for instance, revenues from tourism (many of Cuba's new hotels are joint ventures with foreign firms) almost tripled from 1993 to 1998. Production of petroleum grew from 528,000 tons in 1991 to 1,678,000 tons in 1998, a 200 percent increase (though Cuba still imports 80 percent of its oil).[16] Living standards have improved markedly since the early 1990s. With the advent of private agricultural markets, meat and produce have become more available to consumers, although (in the words of a U.S. Information Agency report) "at prices beyond the reach of most citizens living on peso-only incomes or pensions." More cars can be seen on the streets of Havana, there are more stores stocked with luxury products, and more construction sites can be seen around the city. Private holdings of dollars and other hard currency are increasing; as of the late 1990s, an estimated 30 to 50 percent of Cubans had access to foreign currency—and hence to better-quality consumer goods—via remittances from abroad, Cuban-foreign joint ventures, or tourism-related activities.[17]

Nevertheless, the Cuban economy remains in precarious shape, and future prospects are uncertain. As of early 1999, the economy was still almost 25 percent below the level attained in 1989. Cuba runs a disturbingly large balance of payments deficit; in 1998, exports decreased 11 percent because of lower commodity prices for sugar and nickel, while imports rose 6 percent, widening the deficit from $1.3 billion to $1.7 billion. Cuba's convertible currency debt seems unmanageably large—$10.5 billion in 1996, almost as large as the country's GDP in that year. This figure does not include an estimated $20 million in ruble-equivalent debt borrowed during Soviet times and now owed to Russia.[18]

Viewed overall, the performance of the economy under Castro has been disastrous. In pre-Castro times, Cuba was a center of banking, finance, and insurance, and served as a commercial bridge between the United States and South America. With the socialization of the economy and the emigration of affluent citizens, the bridge function has long since passed to Miami. In many respects the econ-

Table 7.3   Cuba's Economic Growth in the 1990s

Year	Percent
1989–1993	−35
1994	0.7
1995	2.5
1996	7.8
1997	2.5
1998	1.2
1999	6.2

Sources: U.S.–Cuba Trade and Economic Council, <http\\:www.cubatrade.org>; Cuban economic statistics.

omy has stagnated. For example, in the late 1950s, Cuba's per capita income was approximately four times that of Spain; as of the late 1990s, it was less than one-tenth of Spain's. Cuba's exports were almost on a par with Mexico's in 1958 ($732 million and $736 million, respectively); by 1997, exports from Cuba had increased a mere 160 percent to $1.9 billion, whereas Mexico's had increased 150-fold to $110 billion. Cuban rice production actually declined from 1958 to 1996. Pre-Castro Cuba ranked third in Latin America in per capita food consumption, but today it ranks last. There are fewer cars in Cuba today than in the 1950s, the only Latin American country in which this is the case.[19]

Poverty still is ubiquitous on the island. In terms of purchasing power, Cuba's eleven million citizens are the second poorest in the Western Hemisphere after the Haitians. The average Cuban salary, according to Cuba's Central Bank, is the equivalent of only $10 per month. A doctor earns a meager $20 per month, a nurse $17 to $18, a librarian $15, and a sales clerk in a government store $7 to $8. (Admittedly, remittances and other hard-currency income add significantly to the real incomes of some Cubans.) Unemployment is also rife; the Cuban government's own figures indicate that an astonishing 55 percent of Cubans over the age of twenty have no viable means of employment—that is, they are not working in the formal labor sector (such as state organizations, cooperatives, mixed enterprises, political organizations, private associations, and self-employment). Undoubtedly, this 55 percent figure includes Cubans who are unregistered self-employed or who are engaged in various black market or criminal activities. Many others, though, simply may be jobless.[20]

Overall, Cuba's economic outlook remains bleak, even while the economy continues to grow. Over the long run, economic performance is likely to be constrained by two main factors. One is simply the nature of Cuba's government. Cuba is still a socialist country, and its economy is mostly state run. Private enterprise in the classic sense of the term is confined to individuals and families and exists only at the margins of society—there are no companies or corporations in private Cuban hands. Privatization of state enterprise, in fact, was specifically repudiated at a recent (1997) Communist Party Congress. Foreign companies' only choices of joint venture partners are state-controlled entities (even if these entities have acquired more autonomy and flexibility in recent years). This anachronistic structure breeds inefficiency, constricts investment, and jeopardizes economic growth. Reform, in other words, has not proceeded far or fast enough. Some of Cuba's technocrat-types, like Carlos Lage, vice president of the Council of State, and Ricardo Alarcon, a Politburo member and president of the National Assembly of People's Power, are reputed to favor further economic liberalization (though whether they could support transformation to a full-scale market economy is unclear). However, most of the power structure in Cuba, including the military, the upper echelons of the Communist Party, and Fidel and Raul Castro display little enthusiasm for the economic reform movement, regarding it as a temporary expedient, rather than a long-term development strategy.

An additional constraint on Cuban economic growth, which is rooted in America's historical antipathy toward the Castro regime, is the U.S. trade embargo with Cuba. In place since the early 1960s (though in various permutations since then), the embargo prohibits most forms of commerce with Cuba by U.S. companies and their foreign subsidiaries and effectively disallows U.S. private investment on the island. With American businesspersons all but shut out of the Cuban market, limited as it is, Cuba must look farther afield for commercial partners. Also, the embargo and reinforcing legislation practically exclude Cuba from membership in international organizations such as the World Bank and the Inter-American Development Bank, and hence from access to low-interest loans from these bodies. The full impact of the embargo on Cuba's economy cannot be estimated precisely—the subject is widely debated—but in the aftermath of the loss of Soviet subsidies, the costs probably have been considerable. The Cuban government estimates that the embargo's opportunity costs, calculated in terms of additional freight charges (say, importing rice from Vietnam instead of Louisiana), higher borrowing costs (taking out loans at commercial rates of interest), and associated losses in foreign exchange transactions were $800 million in 1998 alone.[21] Many U.S.–based observers, though, believe that the main obstacle to progress in Cuba is the state-controlled economic system, not the U.S. embargo. In any event, the embargo and Communist rule in Cuba are inextricably linked and (to some extent) mutually reinforcing, as will be discussed later on. This, of course, is a tragedy for Cuba. As one American Cuba specialist observes, "Simply put, since 1990s Cuba has reverted to its historic economic position: a small island with few resources, a minuscule market of 11 million poor people whose 'natural' partner is the United States."[22]

Some dysfunctions of economic reform in Cuba also need to be addressed. Reform has resulted in economic gains, at least for the time being, but the gains have been accompanied by significant social costs. One obvious result has been the emergence of a new type of social stratification based on access to hard currency. Beneficiaries have been Cubans in the nonstate or foreign-oriented sectors and Cubans with Miami connections. Core elements of the bureaucracy and the political elite have been the losers. As a recent article in *Foreign Policy* explains this process: "The self-employed owners of paladares [private restaurants], farmers, artisans, joint venture employees and prostitutes are enjoying their taste of capitalism and want more. But doctors, educators, scientists and government employees who have sacrificed years climbing up the traditional socialist ladder rightly feel left behind. For them, still trapped in the peso economy, it is the end of the revolution."[23]

Such a bifurcation of the economy is understandably generating resentment and discontent among traditional professional and official elites. Moreover, officials are becoming increasingly susceptible to bribery, especially those working in the international sector of the economy. Recent punitive dismissals of the director of the Villa de Berroa Free Trade Zone (managed by CIMEX), the director of the Hotel Division of Cubanacan (the umbrella Cuban tourist agency), and of warehouse managers of Cubalse (a government-operated trading company) are apparent cases in point.[24]

Furthermore, the reform dynamic is weakening grassroots' political controls and eroding the ideological legitimacy of the regime. A consequence has been a "creeping moral laxity," reflected in significant increases in lawbreaking, including street crime, armed robbery, prostitution, currency speculation, people smuggling, and narcotics trafficking.[25] Economic motivations are, of course, central to the growth of criminal activity, but other factors—including impatience with the utter tedium of Cuban daily life—help explain the trend. As one high-priced Cuban call girl explains, "If I were not a prostitute I would be bored to death. How else would I spend my nights? I suppose watching television with my neighbors because I do not have a TV."[26]

A particularly unsettling manifestation of the unraveling of the Castroite revolutionary order has been Cuba's growing importance in the hemispheric drug trade both as a transshipment center and as a market for drugs in its own right. Cases of collusion between high-ranking Cuban officials and Colombian trafficking organizations had been documented in the late 1980s. According to Cuban government sources, the Ministry of Interior orchestrated fifteen successful smuggling operations moving approximately six tons of Colombian cocaine through the island between 1987 and 1989. Although the responsible officials were executed or purged, the flow of drugs continues, possibly with some government connivance.[27] For instance, in early December 1998, Colombian police in the Caribbean port city of Cartagena intercepted 7.25 tons of cocaine hidden in false bottoms and walls of six containers that were to be loaded onto a ship bound for Cuba. The consignment—destined eventually for Spain, according to most accounts—was addressed to a Havana company, Artesania Caribena Poliplast y Royo, that was reportedly a joint venture of two Spanish businessmen and "several Cuban state companies."[28] In a 1999 incident, reported by informants inside Cuba, Cuban customs officials allegedly received $20,000 in bribes to permit the offloading of two tons of cocaine and the temporary storage of the drugs in an "industrial warehouse" in a port on the south side of the island; that particular shipment apparently was on its way to the southeastern United States.[29]

Moreover, Cuba itself is probably ripe for penetration by organized drug mafias. According to Cuban health authorities, roughly 140 Cubans have sought treatment for drug abuse in the past year, compared with almost none in the mid-1990s. In Havana as of mid-1999, cocaine sold for $20 per gram and $7,000 to $10,000 per kilo. In a two-tiered price structure, imported and domestically grown marijuana sold for $70 and $35 per ounce, respectively. Reflecting the progressive disintegration of the Communist control structure, parts of Havana Vieja (Old Havana) and San Miguel del Padron have reportedly become virtual free zones for drug dealers and other criminal elements. Cuba in the 1940s and 1950s, it will be recalled, was a playground controlled by North American Mafia families and a haven for drug trafficking, prostitution, and casino gambling. With drugs and prostitution on their way back to Cuba's hotels, nightclubs, and streets, Cuba again could become the criminal paradise that it was in pre-Castro times.[30]

THE INVESTMENT PICTURE

Despite intractable economic problems and apparently increasing societal tensions, Cuba is managing to attract some foreign investment. As of early 1999, as noted earlier, investment funds committed or delivered to Cuba had reached some $1.7 billion to $1.8 billion. Companies or government entities representing twenty-four countries had invested in the island (see table 7.4). The four largest country-investors in Cuba—Canada, Mexico, Italy, and Spain—accounted for 87 percent of this capital influx. Unsurprisingly, the United States is not represented in Cuba; more surprisingly, perhaps, is the absence of Russia and eastern European countries from the list, given the multiplicity of Cuba's former economic ties to the CEMA countries. Investment in Cuba was concentrated in four sectors: telecommunications, mining and petroleum extraction, tourism, and accounting, which accounted for 37 percent, 20 percent, 20 percent, and 11 percent, respectively, of the total influx of funds. This investment configuration, though, is changing. In a major, recently announced deal, a Madrid-based company acquired a 50 percent share in Habanos S.A., the government cigar and tobacco marketer for a reported $500 million.

Under current U.S. legislation, the Cuban market is largely closed to American corporations and their subsidiaries outside the United States. U.S. firms cannot invest legally in Cuba or form joint ventures with Cuban entities. Indeed, the 1996 Cuban Liberty and Democracy Solidarity ("Helms-Burton") Act seeks to discourage even non–U.S. businesses from setting up shop in Cuba; specifically, it exposes foreign investment in nationalized Cuban properties (termed "trafficking in confiscated property") to the possibility of legal challenges in U.S. court by American citizens (including former Cuban nationals) who at one time owned these properties. Some U.S. trade with the island, nevertheless, is permitted. The Cuban Democracy Act (CDA) of 1992 tightened the embargo by disallowing most forms of trade between third-country U.S. subsidiaries and Cuba; however, a section of the CDA entitled "Support for the Cuban People" set the stage for possible U.S. exports of food, medicines, and informational materials to the island, as well as for the establishment of direct U.S.–Cuban postal and telecommunication links.[31] (A recent piece of legislation for humanitarian aid just passed the House.)

The current U.S. regulatory regime in theory permits U.S. businesses "to execute and implement contracts" in twenty different fields (see table 7.5). U.S. businesspersons are also permitted to travel to Cuba to identify commercial—that

Table 7.4 Foreign Investment in Cuba, early 1999

Country	Announced (in millions of U.S. dollars)	Committed–Delivered (in millions of U.S. dollars)
Australia	500	N/A
Austria	.5	.1
Brazil	150	20
Canada	1,807	600
Chile	69	30
China	10	5
Dominican Republic	5	1
France	100	50
Germany	10	2
Greece	2	.5
Honduras	7	1
Israel	22	7
Italy	397	387
Jamaica	2	1
Japan	2	.5
Mexico	1,806	450
Netherlands	300	40
Panama	2	.5
South Africa	400	5
Spain	350	100.3
Sweden	10	1
United Kingdom	75	50
Uruguay	.5	.3
Venezuela	50	3
TOTAL	**6,077**	**1755.2**

Source: U.S.–Cuba Trade and Economic Council, <http\\:www.cubatrade.org>.

is import-export—opportunities in their areas. In practice, commerce with Cuba is still heavily embargoed. No export financing is authorized, and most deals require licenses from the Treasury Department's Office of Foreign Assets Control or from the Bureau of Export Administration of the Department of Commerce or both. Obtaining such approvals can be costly and time consuming—though a number of U.S. companies seem willing to make the effort.

In this regime, for example, regulations allow sales of food or agricultural imports only on "a case-by-case basis," and licenses will only be issued for exports to entities "independent of the Cuban government" such as family-owned restaurants, private farmers, and religious groups. The burden of proof that sales will reach their designated targets is on the seller. Would-be exporters of medicine must also demonstrate that such products will be used for the benefit of "the Cuban people," which obviously creates enormous problems of interpretation.

Table 7.5   Permitted Areas of Business Activity in Cuba, 1999

Agricultural products
Air charter services
Artwork
Communications
Cultural events
Entertainment
Exhibitions
Farm supplies
Food sales
Informational materials
Medical instruments
Medical supplies
Medicated products
Medicines
Money transfer services
Package delivery services
Pharmaceuticals
Telecommunications
Travel services

Selling can be an arduous process.[32] In January 2000, U.S. firms sponsored an exhibition in Havana designed to promote exports to Cuba of U.S.–made health care products, medical equipment, and medicines. Representatives of the exhibitor companies needed licenses to travel to Cuba. A license also had to be issued for each individual product displayed by the companies, and an additional license was required if that display model was to be sold to Cuban entities upon termination of the exhibition.[33]

Despite these bureaucratic obstacles, U.S. corporate interest in the Cuban market has been growing in the 1990s. One indication of such interest is the number of visits to Cuba by U.S. business executives, which grew steadily between 1994 and 1999 (see table 7.6). The actual volume of permitted business activity with Cuba has so far been small (an estimated $750 million worth from October 1994 through December 1998), but a few commercial highlights—deals or deals-in-the-making—can be mentioned. One of the most important is an agreement between Smith-Kline-Beecham (a Pennsylvania-based U.S. subsidiary of the British firm of the same name) and Cuba's Carlos Finlay Institute for testing, chemical trials, and marketing of a meningitis-B vaccine developed by the institute. Smith-Kline-Beecham would make an initial payment to Finlay of $10 million to $20 million, apparently in health care and food products, for the exclusive right to market the vaccine, and would pay the Cubans an undetermined amount of royalties on international sales thereafter. (U.S. licensing approval for this transaction, incidentally, took a total of eighteen months.) Moreover, as of 1999, the Office of Foreign Assets Control had issued 214 licenses to 115 U.S. companies to provide Cuba-related travel services, air carrier services, and electronic funds transfers to individuals "subject to U.S. law"; some of the beneficiaries include American Express, Western Union Financial Service, and Money Gram Payment Systems. Several companies, including AT&T, MCI, Sprint, and IDB World Com now provide long-distance telephone and data transmission services between the United States and Cuba. Executives of Time-Warner and other media companies have traveled to Cuba to discuss opportunities for export and import of movies, films, and other types of publications. Trade in such informational materials, which (unlike food or medicines) are subject to few if any licensing restrictions under U.S. law, should develop fairly rapidly in future years.[34]

Finally, pressures from the U.S. business community and from the farm belt have occasioned changes in political thinking on Cuba. One manifestation is recent (1999) visits to Cuba by prominent U.S. politicians such as Senator Arlen Specter and Governor George Ryan of Illinois. (The latter's stated view of the embargo is that "isolating Cuba is not in the best interest of the United States.") Furthermore, in the fall of 1999, the Senate voted seventy to twenty-eight to add an amendment to the annual agricultural appropriations bill that would eliminate existing restrictions on foreign sales of food and medicine (including, of course, to Cuba). The amendment, though, was defeated in the House, where anti-Castro sentiment runs strong. As of this writing, Congress is contemplating bills that would facilitate such sales; unfortunately, export financing would be disallowed.[35]

Quite obviously, the embargo makes little sense from a purely economic perspective, since both geography and tradition make Cuba and the United States natural trade partners. U.S. companies and their subsidiaries have lost markets to western European, Canadian, Latin American, and Asian competitors. Cuba must pay additional carrying costs to import necessities such as foodstuffs and agricultural inputs (e.g., rice from China and Vietnam and fertilizer from Russia) from faraway countries. Two Michigan-based consultants, Donna Rich and Michael Kaplowitz, argued in a congressional testimony that without the embargo, U.S. companies "could sell about $500 million worth of grain to Cuba each year; U.S. chemical companies could supply up to 100 percent of Cuba's

Table 7.6 U.S. Corporate Executives Visiting Cuba

Year	Number
1994	500
1995	1,300
1996	1,500
1997	2,000
1998	2,500
1999 (estimated)	2,800

Source: U.S.–Cuba Trade and Economic Council.

fertilizer needs of about $150 million annually [and] U.S. medical suppliers could sell about $90 million worth of medical products to Cuba every year." Rich and Kaplowitz also pointed out, correctly in this writer's opinion, that *some of the damage done to U.S. business interests by the embargo may be irreparable*; in their words, "Cuba's beachfront property is being divided up among our major competitors, as well as oil and mineral rights."[36] The self-centered and revanchist behavior of the Cuban-American lobby and their allies in Congress are largely to blame for this unfortunate state of affairs.

Still, the total size of the Cuban "pie" is relatively modest, and Americans may not be missing much by being excluded from that market. Consider the economic constraints. Cuba is poor—in terms of purchasing power parity, its per capita income exceeds only Haiti's in this hemisphere. Cuba's imports in 1998 were only $3 billion, approximately 80 percent those of the neighboring Dominican Republic, which has 30 percent fewer people. Its grain imports averaged only about $250 million in the mid to late 1990s. Cuba's foreign indebtedness, which stands at anywhere from $10 billion to $30 billion depending on how it is calculated is virtually unmanageable for a country that size; in effect, the country is bankrupt. Finally, Cuba's principal exports—citrus, shrimp, sugar, nickel, and cigars—are produced domestically in the United States or are available in ample quantities from other suppliers in the hemisphere. Such factors necessarily limit prospects for expanded trade with Cuba, at least in the short and medium term, although U.S. firms would be well positioned to capture existing markets for certain products—grain and fertilizers, for instance.

Lifting the embargo, of course, would allow U.S. private investment in Cuba, but here also the prospects for growth are uncertain. As noted, Cuba's socialized economy is itself a constraint—virtually the only opportunities for investment are in joint ventures with the government. (Although Cuba permits 100 percent foreign ownership in theory, such entities pay significantly higher taxes on profit and on "utilization of the labor force" than do joint ventures; hence, the latter is the preferred vehicle for foreign investing in Cuba.[37]) While a state-controlled economy offers advantages (little or no labor unrest and relative social tranquility), the bureaucracy can be stifling. Investors, for example, complain about a huge paperwork burden on foreign companies; inability to hire and pay Cuban workers directly—that is, without going through state enterprises—and Cuba's underlying culture of hostility to private enterprise. Cuba's obsolete communications (including a forty-year-old telephone system), atrociously maintained roads, and decrepit electrical power systems add to the frustration. Ian Delaney, chairman of the Toronto-based Sherritt International Corporation—a company heavily invested in mining, agricultural, and tourist ventures in Cuba—declared in a recent speech that "There's a limit to the rate at which you can invest in Cuba that is defined by the infrastructure." Apparently referring to the company's overall experience in that country, he added, "We would not want to leave anyone with the impression that this has been a satisfactory investment. It has not."[38]

To be sure, the Cuban market's limited potential for exporters and investors largely reflects the direct and indirect effects of the embargo itself. Yet trade and investment would not necessarily flourish even without it. As the head of the U.S. Chamber of Commerce, Thomas Donohue recently observed, "The embargo has no doubt been a hardship—but more than any other factor, *the lack of independent, private enterprise has held Cuba back*"[39] (italics mine). Sustained progress on the economic front will require extensive reconstruction of the Cuban economy as well as the dismantling of statist controls on the private sector. This in turn must be accompanied or preceded by significant liberalization in the political sphere, including the departure from power of the more hard-line (and anti-free enterprise) elements of the Cuban leadership. These are longer-term prospects. In the meantime, the real U.S. economic stake in Cuba must be considered problematic, even if intriguing business possibilities exist in some areas.

Indeed, the core argument against the embargo should be more strategic than economic—it relates to overall U.S. security concerns vis-à-vis Cuba and the hemisphere. On the one hand, in the post-Soviet era Cuba is no longer in a position to foment revolution around the globe or to challenge U.S. preeminence in this hemisphere. Moreover, as the Defense Intelligence Agency noted in a 1997 report, "Cuba's weak military poses a negligible conventional threat to the United States or surrounding countries."[40] The essential national security justification for the embargo has thus evaporated. The new justification, embodied in both the Cuban Democracy Act and the Helms-Burton Act, is to hasten the demise of the Castro regime and the advent of democratic government in Cuba. Helms-Burton, in fact makes Castro's departure from power a precondition for normalization of U.S.–Cuba ties. Whether or how much the embargo has weakened Castro's leadership is uncertain. Like other recent visitors to Cuba, this writer is struck by the increasingly vocal criticism of Castro (though not public criticism or organized protest) by educated Cubans. Certainly, events of the past decade—the end of Soviet subsidies, the tightening of the embargo, and the Cuban regime's small steps toward economic liberalization—have highlighted the failures of socialist economic policies, throwing into question much of the Castroite revolutionary legacy. The embargo, on the other hand, is a blunt instrument. To the extent that it generates opposition to Castro's rule, it increases Cuban economic misery and therefore poses risks of a new kind for the United States.

In the post-Soviet, post–cold war era, Cuba is increasingly reverting to the status of "just another" Caribbean country. Core U.S. strategic interests in the Caribbean are largely negative—policymakers traditionally have perceived the region as a geographical nuisance and a perennial source of trouble for the United States. The regime's endemic economic and political problems create spillover effects that tend to gravitate northward. One bottom-line U.S. concern is the prospect of uncontrolled mass migration to the United States. As a recent Council on Foreign Relations report on Cuba observed, "Having tens or hundreds of thousands of Cubans fleeing across the United States would create both humanitarian and political emergencies for the United States."[41] Already we see harbingers of Cuba's economic crisis; more than 23,000 Cubans have "fled to Florida on makeshift rafts, inner tubes and boats."[42] "Boat people," of course, continue to arrive on Florida's southern shores, and pressures to emigrate from Cuba, as reflected in the number of Cuban applications for U.S. visas, appear to be intensifying according to U.S. diplomatic sources in Havana. A related concern is the threat of economically driven internal unrest, leading to increased antigovernment violence and perhaps a complete breakdown of civil order. In such a scenario, the United States might have to intervene militarily to restore order and to install a new political regime. While the United States has intervened in the internal affairs of Caribbean states before in this century (most recently in Grenada, Haiti, and the Dominican Republic), the costs of a military operation in Cuba would be almost unimaginably high—no U.S. presidential administration would be anxious to undertake such an adventure.

A third priority issue for U.S. and foreign business interests in Cuba and in much of the rest of the Caribbean is the ascendant power of organized crime, especially the illicit drug industry. Cuba, it should be stressed, occupies a favored strategic position from a drug trafficking perspective. The island lies only ninety miles south of Key West, Florida, on a direct flight path between Colombia's Caribbean coast and the southeastern United States. Potent economic or socioeconomic forces—deteriorating living conditions for most Cubans, increasing relative poverty of the official class, and visible increases in crime and corruption—also make Cuba a target of opportunity for drug dealers. Indeed, tons of Colombian cocaine may already be flowing through the island, possibly with the connivance of corrupt government officials. This is not the kind of outcome favorable to a relationship with the Cuban government. The cozy partnership between the U.S. Mafia and the Cuban political elites in the 1940s and 1950s may be recalled here. The emergence of a bastion of organized crime and drugs ninety miles from U.S. shores operating smuggling ventures and other illegal activities is hardly in the best interest of the United States, other countries in this hemisphere, or the businesspersons who have to operate and make legitimate deals there.

In sum, Cuba's economic plight and its side effects run counter to important U.S. objectives and interests vis-à-vis that country. To the extent our embargo against trade with Cuba has damaged its economy, Americans may suffer. Cuba's problems have significant stateside repercussions. Trashing Cuba's economy also diminishes future U.S. business opportunities on the island. Admittedly, the Castro regime remains a noxious influence, if no longer a serious threat within the hemisphere. However, the safest and most humane way to advance the cause of peaceful democratic transition is to reduce the country's economic and political isolation, not to increase it.

Normalizing trade and investment ties, extending U.S. diplomatic recognition, establishing a credible U.S. commercial and official presence on the island, and cultivating extensive links to Cuban officials on matters ranging from economic policy to narcotics control—in the longer term all would generate pressures for a more open and (eventually) for a dismantling of Castroite rule. In the absence of the U.S. embargo alone, Cubans would see more clearly the utter irrelevancy of their current system; with the support of the international community, they can then proceed to make the appropriate adjustments.

If infrastructure conditions are ample in a given area, or can be made satisfactory through amenable contract negotiations, the forward-looking investor (particularly in service industries and basic commodities) would do well to begin planning. Businesspersons in industries of key potential should look beyond their immediate bottom line and begin planning now. They should make an effort to join the raft of new pioneers who have taken advantage of more relaxed travel restrictions to scout opportunities and size up the situation for themselves. The investor should become an advocate in the United States for reform of our official—and somewhat dogmatic—posture toward Cuba, and lay the groundwork for doing concrete business in the near future.

The process of change can move quickly, especially once Castro has departed. Businesspersons should focus their attention now on potential local partnerships with technocrats, with good connections, who are not wedded to the Castro orthodoxy and seem to favor a broader and freer market.

NOTES

1. Archibald M. Ritter. "Challenge and Policy Imperatives to the Economy," in Irving Lewis Horowitz, ed., *Cuban Communism, 1959–1995* (New Brunswick, N.J.: Transaction, 1995), pp. 345–51. Ritter's estimates do not include subsidized prices that paid for Cuban nickel. In addition to the subsidies, the Soviet Union also lent money to Cuba for long-term development projects. Total Soviet assistance to Cuba has been calculated at more than $6 billion annually.

2. In pre-1991 times, terms of trade with the Soviet Union were highly favorable to Cuba. Cuba could import 6 to 8 million tons of oil in exchange for 1 ton of sugar. By the end of 1991, calculations based on world market prices indicated that Cuba would get only 1.3 to 1.4 million tons of oil for 1 ton of sugar. See Yuriy Pavlov, "The End of the Road," in *Cuban Communism*, 9th ed., ed. Irving L. Horowitz and Jaime Suchlicki (New Brunswick, N.J.: Transaction, 1998), pp. 840–41.

3. See for example Peter Schwab, *Cuba: Confronting the U.S. Embargo* (New York: St. Martin's Press, 1999), pp. 38–41, 90–91.

4. Ana Julia Jatar-Hausmann, "What Cuba Can Teach Russia," *Foreign Policy*, no. 113 (Winter 1998–1999), pp. 87–94.

5. Jatar-Hausmann, "What Cuba Can Teach Russia"; Jorge F. Perez Lopez, "Cuba's Underground Economy," in *Cuban Communism*, 9th ed., ed. Irving L. Horowitz and Jaime Suchlicki (New Brunswick, N.J.: Transaction, 1998), pp. 253–54.

6. Author interview with U.S. diplomats in Havana, July 30, 1999.

7. Perez Lopez, "Cuba's Underground Economy," pp. 249–51; Jatar-Hausmann, "What Cuba Can Teach Russia," pp. 94–96; Tim Johnson, "Firms Invest in Cuba . . . but

Cautiously," *Miami Herald*, 21 March 1999, cited in U.S. Information Agency, "Cuba Update" (March 1999), p. 31; Schwab, *Cuba*, p. 93.

8. Carmelo Mesa-Lago, "Cuba's Economic Policies and Strategies for the 1990s," in *Cuban Communism*, 9th ed., ed. Irving L. Horowitz and Jaime Suchlicki (New Brunswick, N.J.: Transaction, 1998), p. 187.

9. Central Intelligence Agency, *World Factbook, 1998* (Washington, D.C.: Central Intelligence Agency, 1999), p. 123.

10. U.S.–Cuba Trade and Economic Council (USCTEC) web site at http\\:www.cuba-trade.org. See especially sections on "1999 Commercial Highlights," "Realities of Market: Cuba," and "Foreign Investment and Cuba." Last accessed: September 19, 2000.

11. Perez Lopez, "Cuba's Underground Economy," pp. 46–49.

12. Consultores Asociados, S.A., *Legal Profile of Foreign Investment in Cuba* (Havana: Ediciones Ponton Caribe, S.A., November 1996), pp. 59–101; "Nueva Ley de la Inversion Extranjera," *Business Tips in Cuba* (Havana), undated, pp. v–xv. Law originally published in *Gaceta Oficial Extraordinaria*, no. 3 (6 September 1995).

13. Pascal Fletcher, "Expansion Plans Are in the Pipeline: Oil," *The Financial Times*, 24 March 1999, p. 4; USCTEC.

14. Perez Lopez, "Cuba's Underground Economy," pp. 248–49.

15. *The Cuban Democracy Act of 1992, S.2918*. Hearing before the Subcommittee on Western Hemisphere and Peace Corps Affairs of the Committee on Foreign Relations, United States Senate, August 5, 1992 (Washington, DC: U.S. Government Printing Office, 1992), pp. 62, 71–76.

16. Jose Rodriguez, minister of Economy and Planning; Osvaldo Martinez, president of the Commission on Economic Affairs. "Cifras y Datos de la Economia Cubana en 1998," *Havana*, 21 December 1998, pp. 1–8.

17. Juan O. Tamayo, "Troubling Changes Fan Fear, Anxiety in Havana," *Miami Herald*, 17 March 1999, cited in U.S. Information Agency, "Cuba Update," p. 27; Johnson, "Firms Invest in Cuba . . . but Cautiously."

18. Johnson, "Firms Invest in Cuba . . . but Cautiously"; Central Intelligence Agency, *World Factbook*, pp. 121–22; "Cifras y Datos," p. 2.

19. Fletcher, "Expansion Plans Are in the Pipeline"; Department of State, Bureau of Inter-American Affairs, "Zenith and Eclipse: A Comparative Look at Socio-economic Conditions in Pre-Castro Cuba and Present-day Cuba," February 9, 1999, cited in U.S. Information Agency, "Cuba Update," pp. 11–21.

20. Central Intelligence Agency, *World Factbook*, relevant pages; "Cuba 1996: Employment and Population Rates—Ages 20 and above," cited in U.S. Information Agency, "Cuba Update," p. 23; author's street interviews, Havana, July 29–30, 1999.

21. "Cifras y Datos," p. 5.

22. Michael Radu, "Don't Reward Castro, Keep the Embargo," *Orbis*, vol. 42, no. 4 (Fall 1998), p. 549.

23. Jatar-Hausmann, "What Cuba Can Teach Russia," p. 97.

24. USCTEC.

25. Mireya Navarro, "As It Opens to Outsiders, Cuba Is Infected by Crime," *New York Times*, 4 April 1999, p. 3.

26. Serge Kovaleski, "Havana Daydreamin'," *Washington Post*, 5 March 1999, p. A27. For an excellent Cuban account of the rise of prostitution in Havana based on interviews with prostitutes and law enforcement officers, see Pedro Juan Gutierrez, "Cuantas Caras

Tiena Eva," *Bohemia* 19 December 1997, reprinted in Centro de Estudios Sobre America, *Cuba es el Unes* (December 1997), pp. 123–25.

27. Rensselaer W. Lee III, "Cuba's Drug Transit Traffic," *Society*, vol. 34, no. 3 (March–April 1997), pp. 51–52.

28. For example, see Tim Johnson, "Drug Trafficking through Cuba on the Rise, Investigators Say," *Miami Herald*, 27 January 1999, p. 17A; "Colombia: Implications of Castro's Charges against Spaniards," Foreign Broadcast Information Service, Daily Report, FBIS-LAT-99-016, January 11, 1999 (electronic version); "The Disputatious Diplomacy of Drugs," *The Economist*, 11 September 1999, p. 37.

29. A western diplomat based in Barbados reported this incident; author interviews, Miami, Fla., July 23–24, 1999.

30. Author interviews with Cuban health authorities and with drug addicts undergoing treatment, Havana, July 28, 1999.

31. *National Defense Authorization Act for Fiscal Year 1993*, Public Law 102-484, 102nd Cong., (23 October 1992), Title XVII, "Cuban Democracy Act of 1992," pp. 2575–81. See especially Section 1705, "Support for the Cuban People," pp. 2577–78, which outlines conditions for exports of food, medicine, and medical supplies, and also authorizes telecommunications services between the United States and Cuba. Wording of this law emphasizes that the U.S. objective is to foster a "peaceful transition" to representative democracy in Cuba. See also *Cuban Liberty and Democracy Solidarity Act of 1996*, Public Law 104-114, 104th Cong., (12 March 1996), pp. 785–824. See especially Title III, "Protection of the Property Rights of United States Nationals," pp. 814–22. The act authorizes the president to suspend implementation of the provisions of Title III at six-month intervals, which President William Clinton so far has done. Title IV of the act bars entry into the United States of foreigners said to be trafficking in expropriated U.S. property, a category that includes business executives of many companies invested in Cuba. Needless to say, Helms-Burton elicited a storm of international protest, disrupting vital relationships with Canada, Europe, and Mexico. For a good commentary on the embargo legislation, see Wayne Smith, "Our Dysfunctional Cuban Embargo," *Orbis*, vol. 42, no. 4 (Fall 1998), pp. 533–44.

32. State Department, Bureau of Inter-American Affairs, "Fact Sheet on U.S.–Cuba Policy Initiatives," in *U.S.–Cuba Relations in the 21st Century*, p. 62.

33. USCTEC.

34. USCTEC.

35. USCTEC; "Seven Hours with Fidel," *The Economist*, 30 October 1999, p. 32.

36. "Prepared Statement of Donna Rich Kaplowitz and Michael Kaplowitz," in *The Cuban Democracy Act of 1992*, pp. 111–12.

37. *Legal Profile of Foreign Investment in Cuba*, pp. 85, 93.

38. USCTEC.

39. Thomas Donohue, "Market Foothold in Cuba," *Washington Post*, 26 July 1999, p. A19.

40. Defense Intelligence Agency, "1998 Report on the Cuban Threat to U.S. National Security," November 18, 1997, in *U.S.-Cuban Relations in the 21st Century*, pp. 67–72.

41. *U.S.–Cuban Relations in the 21st Century*, p. 6.

42. Schwab, *Cuba*, p. 90.

III

Calculated Risks

8

Political Risk Investment Insurance: A Back-up Option for Risk Transfer

Felton "Mac" Johnston

As little as ten years ago, the political risk insurance landscape, especially that for investment exposures, bore only slight resemblance to that of today. In scope of coverage, capacity, proliferation of sources, and product development, much has changed. To a considerable extent, the changes represent the private market's recognition of the legitimacy and profitability of the business, propelled in substantial part by the pursuit of profitable outlets in a soft market environment. Recently, worldwide economic reform, privatization, and the collapse of the Soviet system have created burgeoning demand to which public- and private-sector participants in the marketplace could respond. The market continues to be characterized by innovation, growth, competition, and cooperation. Even if it (like all markets) experiences setbacks, they are likely to be temporary.

WHAT POLITICAL RISK INSURANCE IS

In general, political risks are categorized by insurance buyers and sellers according to the type of exposure to loss—sales and contracting overseas and investment—and by the type of coverage available for such exposures. The primary focus of this chapter is insurance for investment—equity and term debt for private projects. Table 8.1 provides a general description of these exposures for which political risk coverage is available. The coverages are generally one form or another of loss due to (a) inconvertibility or transfer risk coverage; (b) expropriation, confiscation, or other "wrongful" and harmful behavior by a government; and (c) various forms of political violence along a spectrum from international war to strikes, riots, and civil commotion. If it occurs to the reader that the latter two categories are not peculiar to other people's countries, this simply confirms the reality that "political" risks are not peculiarly foreign by nature. Nevertheless, that is the way the market, for the most part, treats them.

One of the notable developments in the marketplace has been the development of "breach of contract" coverage that applies to host government nonperformance of obligations undertaken to private projects. The obligation could be the maintenance of a concession grant or license, but in most cases it involves a government agency's promise to provide vital inputs to a project, or to pay for its

Table 8.1   Insurable Perils

I. Selling and Contracting Abroad
  A. "Wrongful" calling of bid, performance, advance payment, and similar guaranties or other "on demand" instruments posted by a seller in favor of a buyer.
  B. Contract Frustration: action taken by a government, not allowed by the terms of the contract itself, including:
      i. contract repudiation
      ii. export embargo/license revocation
      iii. import embargo/license revocation
  C. Nonpayment or other default due to:
      i. currency inconvertibility (active or passive)
      ii. political violence
  D. Loss due to other causes:
      i. confiscation or deprivation of equipment or inventory
      ii. damage or nonpayment due to political violence

II. Investment Abroad
  A. Currency inconvertibility due to active or passive measures (devaluation protection is unavailable). Coverage may extend to repatriation of capital, earnings, debt service, and various contractual payments.
  B. Expropriation
      i. nationalization or confiscation of an enterprise or of assets without adequate, effective, and timely compensation
      ii. "creeping" expropriation (government actions having the effect of depriving the investor of its interest or benefits of the investment even if not expressly for the purpose of expropriation)
      iii. other governmental action or condonation of actions, resulting in deprivation of the investor's assets, rights, or ability to operate
  C. Breach of contract/Nonhonoring of guaranties: failure of the host government to pay an arbitral award arising out of its breach of an undertaking to an investment project or the investors.
  D. Political Violence
      i. damage loss
      ii. nonpayment or default on account of political violence
      iii. other losses consequential to political violence
      iv. kidnap and ransom (available from private carriers only)

output, such as a commitment to supply fuel or take or pay for project-generated electricity. Most such coverage is linked to government default on an arbitral award based on a finding of the nonperformance. It may be deemed by insurers to be a subset of expropriation coverage or a separate coverage.

Although insurers tend toward convergence in the terms and wordings of their standard policy forms, they are not identical, and buyers of insurance need to be alert to differences in language and practice. More importantly, policy forms have many blanks to be filled in, and adaptation of standard terms to specific situations is common. This can work to the insurance buyer's advantage, as it may be possible to negotiate improved terms or at least language that is appropriate to the specific situation. However, a word—or a number— or two can profoundly affect the quality of coverage. Particularly but not exclusively for inconvertibility coverage, waiting periods (prior to which a claim does not mature), percentage of coverage, recovery limits per period or event, limits (if any) on the time an insurer has to settle a claim, and many other particulars affect the value of coverage.

WHO BUYS (OR DOES NOT BUY) POLITICAL RISK INSURANCE AND WHY

The motivations of the buyers of political risk insurance are varied and, at least in the case of investment risk coverage, not always based on logical analysis. Perceptions of political risk and of the utility of insurance to deal with it vary widely, as do the circumstances facing the companies contemplating its purchase. The decision to purchase investment insurance is often a matter of corporate policy rather than the result of an analysis of specific need. There may be good reasons for this thinking. Advocates of a specific project may resist burdening its profitability with the cost of insurance, regardless of risk. Insurance may satisfy a strategic need. A global approach may be critical to obtaining insurance when it is most needed and least available to a case-by-case buyer. A corporate policy may also dictate that insurance should never, or rarely, be purchased. Very large firms with widely spread exposures may safely and economically be self-insurers.

An example of the confusion that sometimes characterizes investors' thinking about political risk insurance is the common tendency to subject investment decisions to "hurdle-rate" analysis that imputes greater risk to cross-border investments. Typically, the analysis factors in the cost of political risk insurance without any corresponding offset to the hurdle rate. What value should be attached to insurance is a challenging issue both in the abstract and case-by-case. Complicating the value question is the perception that insurance from public agencies may be as important as a prophylactic against loss as a source of partial recovery of losses.

For some firms, recoveries from insurance in relation to the market or strategic value of their investments do not justify the cost, or the terms of coverage cannot be made to address the most serious and likely risks. Some investors may decide that the involvement of a major multilateral agency or other potent investors provides adequate protection from harmful sovereign behavior.

The purchase of coverage for trade transactions may be driven by a desire to cushion the potential effect of exchange crises and other noncommercial causes of nonpayment. Insuring trade transactions against political risks (with that coverage increasingly being combined with credit risk insurance) facilitates financing and expanded sales.

Demand for investment risk coverage has expanded with global economic reform and the opportunities that they have yielded for investors and lenders to private projects. New opportunities that require long-term investment in "reforming" but unsettled and untested environments have spurred much of the growth in demand. These opportunities have arisen especially in privatized infrastructure—hence the demand for "breach of contract" coverage. But interest is every bit as keen in obtaining convertibility/transfer risk coverage for these exposures; infrastructure projects typically do not generate foreign exchange, but they do consume it.

Bank lenders are major buyers of political risk coverage. Their demand is partly to cover "project" term loans to infrastructure and other private projects, but banks also utilize insurance to cover loans to their developing country affiliates for on-lending locally. Coverage is required not merely to offset perceived risk; even where risks may be perceived to be low, prudential limits (regulatory or internally-generated) on per-country exposure drive lenders to use insurance as a mechanism to "score" their cross-border exposures at lower levels.

WHO SELLS POLITICAL RISK INSURANCE AND WHY

The great marketplace divide is between public- and private-sector insurers. On the trade side, in recent years public agencies have yielded much of the short-term business to private insurers—in some cases by privatizing themselves. On the investment side, private insurers have aggressively increased their presence and competitiveness with greatly increased capacity (amounts of insurance available), longer tenures, broader coverage, more players, and the abandonment of assorted constraints and taboos.

The public or official markets are made up principally of the export credit agencies whose purpose is to facilitate national export sales. While these agencies principally serve to offset export risks rather than investment risks, more often than not they double as investment insurers (although the United States and Germany utilize separate agencies for this purpose). And of course "export" and "investment" risks are not entirely exclusive categories. In some cases, private entities conduct business partly for their government, and partly for their own account.

With the expansion of opportunities for private investment and policy emphasis on that means of economic development, multilateral institutions are playing an increasing role in political risk insurance (usually styled by them as "guaranties"). Most prominent among these is the World Bank–affiliated Multilateral Investment Guarantee Agency (MIGA), a ten-year-old institution marked by rapid growth and aggressiveness market penetration. Other multilateral institutions have or are developing "partial risk guarantee" programs to respond to demand for coverage in their respective regions.

The private market, once made up of Lloyd's of London, American International Group (AIG), and a handful of marginal players, continues to have those major institutions as leading sources, but in addition to the expansion of their own activities in the field, new or newly energized insurers have added substantially to the quantity and quality of available private coverage.

Although competition between public and private sources of political risk insurers is often keen, there is also considerable cooperation to muster large amounts of capacity for single exposures, to manage country exposure levels, and to leverage each other's special strengths, as discussed later in this chapter. In the process, while differences between the public- and private-sector insurers remain, they tend to diminish.

WORKINGS OF THE MARKETPLACE

What Motivates Private Insurers

Fundamental to understanding the private insurance marketplace is recognition that insurance markets are similar to commodity markets—highly responsive to supply and demand and subject to episodes of under- and overcapacity affecting price—and that spreading risk across countries is essential to the business. Thus, although the private market takes account of risk differentials, the price and availability of coverage for a particular transaction may be profoundly affected by alternative demand and available supply for coverage in one particular country. In fact, a "good" risk in a country like Brazil, where demand is typically very high, may be more costly to insure than an inferior risk in a country where demand is limited.

So how a private insurer greets a request for coverage will depend partly on the "market" rate for insurance in a particular country, that is, competition setting some ceiling on what he can charge and a dearth of market capacity for that country making it competitively possible to charge a higher rate than elsewhere. The insurer's own capacity—dictated in most cases by the terms of his reinsurance support and by how much of his capacity remains unused—is also important.

This is not to say that risk perception plays no role. Insurers will reject business that is deemed unsound, and rates will reflect differences in risk perception.

Still other factors affect the insurer's price for coverage and how much coverage he offers for a particular risk exposure. Relationships remain important in the insurance business. The insurer's view of a transaction or group of transactions will be colored by his attitude toward the prospective insured. Is the company one with which the insurer does a large volume of business, or is the insurer seeking to win business from the company? Is that company's business particularly desirable? Conversely, is the prospective insured not a regular customer, merely shopping for the lowest rate, seeking to cover only the biggest risks, and perhaps known to be a troublesome or accident-prone insured? A new or irregular customer not particularly sought after may nevertheless obtain reasonably priced coverage for an acceptable risk, especially if the customer is represented by a skillful, vigorous, and influential broker specializing in this risk.

Investors who are able and willing to purchase coverage from an insurer for a number of exposures that bring the insurer a desirable spread of risk across countries should be able to obtain insurance at a lower unit cost than they would by insuring each item separately, and may win capacity and tolerance for their least desirable risks that otherwise would not be obtainable.

What Motivates Public Insurers

Public-sector insurers are not involved in political risk insurance primarily to make money, but they are increasingly interested in enhanced revenue generation, loss avoidance, and loss control. Their involvement principally serves national or international objectives, such as export promotion, economic development of emerging market countries, or other policy goals. They commonly have subsidiary objectives that may or may not favor the investor. For instance, most public entities will do business with smaller domestic firms on terms at least equal to those offered to larger firms even though the smaller firms' business is not as profitable, or is unprofitable. The public entity will be willing to consider insuring individual items (i.e., to be the victim of adverse selection) if those items otherwise fit its criteria. And the public entity may be willing to assume some (but not all) risks that private insurers would shun for underwriting or other reasons, and to write business at or below "market" prices.

Still, public agencies increasingly resemble private insurers in moving toward market pricing, discounting for spread of risk, and general commercial practice. Governments are not keen to lose money on insurance schemes. Public agencies increasingly use private reinsurance to manage exposures and increase capacity, and private reinsurance terms tend to enforce commercial behavior. In spite of having differing objectives and capabilities, public and private markets increasingly cooperate as well as compete for their mutual benefit.

Working with Both Markets

It serves the interests of buyers of political risk insurance, as well those of the public and private insurers, that the two markets should both compete and cooperate. Competition draws forth better terms and greater responsiveness. Private insurers have become more competitive with public insurers by offering longer term coverage, less restricted coverage for land-based war risks, greater willingness to cover convertibility and transfer risks, and larger volumes of coverage per risk. In turn, public agencies have recognized the need to improve their responsiveness and to adopt means of cooperation with private insurers for customers' benefit.

Cooperation yields greater capacity, the opportunity to optimize the special strengths of both sectors, and the avoidance of gaps, overlaps, and friction arising out of uncoordinated insurance purchases. An individual insurer's capacity to write business can be augmented either through reinsurance or some form of coinsurance. Private insurers invariably are reinsured by other private reinsurers on a global ("treaty") basis that involves sharing losses relating the insurer's whole portfolio, and public agencies may utilize such treaty reinsurance as well. As the need arises, public and private insurers can also increase their capacity to write more coverage than they otherwise could by reinsuring "facultatively" (case-by-case) particular large transactions. (Because of public agencies' normally superior ability to deter claims and manage recoveries, and other policy and logistical considerations, private insurers usually reinsure public agencies, not the other way around.)

Coinsurance can yield the same capacity augmentation as reinsurance arrangements do, but liability is separate, and separate policies can lead to difficulty in claims and recovery situations. For these reasons, it is common for coinsurers to enter into claims cooperation agreements, and to bring their policy language into substantial conformity. Coinsurance arrangements are common among public and private insurers, and between them.

Another mode of cooperation between public and private insurers is a "fronting" arrangement in which liability is separate, but a fronting public agency agrees to share recoveries pro rata with a cooperating private insurer, thereby effectively sharing both its superior claims deterrence and recovery status with the private insurer—but at some cost.

For the investor lacking the right staff and/or experience in this field, recourse to a specialist insurance broker may be essential. Some markets, like Lloyd's of London, can only be approached through an insurance broker; others do not have this requirement. Brokers (for a commission or fee) can stimulate competition and achieve better terms, help investors understand the protection available, and manage the mechanics of meshing two or more insurers when that becomes necessary.

ISSUES AND TRENDS

The political risk insurance field is replete with issues and change. Here are a few areas of special interest to buyers and sellers alike.

Convertibility and Transfer

For banks in particular, this coverage is the most necessary and often the only coverage they seek. The risk of blocked remittances is what compels lenders and others to mark exposure as "cross-border" risk, and removal of that risk through insurance may enable the lender or investor to count the risk as domestic. There can be wide variations in coverage terms and conditions that profoundly affect the value of the coverage.

Once available from the private market in very small portions and only for a short term, convertibility/transfer coverage is increasingly available, although insurers may not be prepared to offer it without expropriation coverage as well (or without an equivalent charge). Expropriation coverage is generally less in demand at this time as the incidence of expropriation activity is believed to have become rare. Such a judgment may rely too much on recent history.

Breach of Contract

Breach coverage deals with the prospect that a government may be unable or unwilling to meet its obligations, whereas expropriation coverage generally involves a lesser likelihood—that of a government taking positive steps that harm the project or the investor. Breach coverage is particularly useful in facilitating the financing of private infrastructure projects, which have proliferated as governments have privatized economic sectors previously reserved for public investment. The linkage of breach coverage compensation to a government's failure to honor an arbitration award promises a substantial delay between the government's nonperformance of its commitment (of whatever nature) and the point when insurance compensation is yielded. It may be possible to obtain from some insurers a provisional payment pending the outcome of arbitration.

When a government's obligation involves payments in foreign exchange or in local currency indexed to foreign exchange, it may be very difficult for the government to keep its commitments during an exchange crisis.

Exchange Rate Risk Dilemma

Political risk insurance does not include protection against exchange rate risk. However, insurers are very much exposed to the consequences of changes in relative currency values. Blocked or significantly delayed remittances usually result from the authorities' efforts to ration foreign exchange when the domestic currency is overvalued. If a devaluation follows, the insurer who previously paid a claim for delayed remittances and received local currency in return may absorb the loss; insurers try to avoid this.

Once a devaluation occurs to bring currency values into balance, there is less likelihood that inconvertibility claims will arise. For those who believe that floating rates and timely devaluation are the wave of the present and the future, this diminishes the need for convertibility/transfer coverage. But the impact of a significant devaluation will reverberate onto infrastructure projects with government-backed obligations linked to foreign currency values. Thus, in the context of infrastructure projects, when foreign exchange crises loom, the risks are heightened that a loss associated with either convertibility/transfer, or breach of contract, will occur. Nowhere is it written that governments will forever bind themselves to either fixed or floating exchange rate systems.

Capital Markets Coverage

Several public and private political risk insurers have recently developed special policy forms to cover bond market financings, addressing the critical "timeliness of payment" issue by triggering claims to blockage of transfers to prefund payment reserve accounts. The vagaries of the bond markets and pricing constraints limit the scope for capital markets coverage. However, where circumstances are favorable, political risk insurance can justify upgrading a developing country project borrower's credit rating above the sovereign foreign debt ceiling up to or near the borrower's local currency borrowing rating. If that yields an investment grade rating, insurance may open the door to an important alternative to bank financing.

Preferred Creditor Status

Multilateral agencies like MIGA and regional development banks claim "preferred creditor status" that historically has exempted them from debt reschedulings following an exchange crisis, and the influence these institutions enjoy also helps to insulate them also from acts of expropriation or other "sovereign risks." Multilaterals leverage their privileged status through so-called "B-loans" for which they are lenders of record but whose risks are borne by private lenders. The multilaterals accord the B-loans equal treatment with their own, so that a host government cannot withhold exchange for such loans without correspondingly withholding it from the preferred multilateral creditor. The corresponding practice of multilateral insurers is the fronting insurance arrangement with a private coinsurer described earlier. A somewhat similar effect can be achieved through formalized coinsurance arrangements between public and private insurers. The volume of this kind of activity appears to be increasing rapidly. Some observers fear that excessive use of multilaterals' privileged status could discourage activity by lenders not enjoying such preference, and could reach a country-by-country magnitude that stretches the exchange authorities' ability to honor their obligations to all of their preferred creditors.

Pledge of Shares and Lender Priority

Although both political risk insurers and project lenders contribute mightily to the realization of new private projects in emerging markets, and indeed project lenders often rely on the insurer's product, they can also be at cross-purposes. In order to secure their interests in the event of a borrower default, project lenders typically demand that project sponsors pledge their ownership shares in the project to collateralize the debt. Most public-sector political risk insurers (and many private-market insurers also) will not pay an expropriation claim to an equity investor unless the insured can assign his ownership interest—unencumbered—in exchange. Lenders have generally refused to make exceptions to their requirement that the shares remain pledged to them. Some arrangements to reconcile lenders and insurers have been manuscripted, but overall this remains a stubborn issue over which much heat and little light has been generated.

Another potential difficulty is that the "waterfall" provisions of the loan agreement (intended to assure that borrower resources go first to pay out lenders) may be used by lenders to deny equity investors the ability to transfer blocked local currency to their insurers in order to perfect a convertibility claim.

Changing Insurance Techniques

The insurance industry is generally undergoing significant transformation as new techniques of buying and selling coverage evolve and as the boundaries between insurance and finance erode. Different coverages—such as political and credit risks—are bundled together so that insurers get economies (you cannot pay twice on the same transaction) and those insured do not have to decide which risk of loss most needs to be insured. Private insurers provide political risk global "umbrella" packages that fill gaps left by public agencies in terms of amounts or types of coverage. Captive insurance companies (individually owned or group captives) can provide access to insurance on better terms than direct purchase. Captives can be vehicles for sophisticated arrangements, including "alternative risk transfer" policies that permit companies to prefund and smooth out the effects of losses on a tax-deductible basis, with other insurers participating at higher levels of loss.

Sovereign default derivatives are being explored as an alternative to insurance. This kind of derivative is essentially an option to sell to a third party the debt that the public-sector buyer owes it. If the public-sector buyer defaults, the option can be exercised. If indeed there is a market (which may not always be the case), the third party can resell it—at a price.

From an insurer's perspective, overseas political risk is similar to domestic risk. The international businessperson's main concerns, particularly in the third-world and reemerging countries of eastern Europe and the former Soviet Union, will be expropriation and exchange transfer risks, as well as a host government's reneging on supportive infrastructural commitments. All these defaults must stem from the actions of the governments in question. Political risk analysis can be the guide to seeking protection, but it should be considered no more exact about predicting outcomes than good market analysis. If an investor's choice is to leverage his or her position in a strange overseas market, public and private risk insurance is a good option. Any corporation expanding overseas may find it relatively costly unless it can accept coverage in a basket of countries, but the advantage now as the field becomes more sophisticated is that the businessperson gets a step up on financing as well. The distinction between financing and insurance now is often blurred. The right insurer, sometimes brokered in combination with public agencies, can offer stopgap partial payments before in-country disputes have been arbitrated, can raise a customer's credit rating in-country, and can offer prefunding against losses. Moreover, if a broker puts together a package with a public insurer involved, the insurance customer is likely to benefit further from the deterrent effect of being guaranteed by a multilateral or his government.

9

Conclusion: A Final Word about Setting up Shop

Take calculated risks;
That is quite different from being rash.

—Gen. George S. Patton

In an era of so-called "globalization," a trend has been developing for intermediate-size corporations to expand their frontiers overseas, and to even take a look at some of the less well-trodden areas. For an American company, learning to adjust to an international environment (particularly one of the less developed countries of the third world, eastern Europe, or the former Soviet republics) is a matter of commitment and patience. The company that chooses this route must appreciate that other peoples and systems may behave differently from us in the negotiation and implementation of business transactions.

The new international topography of less developed countries and the newly independent states of the former Soviet bloc varies in ways that this book, through its manifold illustrations and in-depth case studies, has tried to demonstrate. International businesspeople should never forget that they are identified with their country. They should assume the characteristics of neither explorer nor missionary. Most important, international businesspeople—whether planners or marketing officers—should not perceive themselves as scaling the Matterhorn—either for glory or great profits.

Be circumspect and look at each new and unfamiliar market through the sort of prism that we have tried to present here. Apply the principles well and let intuition and cross-cultural sensitivity temper the numbers and hard facts. You will find as many commonalities among developing countries as unique features. In most cases, the nuisances to you may be viewed as symptomatic of the process of transition and change, and you can look to the future that you, as an investor, will help shape. Political/social risks should not be represented necessarily as a "red flag" from which to run. In fact, we prefer to refrain from using the term "political risk." But you will notice that the extractive industries, like oil companies and others that require a lot of front-end capital and a longer term for development in a country, are most always prepared for a damaging political or social crisis. They make it part of their business, one way or another, to continuously monitor events that could jeopardize their own enterprise. They are concerned about accidents of their own that could generate bad publicity in the host country and among environmentalists at home. Furthermore, at the negotiating phase, they do not mind talking explicitly with their "opposite numbers" about the trade-offs between risk and return.

Our use of the concept "business environment conditions" or something like it is meant to be interpreted broadly. It is relatively neutral emotionally and in concert with the general practice of rational corporate strategic planning and good marketing savvy. In an age of "political correctness," it is politically correct! If the marketing executive will allow himself to think in terms of our framework, retaining a knowledge of the implications of the discussion of such issues as political legitimacy and elites in an elitist country, for example, or inflation and a drain of a country's hard currency reserves, he will position himself to assimilate information and be better informed. Not only will he be reacting to problems or catastrophes in the social/political milieu or economic/commercial sphere in a knowledgeable manner, but he will also be able, under certain circumstances, to gradually take the necessary actions to help shape the outcome for his particular foreign enterprise.

How might the corporation establish a mechanism for keeping watch on the business environment in several different countries? Given a specific region of the world, how can senior management intelligently select one particular country for a dual purpose: to serve as the first regional recipient of foreign direct investment and also to act as a fulcrum for additional investments and trade in neighboring countries? The well-heeled outside consultant can provide the general picture, but his or her report will still have to be reinterpreted in-house—even rewritten—in the context of a company's special needs. Otherwise, it is unlikely to have much impact on corporate decisions or actions in the field. One former foreign service officer at Texaco used an outside consulting service for the more comprehensive "reports" on countries ("a group of Oxford dons"), but then had to compose his own short memoranda applying the service's conclusions to the company's needs, and affix them to the nicely packaged, more general academic and untailored documents.

In our opinion, the following guidelines should ideally be followed if the reader in senior management wants to navigate a course with a proper compass, instead of "worry beads," in hand:

First, one must put together a small, in-house department, comprising individuals with a solid background in economics, comparative politics, and international finance. A balance among the disciplines would be good, and they should *interact* whenever possible. The department should be genuinely interdisciplinary.

Second, it is crucial that international business environment people try to establish a communications flow within the corporate entity that will ensure that the real needs of the corporation are being served. Reports written and not read do not represent productivity in a corporation. It is important that this special support and analysis staff at the corporate center leave their desks and do a personal selling job on behalf of their program with operational executives in the subsidiaries and abroad (even if one of the staff must fly to Johannesburg or Lagos to meet with African marketing executives). A give-and-take exchange must ensue over the utility that the marketing people ascribe to the environment analysis services, what factors are most meaningful, and how the reports might be made more practical. Environment analysis services must be sure that its program remains an integral part of strategic planning and that it contributes to both selection of overseas targets and positioning in those markets. The department should try to coordinate with the treasurer's office concerning foreign currencies and their transfer, and work with the insurance office whenever political risk coverage is involved.

A formalized channel of communication might be established on an uncomplicated basis with regional operations officers for the purpose of eliciting input on a given country or area, getting feedback on analysis that the department might have submitted, and just "involving" the operations officers in the *process*. The central purpose should be to educate people, not to predict the future for them! And the best sort of education for all always involves a two-way flow of information. Many larger corporations have mapped out future markets to target offshore, strategies for penetrating them, and ways to reduce the need for, or even avoid, political risk insurance on the basis of proper environmental assessments.[1] If good channels of communication and working relationships cannot be established among different departments at the corporate center or between the international business environment department and the field areas internationally, many interesting reports might be written, but corporate needs will be fulfilled inadequately.

Third, more data are now available—from newspaper accounts to daily terrorist reports that reach us online. We are virtually bombarded, and this poses a problem of collection and assimilation. We even can tap into local newspapers in countries that lack a global perspective. But the analyst must organize all this data and build files in order to be able to answer a query about the present with the advantage of hindsight. Beyond the written resources, the analyst for a corporation must learn how to "work Washington." He or she must regularly cultivate good relations with people at the Departments of State, Commerce, and Treasury, the Overseas Private Investment Corporation (OPIC), Capitol Hill committee staffers, the senior staff of the National Security Council as well as regionally specialized academicians and the right officers in embassies and the World Bank. On one occasion, I had to respond to a fast deadline to provide a background report on Brunei. Panicked at the paucity of available written materials on the island country, I phoned a number of professors in the Southeast Asia field and finally found one who, as an editor of a scholarly journal, had just turned down a piece on Brunei because he "didn't believe the subject was big enough to warrant coverage." After a few carefully timed phone calls to the writer who was roaming the Asian subcontinent after completing his doctorate fieldwork, I was able to piece together a reasonably solid report in a few days. In my own work, I have had to field questions on everything from the state of the economy of Vanuatu to the curious history of a failed construction project involving a small airstrip in Indonesia. The job always got done. My nets were always cast wide, and I kept a firm hold of them.

We have noted that some international corporations, taking a proactive stance with regard to political and economic risk, have incorporated country analyses into the process of strategic planning, that is, targeting overseas markets and developing strategies for positioning the corporation in that market.

Sometimes the process is informal and responsive on an ad hoc bias. The country business environment department, under any label, should be ready to tackle questions from the General Counsel and legal department or the troubled marketing people in the field concerned with such matters as the backgrounds of local personalities, the identity and background of a local agent or liaison, or the implications of a political change.

Ultimately, the midsized corporation that wants to expand internationally will be in greatest need of such country business environment analyses as a first indication of whether to proceed. When war, insurrection, civil strife, and expropriation or default become real and potential threats, the corporation may opt for political risk cover or avoid the business opportunity altogether. A survey that OPIC commissioned several years ago noted that firms "whose strategy and structure is global" and have a greater and more diversified spread of international operations "may well decide to absorb the cost of risk because of the diversity of the portfolio of its subsidiaries."[2] But what about the smaller-scale, newly internationalizing corporation? The key to deciding early in the game whether to avoid a particular international opportunity, whether to choose one opportunity over another, or whether to pursue a specific strategy as opposed to another to protect oneself is at bottom good intelligence and more good intelligence. Country business environment analysis and the access to the right political and economic information on the spot might not reduce the risk of running into serious difficulty, but it can reduce uncertainty and allow the company to think through its options.

NOTES

1. Arthur Young and Company, "A Study of OPIC Assistance to US Private Direct Investment in Developing Countries," unpublished paper for the Overseas Private Investment Corporation, May 28, 1982, p. II-17.

2. Arthur Young and Company, "A Study of OPIC Assistance," p. II-22.

Index

About the Author/Editor

David M. Raddock, a specialist in Chinese politics and developing countries, is currently the principal officer of David M. Raddock Associates International in Brooklyn Heights, New York. Formerly, he was director of international affairs for the multinational ENSERCH Corporation, with headquarters in Dallas, and managing partner of KCS&A Public Relations, Inc., in New York. In nearly a decade at ENSERCH, Raddock put together a system for monitoring political risk in thirty countries on a semiannual basis.

He received his undergraduate degree with honors from Cornell University in Asian studies and government, a master's degree in international relations and a Certificate of the East Asian Institute, and a doctorate in comparative politics and political psychology from Columbia University. With a knowledge of Chinese, Russian, and French, he has conducted research in East Asia, Southeast Asia, North Africa, the Middle East, and Latin America. Raddock began his career on the faculty of the Graduate School of International Management at the University of Texas in Dallas. He has been a senior research associate at Columbia's East Asian Institute and at the Shanghai Academy of Social Sciences. He also serves as an adjunct professor of international affairs at Columbia.

He has been a frequent contributor to such academic and popular publications as the *New York Times Magazine*, *Journal of Commerce*, *Far Eastern Economic Review*, *China Quarterly*, *The Weekly Standard*, *Art News*, *New York Newsday*, and *New Art Examiner*, among others. His first book, *Political Behavior of Adolescents in China* (1977), discussed social change in the People's Republic of China at the outset of the Cultural Revolution. He is currently at work on his first novel, which examines the effects of a pervasive police state environment on the mind of an American in China.

About the Contributors

John P. Entelis is a professor of political science and director of the Middle East Studies Program at Fordham University. Author and coauthor of several books on the Middle East and North Africa, he appears frequently on television and has lectured overseas at summer institutes and at the Foreign Service Institute in the Washington, D.C., area. His most recent work is *Islam, Democracy and the State in North Africa* (1997).

Felton McL. Johnston III is the president of FMJ International Risk Services, LLC in Chevy Chase, Maryland. His career includes thirteen years as a vice president for insurance of the Overseas Private Investment Corporation (OPIC), the independent U.S. government agency that provides coverage and financing for political risk to U.S. corporations overseas. He was OPIC's representative at the Berne Union and served on OPIC's management committee. He is a graduate of Colgate University, the Fletcher School of Law and Diplomacy, and the Harvard Business School.

Rensselaer W. Lee III is the president of Global Advisory Services, in Alexandria, and is also an associate scholar at the Foreign Policy Research Institute in Philadelphia. He is the author of two books on nuclear smuggling and on the politics of the narcotics trade. He taught much earlier at the City University of New York. He received his bachelor of arts from Princeton University, his master of arts from Columbia University, and his doctorate from Stanford University.

Stephen I. Levine is a professor of political science and director of the Asian Studies Center at the University of Montana in Missoula. He is particularly well known for his work in the modern history of Russia and China and is fluent in both languages. He has spent time in China and created the award-winning *China Box* as an educational tool for children. Having taught formerly at Columbia University, American University, and the University of North Carolina, he is the author of several books and articles including, *America's Wars in Asia: A Cultural Appraisal to History and Memory* (1998).

Michael Newcity is the coordinator of the Center for Slavic, Eurasian, and East European Studies at Duke University and a senior lecturing fellow at the law school. A specialist in the Russian legal system and intellectual property law, he is the author of two books and numerous articles on related subjects. He has also been called as an expert witness in federal and state courts in the United States. He received degrees with distinction in political science and Russian studies and was awarded the JD from George Washington University.